Art and Authorship in the AI Spring

"As AI opens up new pathways for authorship, cultural production and artistic creation, we desperately need broader historical and theoretical trajectories to make sense of the ongoing changes. *Art and Authorship in the AI Spring* provides just this. Looking back at the decade preceding the emergence of ChatGPT and the AI hype, and activating a rich theoretical tradition centred around the work of Brazilian media philosopher Vilém Flusser, this acute and thoughtful book is the ideal compass for anyone interested in exploring from a novel angle the intersections between AI, art and communication."

—Simone Natale, *Associate Professor in Media Theory and History, University of Turin*

"Opening the black box of generative AI, but at the same time resisting mere technological determinism, McIntyre reveals its socio-technical agencies, both in terms of creative authorship and big tech companies authority. Focusing on the incubation phase of generative AI "before the hype" (when its structures were still intelligible in creative usage), this study—in media-phenomenological alliance with Flusser—addresses the "gestures" of AI in terms of authorship with precise analytics and ethical concern. With his final warning against "cultural extinction" as a collateral damage of displaced human authorship by AI, McIntyre carries media philosophy beyond the subsymbolical AI turn."

—Wolfgang Ernst, *Former Chair of Media Theories at Humboldt University of Berlin*

"Both highly original and rigorously argued, this book outlines the way concepts of authorship and creativity are bound up with advanced technological systems. McIntyre develops an entirely new take both on the old humanist concept of authorship as well as the technical images produced by AI. It is a must read for anyone interested in understanding the power of technology to reshape culture and what it means to be human amongst artificially "creative" systems."

—Timothy Barker, *Professor of Media Technology and Aesthetics, University of Glasgow*

"We urgently need more interventions like McIntyre's that remind us of the short yet already strangely forgotten history of generative AI amid today's relentless hype. This book recovers the past decade of developments that too often vanish from public debate to understand where we are and how we got here. It resists narrowing the ethical frame of generative AI to solely legal terms, instead opening up its wider societal and philosophical implications. We can all learn from McIntyre's creative conceptualisations, such as "weird media", to better understand how generative AI reshapes authorship, creativity and our cultural consumption and production."

—Tobias Blanke, *Professor of Artificial Intelligence and Humanities, University of Amsterdam*

Andrew McIntyre

Art and Authorship in the AI Spring

A Media-Philosophical Approach

palgrave
macmillan

Andrew McIntyre
Media Studies
University of Amsterdam
Amsterdam, The Netherlands

ISBN 978-3-032-18573-0 ISBN 978-3-032-18574-7 (eBook)
https://doi.org/10.1007/978-3-032-18574-7

This Palgrave Macmillan imprint is published by the registered company Springer Nature Switzerland AG
The registered company address is: Gewerbestrasse 11, 6330 Cham, Switzerland

For Pip and John

Acknowledgements First and foremost, I would like to express my sincere thanks to Professor Timothy Barker and Dr. Michael Bachmann of the University of Glasgow who supervised my doctoral research upon which this monograph is based. Without their kind support, invaluable feedback and continual guidance, this work would simply not exist.

While completing my doctoral research, I also had the pleasure of studying under the temporary supervision of Professor Wolfgang Ernst at Humboldt University of Berlin. I would like to thank Professor Ernst and his staff, particularly Dr. Stefan Höltgen, for their warm welcome and the time they dedicated to aiding my studies.

In Berlin, I also had the opportunity to visit the Vilém Flusser Archive, and I would like to thank the staff, especially Dr. Anita Jóri, for kindly providing access to archive documents and unpublished manuscripts that have significantly influenced the ideas discussed in this monograph.

I am also grateful to the Scottish Graduate School for Arts and Humanities for funding my doctoral research through the UK Arts and Humanities Research Council Doctoral Training Partnership.

Parts of this book are based on previously published material that has been substantially revised. I thank the original publishers for granting permission to reuse material from the following:

- McIntyre, Andrew. 2023. Weizenbaum's nightmare: the decay of language in AI-generated communication. *Journal of Pervasive Media* 8.1.
- McIntyre, Andrew. 2022. The infinite portrait: a case of post-human authorship. In *Materializing Digital Futures: Touch, Movement, Sound and Vision*, eds. Toija Cinque and Jordan Beth Vincent, 141–162. London: Bloomsbury Academic.

Finally, I want to thank my friends and family for their constant support and encouragement over the many long years it has taken to develop this work.

Competing Interests The author has no competing interests to declare that are relevant to the content of this manuscript.

Contents

About the Author

Andrew McIntyre is a media theorist based in the United Kingdom. His work explores the social, cultural and political implications of AI-generated media and sits at the intersection of media philosophy, philosophy of technology and AI ethics. McIntyre holds a PhD in Film and Television Studies from the University of Glasgow, and he has lectured and conducted research at the University of Amsterdam, University of Stirling and Humboldt University of Berlin.

List of Figures

CHAPTER 1

Before the Hype

In a landmark hearing on 11 October 2022, members of the UK Parliament House of Lords directly questioned an artificial intelligence (AI) system as a formal witness for the first time in history (Hern 2022): the humanoid machine dubbed "Ai-Da". Created by Aiden Meller and named after the pioneering mathematician Ada Lovelace, Ai-Da was capable of creating detailed and aesthetic sketches, paintings and sculptures of the people or objects it "saw" using a camera system and mechanical arms. Since its construction in 2019, Ai-Da had made numerous media appearances, while its artworks had been featured in galleries and museums around the world, including a solo show of self-portraits at the Design Museum in London in 2021. Earlier in 2022, the machine had also been commissioned to produce a portrait of Queen Elizabeth II for the monarch's Platinum Jubilee. Having gained international attention as a so-called "AI artist", Ai-Da and Meller were invited to give evidence to parliament as part of the Communications and Digital Committee's inquiry into the future of the creative industries.

Though the hearing followed all the usual formalities and committee chair Tina Stowell insisted it was a serious matter, the absurdity of the situation was quite apparent to all involved. Placed in front of the committee, the machine wore a rubber mask with the features of a woman and sported a bob haircut, floral shirt and dungarees over the mass of electromechanical parts that formed its body. When questioned by the

A. McIntyre, *Art and Authorship in the AI Spring*,
https://doi.org/10.1007/978-3-032-18574-7_1

barons and baronesses of the committee, Ai-Da replied in a toneless voice, failed to respond at times, and at one point abruptly malfunctioned and required re-booting by Meller. Ultimately, the evidence provided by Ai-Da itself amounted to three brief responses (UK Parliament, 2022).

Despite Ai-Da's somewhat lacklustre insights, the machine's appearance before the committee nonetheless inspired much discussion among the members present. Some expressed concern that AI systems might one day replace human artists, some argued that the technology would allow artists to produce "better" art, while others questioned whether or not AI could ever create "true" art at all. A few members even voiced anxiety that AI systems such as Ai-Da might eventually break free from human control and take over the world, though they did so somewhat humorously. The hour-long session became a microcosm of the wider debate on AI and creativity at the time, reflecting questions around creative practice, the difference between human and AI art, and the impact of technology on culture.

The most striking contribution to the discussion came from Meller himself who in his closing remarks stated that "AI machine learning will be very capable of language, image creation and music creation. We are going into a world where those processes will be mimicked extraordinarily well… we are going into a world of non-human creativity" (Ibid., Q29). Meller's words proved to be rather prescient. Just one month later, the launch of ChatGPT introduced far more sophisticated AI systems to the world at large, hyper-charging these debates around AI and creativity, and igniting an intense fascination with these technologies that continues to this day.

Released in November 2022, OpenAI's now-famous chatbot ChatGPT demonstrated such human-like fluency and comprehensive knowledge in its responses that the potential of AI suddenly appeared almost limitless. While earlier systems like Ai-Da appeared as novelties or gimmicks, ChatGPT seemed to present a technology that could fundamentally transform how people communicate, generate ideas and arguments, engage in creative activities and access information about the world. Within just two months, ChatGPT gained over 100 million users, becoming the fastest-growing consumer software application in history and has since seen rapid adoption across various sectors including business, education, research, journalism and policy (Milmo 2023). Though certainly not the first or last system of its kind, ChatGPT marked a decisive turning point in AI history. Not only did the chatbot prompt widespread use of AI systems in both professional and personal contexts, it also inspired an unprecedented public fascination in the technology. The arrival of sophisticated machines apparently capable of convincingly mimicking human thought and expression fed into long-standing fantastical narratives of technological singularity, AI apocalypses and science fiction-inspired futures driven by intelligent machines. While AI had long been a subject of public curiosity and speculation, the release of ChatGPT brought about a wave of intense excitement, anxiety and existential fear fuelled by visions of utopias and dystopias on the horizon. Even now, the world remains gripped by this so-called "AI hype".

Spurred on by this wave of public fascination and hype, AI research has since experienced a drastic surge in financial investment from governments and private businesses. The AI industry has now become one of the wealthiest and fastest-growing industries in the world with companies such as OpenAI and Nvidia rapidly reaching record market valuation (Criddle 2025; Roush 2025). Similar AI systems have also emerged from other technology companies including Google Gemini, Microsoft Copilot and DeepSeek, among others. Meanwhile, text-to-image generators and text-to-video generators such as Midjourney, DALL-E and Sora have also gained greater public attention and use. Due to their capacity to produce human-like content, these generative AI technologies have been increasingly integrated into corporate, government, media, education and advertising practices. For example, these systems are used for customer relations, report writing, data visualisation, generating visual marketing material and developing lesson plans. Of course, AI technologies are not limited to content generation and the past few years have also seen a significant increase in the use of AI systems for financial forecasting, facial recognition, strategic decision-making and data analysis and modelling. However, it is these generative AI systems that mimic human modes of communication (e.g., writing, music, images) that have captivated public imagination and that continue to profoundly influence social, cultural and political life.

As Meller and many others anticipated, generative AI has emerged as a disruptive force within the arts and creative industries as these systems have seen widespread application in visual art, music, literature and performance. A growing number of galleries are exhibiting works created with AI image generators, while Los Angeles will soon see the opening of Dataland, a gallery entirely dedicated to AI art (Rahmanan 2024). Meanwhile, online stores have seen a rise in AI-generated books and novels for sale, with one science fiction writer claiming to have produced and sold over 100 short books using AI (Grant 2023). Similarly, film and television production companies have embraced AI systems with many studios experimenting with AI tools for de-ageing actors, dubbing and promotional imagery, as well as digitally resurrecting deceased actors to reprise their film roles. 2025 saw the arrival of the first so-called "AI actor" with the entirely digital character dubbed "Tilly Norwood", a move that prompted significant criticism within the industry (Morris 2025). Beyond traditional arts, AI-generated images, texts and sounds have now become commonplace online as artificial content has drastically increased in recent years, often referred to as "AI slop".

The sudden emergence of generative AI systems in the arts has prompted significant ethical questions and concerns over labour, image rights and copyright infringement. Even before Norwood, in 2023 the Screen Actors Guild and American Federation of Television and Radio Artists (SAG-AFTRA) launched a strike centred in part on the use of AI-generated digital reconstructions as performers instead of live actors (Horton 2023). Also in 2023, a group of high-profile writers including George R.R. Martin, Jodi Picoult and Jonathan Franzen sued OpenAI for using their works without permission to train their AI systems (De Vynck 2023). Similar lawsuits have also been launched against other AI companies with writers arguing that the unauthorised use of their works as training data constitutes copyright infringement. Later in 2024, a campaign was launched in the United Kingdom urging the government to protect the unlicensed use of artistic works and ensure greater transparency around the training of AI systems, attracting the support of artists such as Kate Bush, Stephen Fry, Thom Yorke and Elton John (Hymas 2025).

There are only a few examples provided above, but there have been numerous other calls and campaigns to challenge the rise of AI in the creative industries in recent years. In spite of these legal challenges and labour disputes, the use of generative AI in the arts has only continued to grow. Not only are these technologies raising issues around labour and copyright, they are also reshaping the nature of artistic practices and redefining authorship.

It is this central question of authorship that this book considers. It is not concerned with legal ownership but, rather, the broader philosophical question of who or what creates a work of art and how this authorship informs the final work, its meaning and its impact on society.

Specifically, this book's discussion examines how AI systems transform cultural production practices and our understanding of authorship. As creativity has long been viewed as a defining mark of humanity, the arrival of creative AI systems is also forcing us to ask uncomfortable questions about humanity's role and significance within culture and society. These are no longer entertaining hypotheticals but, rather, real-world challenges that have drastically intensified in the few short years since the release of ChatGPT.

Looking back on Ai-Da's appearance at the committee in 2022, the spectacle of a humanoid robot artist wearing dungarees in parliament now seems rather quaint and almost silly when faced with the reality of modern generative AI. However, while the watershed moment of ChatGPT brought non-human creativity to the forefront of public discourse, throughout the 2010s and early 2020s many artists were already experimenting with emerging AI technologies. Using systems like Ai-Da, as well as more diverse AI technologies, these artists sought to probe, challenge and complicate traditional notions of authorship and cultural production. They did so at a time when non-human creativity was often dismissed as a novelty or an impossibility, and long before the AI hype that now dominates and distorts public discourse had taken hold. Although Ai-Da and other contemporary AI art systems have largely been forgotten, these early artistic experiments present a lens through which we may come to understand and critique the roots of our current moment. A moment defined by information overload, technological upheaval and apocalyptic anxiety.

As such, this book takes a step back from the modern situation to focus on this decade preceding the release of ChatGPT. By critically analysing various instances of AI art and media during this period, this book explores the question of authorship and the increasingly significant role of AI systems within culture. In this context, the question of authorship goes far beyond simply identifying who or what created a work of art. Rather, to explore art and authorship in the AI spring is to examine how technology is reshaping our society and what it means to be human in a world of non-human creativity.

Thinking of Thinking Machines

While the dramatic emergence of creative AI systems like Ai-Da and ChatGPT has abruptly forced us to reconsider our role in society and culture, these developments are part of a much broader historical trend; what philosopher Luciano Floridi names the *fourth revolution* (Floridi 2014).

For Floridi, the emergence of AI systems represents the latest in a series of key scientific developments that have fundamentally changed human understanding of the world, of our place within it, and of ourselves. The Copernican revolution in the sixteenth century was the first of these developments as the heliocentric model of the solar system revealed that Earth, and thus humanity, was not the centre of the cosmos. The second came in the nineteenth century with the Darwinian revolution in which the theory of evolution by natural selection recast humanity as simply one among many animals, albeit one gifted with consciousness by mere happenstance. The early twentieth century then saw the Freudian revolution as the psychoanalytical notion of the unconscious undermined the idea that humans are fully autonomous individuals. As Floridi claims, there then came a fourth revolution of self-understanding mere decades later with the publication of Alan Turing's seminal paper "Computing Machinery and Intelligence" (Turing 1950).

Published in 1950, Turing's paper questioned whether a machine could so convincingly imitate human behaviour as to be mistaken for or willingly accepted as one of our own; the famous imitation game. In doing so, Turing proposed that intelligent behaviour was not a unique product of the human brain but, rather, a process that could be formalised in mathematics and materialised in a machine. Thus, Turing's ideas followed Copernicus, Darwin and Freud in forcing humanity "to abandon once again a position that we thought was 'unique'" (Floridi 2014, 93) and laid the groundwork for what would become the modern field of AI. For Floridi, Turing's work marked the beginning of a new way of viewing the world in terms of information and of understanding ourselves as informational beings whose behaviours can be replicated in intelligent machines.

Certainly, Floridi's notion of the fourth revolution is not intended as a strict chronology but, rather, a metaphor that highlights how scientific research into computing and AI has brought about an informational worldview. However, the notion of a thinking machine or intelligent mechanism has much deeper roots in cultural narratives, historical myths and artistic practices that long predate Turing's work.

Narratives of thinking machines can be traced back as far as Homer's *Iliad* in which the Greek god Hephaestus created golden handmaidens capable of performing human tasks and of understanding. Similar narratives have been repeated time and time again, for example with the golem myth in Jewish folklore or in the Medieval legends of the brazen head of the Dominican friar Albertus Magnus, as well as stories of the alchemist Paracelsus' homunculi in Renaissance literature. Mere decades before the publication of Turing's paper, popular fantasy and science fiction narratives featured thinking machines and robots as well. Examples include Karel Čapek's 1920 play *R.U.R.*, Thea von Harbou's 1925 novel *Metropolis* and its 1927 film adaptation by Fritz Lang, and Isaac Asimov's early short stories in the 1940s that would later be published in the famous *I, Robot* collection. Furthermore, there are historical examples of early artistic mechanisms and inventions that gave the illusion of machinic intelligence such as Jacques de Vaucanson's automata (e.g., digesting duck, flute player) and Wolfgang von Kempelen's Mechanical Turk. For a deeper discussion of these historical imaginaries of AI, see Cave et al. (2020). I present only a few examples here to demonstrate that the notion of a thinking machine long preceded the founding of AI as a scientific research discipline grounded in mathematics and computation.

It is also important to recognise that Turing's work did not emerge in isolation but stands within a long mathematical and philosophical tradition that stretches back to at least the seventeenth century. This tradition has its roots in the philosophy of Gottfried Wilhelm Leibniz and was developed through the work of later figures such as George Boole, Charles Babbage and Ada Lovelace in the nineteenth century. Furthermore, there were strands of scientific theory outside of mathematics that emerged alongside Turing's work and that also greatly influenced the development of AI as a field of research. These include John von Neumann's computer architecture (1945), Norbert Wiener's cybernetics (1949), Claude Shannon's information theory (1948), Allen Newell and Herbert Simon's cognitive psychology (1956) and also the early neuroscience of Donald Hebb (1949), Warren McCulloch and Walter Pitts (1943) which inspired the development of artificial neural networks, the primary form of modern AI systems.

While Turing's contributions to AI are certainly significant, his work represents only one part of a far broader and more complex evolution of ideas around the nature of human intelligence, the potential of scientific inquiry, and the role of automated machines. In 1956, these various scientific, philosophical, mythical and cultural ideas and narratives coalesced, and the term "artificial intelligence" was formally introduced at the Dartmouth Summer Research Project on AI in New Hampshire. Funded by the Rockefeller Foundation and organized by John McCarthy, Marvin Minsky, Nathaniel Rochester and Claude Shannon, the Dartmouth workshop has since come to be regarded as the official birthplace of AI as a research discipline. One dedicated to the formalisation of human thought and behaviour, guided by the assumption that "every aspect of learning or any other feature of intelligence can in principle be so precisely described that a machine can be made to simulate it" (McCarthy et al. 1955). It is this fundamental assumption underpinning AI research that forms the core of the informational worldview that, as Floridi claims, has since come to dominate the modern world.

Seventy years on, the philosophical, psychological and political fallout from this assumption continues to be experienced at this very moment. Indeed, it has only intensified with the apparent arrival of Turing's hypothesised machines in everyday life. In particular, those modern AI systems that convincingly replicate qualities we once considered to be uniquely human (e.g., artmaking, communication) most clearly articulate this informational worldview.

When considering the complex history of AI, the disparate strands of theory, and the different technologies that have been categorised as "AI", it is understandably difficult to discern what precisely we mean when referring to AI and/or AI systems. This book largely focuses on AI technologies, products and applications that emerged in the 2010s and that are built upon artificial neural networks; computational models inspired by the structure and function of the human brain. These systems came to the forefront of AI research in the 2010s and are direct precursors to today's AI systems.

However, it is important to understand that AI, regardless of the specific technical architecture or application, is fundamentally an expression of this ideological belief that human intelligence and behaviour can be formalised and materialised. A belief that was cemented at the Dartmouth workshop. The AI systems discussed in this book, and those that have since become embedded in our lives, are not simply intelligent mechanisms. They are materialisations of the various different scientific concepts, fantastical myths and ideological beliefs that have been perpetuated over centuries and that eventually crystallised into the modern concept of AI.

Having traced the birth of the idea of AI, let us now consider how this idea materialised as different technologies and how the historical trajectory of AI research shaped the conditions for our modern situation.

Springtime for AI

Since its founding, the history of AI research has often been compared to the changing seasons, seemingly alternating between periods of rapid scientific development, public enthusiasm and financial investment (AI summers) and periods of academic and financial stagnation (AI winters). While this seasonal metaphor presents an overly simplistic timeline and is often only loosely applied, it can be useful to describe the recurring cycles of optimism and pessimism in the history of AI over the past seventy years. I will not provide a comprehensive history of AI here but, instead, I will trace the major seasonal changes to highlight where our current situation fits within these cycles. For a more detailed discussion of the history of AI, see Frana and Klein (2021), Charniak (2024) and Ida (2024).

The period of disparate scientific development and exploration in the 1940s and 1950s that culminated in the Dartmouth workshop has since been described by some as the "AI spring" to highlight the birth of AI as a discipline. Following the Dartmouth workshop, the 1950s and 1960s saw a flurry of scientific activity and financial investment in the field such that this period has been labelled as the first AI summer. Over two decades, AI scientific research became a firmly established discipline with dedicated centres and projects emerging across the world, notable examples being the Artificial Intelligence Laboratory at MIT, the Stanford Carnegie Institute of Technology and the University of Edinburgh's Department of Machine Intelligence and Perception. This period also saw significant investment in AI research from private companies (e.g., IBM, RAND Corporation) and government bodies (e.g., US Department of Defense Advanced Research Project Agency). Such endeavours resulted in key milestones in this period such as McCarthy's LISP programming language, Frank Rosenblatt's perceptron artificial neural network, Simon and Newell's Logic Theorist and General Problem Solver programmes, Joseph Weizenbaum's ELIZA chatbot and Richard Greenblatt's Mac

Hack chess programme, among others. In the 1970s, however, this flurry of activity slowed.

After twenty years, the overly ambitious promises of early AI researchers were not being delivered on. There was also growing criticism of the technical capabilities, philosophical foundations and societal implications of AI from figures such as Hubert Dreyfus (1965, 1972) and Weizenbaum (1972) himself. 1973 then saw the publication of mathematician James Lighthill's report "Artificial Intelligence: A General Survey" which heavily criticised the prospects of AI, ultimately leading the UK government to limit research funding (Lighthill 1973). Similarly, the US government also reduced funding in AI research amid criticism of high financial investment and limited outputs. The decade that followed was then marked by low investment and increased pessimism in AI research such that Minsky and Roger Schank would later describe this period as the first AI winter.

Seasons change, however, and in the early 1980s the winter came to an end with renewed interest in AI, specifically expert systems. These were computer programmes designed to simulate human decision-making in specialist domains such as medicine, finance and engineering. Seeking to capitalise on the potentially significant economic gains, governments and private businesses invested heavily in expert systems. AI research enjoyed a second, albeit very brief, summer. In 1987, the expert systems boom collapsed due to high development costs, narrow applications of the technology, and overly ambitious and often unfulfilled claims. This collapse ushered in another winter as investment was withdrawn, and AI research became somewhat unfashionable in academia through to the 1990s.

It is here that our seasonal metaphor somewhat breaks down. Despite the collapse of expert systems, AI research continued to progress at a steady pace throughout the 1990s and early 2000s. However, advances were incremental, public interest was low, and financial investment was limited. Instead, this period is marked by the arrival of the internet and the rise of the information technology sector which enabled advances in computational power, increased availability of data, and the development of new machine learning algorithms that would eventually contribute to modern AI systems design. AI research became increasingly embedded within large technology companies (e.g., Google, Microsoft, Apple, Facebook) and was applied to the development of digital products and services such as search engines, content recommendation, autonomous vehicles and facial and object recognition. As such, AI research shifted from being a primarily academic pursuit intent upon replicating human intelligence to a commercial endeavour and a significant economic resource in the new digital world.

Having previously fallen out of favour in the 1970s, this period also saw the revival of artificial neural networks as the primary focus of AI research. The work of researchers such as Geoffrey Hinton and Yann LeCun demonstrated that artificial neural networks could be highly effective if using powerful modern hardware and if trained on a vast amount of data. After the leisurely pace of AI research in the 2000s, the field gained momentum again in the 2010s with significant developments in artificial neural network research, particularly with the arrival of the generative adversarial network (GAN) architecture (Goodfellow et al. 2014) and transformer architecture (Vaswani et al. 2017). By the mid-2010s, artificial neural networks were driving rapid progress in various domains and were cemented as the core architecture of modern AI systems. On the back of these advances, OpenAI would go on to develop generative pre-trained transformers (GPTs) in the second half of the decade and in 2022 the company would release ChatGPT, ushering in yet another AI summer.

Following ChatGPT, the early 2020s have seen AI research receive unprecedented private and government investment, while speculation and hype around the technology's potential runs rampant. However, there have been increasing warnings that the current boom is just another bubble ready to burst as scepticism grows around high costs, limited practical applications and unfulfilled claims (Floridi 2020; Toosi et al. 2021; Jones and Arnold 2025). As with the Lighthill report and the expert systems boom, the 2020s may very well see AI research collapse into yet another winter.

As of writing, the summer continues. This book, however, is focused on the decade preceding the release of ChatGPT. Roughly beginning with the arrival of GANs in 2014, this was a period of rapid development and experimentation with artificial neural networks and their potential applications across different societal domains. It was a time before the hype when the modern concept of AI, as we now understand it, was only beginning to take form in the public consciousness and when the societal consequences of such technologies were little understood or largely ignored. I define this historical period as an AI spring.

As mentioned, these seasonal metaphors are rather vague and inaccurate for establishing a comprehensive chronology. However, they are useful for denoting the periods of societal change that frame AI development and for highlighting how AI research is not simply an inevitable march of scientific progress. These changing seasons show that AI is deeply tied to material and economic restraints, public discourse and political attitudes and also the configuration of the broader media and communications environment at the time. To define and explore the 2010s and early 2020s as an AI spring is not simply to discuss a period of accelerated scientific experimentation that set the stage for the current AI summer of innovation and investment. Rather, it is to explore a historical, social and cultural milieu from which this technology grew and in which the dominant narratives, ideas and debates of our time originally began to bloom.

Computers scientists and engineers were not the only ones at play in this AI spring. Indeed, many artists were embracing and responding to these technological developments in their creative practice. These artistic activities included the production of AI-generated paintings, poetry and films but also extended to more experimental practices that utilised so-called "deepfake" techniques, biometric recognition, and early large language models in diverse and unique ways. These artists sought to explore the capabilities of such systems and the questions they raised, in particular reflecting on human self-understanding and the changing role of human beings in an automated culture. While many AI technologies are framed as tools to be used by humans, AI art during this period not only made their technological origins clear but seemed to broadcast and revel in their artificial authorship.

As artmaking is a practice that has long been held as the defining feature of humanity, the use of AI systems in cultural production would seem to undermine the uniqueness of human beings. Such practices exemplified the fundamental change in self-understanding that characterises Floridi's fourth revolution. These practices perpetuate, proliferate and critique the "post-Turing idea that we are not Newtonian, stand-alone, and unique agents…rather, we are informational organisms…mutually connected and embedded in an information environment…which we share with other information agents, both natural and artificial" (Floridi 2014, 94). The arrival of apparently artistic AI systems in the 2010s marked a significant moment as it brought these ideas out of research centres, universities and niche artistic communities and into popular culture and everyday life. It was this artistic experimentation during this period that saw a renewed interest in the long-debated concept of the author.

A Media-Philosophical Approach to Authorship

The arrival of AI-generated images, literature, music and poetry would seem to challenge the long-held belief that artistic expression is an intentional and exclusively human activity. They compel us to ask: how can a system devoid of thought, emotion or real-world experience express anything of meaning? Can an artist be intentionally creative when using an autonomous technology they have little to no control over? Are such works original if they derive from training data or simply follow predefined procedures? Though certainly thought-provoking, the questions and challenges raised by AI systems regarding authorship are not entirely new. Indeed, questions around the relevance and definition of authorship, what practices warrant authorship, and the necessity of human beings in artmaking have been asked time and time again. As will be discussed in more detail in chapter 2, AI art would seem to be only the latest development in a long, expansive tradition of artistic experimentation with technology, rules and randomness.

However, AI art and media cannot be considered in isolation as purely forms of artistic expression or creative activities that are detached from the wider world. Rather, these, AI-generated outputs are cultural products that are the result of industrial production processes and that are situated within a broader social and historical environment. Not only does this context define the aesthetic content of these cultural products, it also influences how such products are received by the public and their socio-political function within society. This book's discussion of art and authorship in the AI spring is primarily concerned with the material conditions that frame AI cultural production practices. This includes the technological and industrial processes behind AI systems, the ideological beliefs embedded within such systems, and the socio-political environments from which they emerge and in which they operate.

To properly account for the significance of AI systems within these cultural production practices, the critique presented in this book progresses a uniquely technologically oriented perspective on authorship. I contend that the question of authorship is not a simple matter of assigning a name to a work of art but, rather, a question of the material processes of production, the relationship between humans and technology within such processes, and the effect these products may have on society as a result. This perspective on authorship is rooted in media philosophy.

Grounded in the foundational work of figures such as Walter Benjamin (2008), Marshall McLuhan (1964) and Friedrich Kittler (1999), media philosophy emphasises how the materiality of different media technologies (e.g., cameras, computers, information networks) structure our reality. From a media-philosophical perspective, AI systems are not viewed as tools, extensions or collaborators of human authors. Nor are such systems considered mechanised versions of human authors capable of expression in the same manner. Rather, AI systems are conceptualised as technical apparatuses that are fundamentally different from human beings and whose material configurations shape human perception, experience and understanding. As such, the critical analysis presented in this book is unconcerned with aesthetics and intentions. Instead, it focuses on the technical processes and conditions of AI systems (e.g., computer architecture, training data) asking how they define the production, experience and meaning of the resulting outputs (e.g., artificial portrait).

By foregrounding the technical conditions of AI systems, this theoretical framework situates authorship in material production processes and emphasises the role such technologies play in mediating both the production and reception of cultural products. Primarily, this framework builds upon the media philosophy of Vilém Flusser (2011 & 2012), whose major theories on the *technical image* are recontextualised here in relation to modern AI systems.

While largely unknown outside of Germany and Brazil during his lifetime, in recent decades Flusser has been "re-discovered" in the English-speaking world as one of the most influential media theorists of the twentieth century alongside Benjamin, McLuhan and Kittler.

Born in 1920 to a Jewish family in Prague, Flusser left the country in 1939 to escape persecution during the Nazi occupation and emigrated first to the United Kingdom then Brazil where he settled and soon gained notoriety as a journalist and lecturer in philosophy at the University of São Paulo. Flusser's nomadic life is reflected in his work as he wrote in four different languages (German, Portuguese, English and French) and this wandering also contributed to his relative anonymity. His writings were dispersed among various publications of different languages and his ideas disseminated among disparate academic groups. This dispersion was further exacerbated by his penchant for translating his own works by literally re-writing them in the new language, thus leading to numerous variations on the same text; a habit that takes on new meaning when considered in relation to his philosophy of language, discussed in greater detail in chapter 7.

In the decades following his death in 1991, however, there has been a concerted effort to gather these disparate writings and to ensure they are publicly available through translation and publication. Central to this effort is the Vilém Flusser Archive in Berlin where much of his publications, unpublished manuscripts, personal notes and letters are stored including his personal collection of philosophical texts. The Archive has helped to solidify Flusser's position as an influential thinker and has further ensured that his work continues to influence further academic research, including the ideas discussed in this book.

While his work spans a variety of topics including language, aesthetics, epistemology, immigration and Zen Buddhism, Flusser has been primarily defined as a philosopher of media in the English-speaking world. This is due in part to this dispersion of material and also the fact that his first major work to be published in English, *Towards a Philosophy of Photography* (2012), proved his seminal contribution to media theory. It is Flusser's unique approach to media philosophy and his particular focus on images as the dominant form of contemporary culture that my own work builds upon in relation to AI art and media in the 2010s and early 2020s.

While this book seeks to explore art and authorship during this period, it is not intended as a chronological historical account. Rather, it traces the emergence of certain technologies, cultural practices, socio-political trends and ideologies through the lens of authorship. In each chapter, I critically analyse key examples of AI art and media including artificial portraiture, media installations, film and videogames. However, the cultural impact of AI systems extends far beyond those singular products that have been identified as artistic. Therefore, my analysis also considers more varied and experimental cases of AI-generated media including early examples of deepfakes, personalised media feeds and biometric readouts produced by facial and emotion recognition systems.

The next chapter sets up the media-philosophical framework on authorship that this book pursues and also introduces Flusser's media philosophy. Later chapters then go on to critically analyse different instances of AI art and media, exploring the key ethical issues they raise and how they relate to the modern situation. The key issues explored include: (i) how the unpredictability of AI systems used in artistic production impacts the way viewers consume and critique images, (ii) how the production of AI-generated images of people distorts human identity, (iii) how the unknowable nature of AI systems influences our understanding of political issues and (iv) how the perception of AI as neutral authorities encourages inappropriate use and deference of responsibility.

Ultimately, I identify an uncritical fascination with AI technologies that emerged during the 2010s and early 2020s and that has since swollen into the AI hype we see today. In a few short years, the public discussion on AI authorship has evolved from one of dismissive incredulity to one of existential fantasy. To end this introduction, I will provide a brief outline of the coming chapters.

AI Art and Media in the 2010s and 2020s

Beginning from the traditional definition of the author, chapter 2 surveys key theories and debates around artistic authorship before introducing the media-philosophical perspective to be progressed throughout this book. This technically oriented perspective on authorship is less concerned with questions of human identity and intention. Instead, it emphasises the technical conditions of cultural production, the human-technology relationship and the broader societal impact. This approach primarily builds upon Flusser's media philosophy and so this chapter also introduces his work and significance to the field. Ultimately, chapter 2 lays the theoretical groundwork for the discussions presented in the following chapters.

Building on the theoretical framework presented in chapter 2, chapter 3 explores the role of AI systems in the production of visual art and how their unpredictability shapes the consumption and critique of images. The discussion in this chapter focuses on a particular artistic trend that emerged in the 2010s and that involved the use of AI systems (primarily GANs) to generate visual art. This trend was characterised by experimentation in aesthetics, artistic techniques and authorial agency but was also marked by an uncritical fascination with AI-generated images and little regard for ethical considerations around consent and appropriation. To illustrate and explore this trend, the chapter provides a close analysis of the art installation *Memories of Passersby I* (Klingemann 2018). The chapter argues that the endless generative outputs of AI systems obscure human authorship and transform aesthetic experience from a contemplative appreciation to a continual consumption. While this argument thread is returned to in the final chapter, the interim chapters explore more varied instances of AI art and media that occurred during this period and highlight different ethical issues associated with AI.

Developing on the previous chapter's discussion of how the arrival of AI art and media began to change the way in which people consume images, chapter 4 considers AI-generated representations of human beings specifically. While the AI art trend was ongoing, the 2010s also saw social media platforms come to dominate public discourse such that the world increasingly came to be defined in terms of online media and into this world came deepfakes. Using examples from political, pornographic and film contexts, this chapter argues that such AI-generated images of people confuse and distort that individual's perceived identity, robbing them of authorial agency over their own image. Where chapter 3 highlighted the impact of AI systems in the artworld, chapter 4 expands this discussion to broader cultural trends and demonstrates how the renewed discussion of authorship links to more explicitly ethical and political issues.

Where the previous two chapters focused on the role and impact of AI systems in cultural production, chapter 5 expands the discussion to explore how such technologies dictate the flow of information between authors and readers in online networks. The socio-political context of the 2010s saw an increased spread of disinformation online resulting in political polarisation and disruption, notably influenced by the use of AI systems to moderate, recommend and personalise content for social media users. While ostensibly neutral authorities that function "for us" by recommending personalised content, these systems actually contributed to the post-truth confusion, division and mistrust of the 2010s that has only been exacerbated in the modern day. This chapter argues that personalised newsfeeds are a form of ***weird media*** i.e., a mediation between the known human world and the unknown non-human world of the machine itself. Therefore, AI recommendation systems do not simply dictate flows of information but, rather, they construct coherent but entirely fictitious visions of the world for individual social media users. To fully appreciate how these systems influence the production and distribution of information, particularly in socio-political contexts, this chapter focuses on instances of apparently malfunctioning systems. By no longer functioning "for us", these broken systems reveal the nonsensical and non-human nature of AI authorship.

Chapter 6 elaborates on the notion that AI systems are perceived as neutral and impartial authorities. In particular, this chapter focuses on biometric recognition systems that emerged in the 2010s and that came under increasing scrutiny and criticism for relying on dubious scientific theories and practices. There are numerous instances of human decision-making and responsibility being deferred to such systems and resulting in unethical practices that disproportionately impacted vulnerable groups. While the conscious and unconscious biases of human programmers are of concern, this chapter argues that this deference of responsibility arises, first and foremost, from the ideological belief that AI systems are neutral authorities and the long-established myth that such technologies are thinking machines equivalent to human brains. Using instances of AI art and media that challenged these ideas, this chapter further explores how this notion of the thinking machine invites others to reconsider themselves and others in relation to AI as an authority.

Finally, chapter 7 returns explicitly to the topic of authorship and artistic production presented in chapter 3 and directly links this topic to the previous discussions on perceptions of AI and deference of responsibility. Specifically, this chapter considers examples of large language models and chatbots that emerged before ChatGPT, particularly Google's research activities in this area. Considering the design and use of such systems in relation to Flusser's unique philosophy of language, I argue that these systems only appear to produce coherent communications while adhering to the purely formal language of mathematics. As such, these systems are not bound by the same moral and syntactical rules that human speakers recognise and abide by in cultural communication. To use such systems to communicate is to bypass the process of articulation and to defer responsibility of one's own self-expression to the machine. By deferring the labour of communication to such AI systems, the human as author retreats ever inward and chooses not to participate in dialogue, thus leading to a culture filled only with illusions of self-expression and where there is no evidence of humanity at all.

Finally, the book concludes with a brief reflection on where these trends might lead if we continue to consider AI systems uncritically as something akin to human beings and continue to defer cultural communication to technology. To be enamoured by the spectacle of AI is to indulge in the fantasies and illusions that surround AI, rather than addressing the materiality of these technologies and how they are fundamentally changing the role of humanity within culture.

References

Benjamin, Walter. 2008. *The work of art in the age of mechanical reproduction.* Translated by J.A. Underwood. London: Penguin Group.

Cave, Stephen, Kanta Dihal, and Sarah Dillon. 2020. *AI narratives: A history of imaginative thinking about intelligent machines.* Oxford: Oxford University Press.

Charniak, Eugene. 2024. *AI & I: An intellectual history of artificial intelligence.* Massachusetts: MIT Press.

Criddle, Cristina. 2025. OpenAI secures $300bn valuation after $40bn SoftBank-led funding round. *Financial Times*, March 31.

De Vynck, Gerrit. 2023. 'Game of Thrones' author and others accuse ChatGPT maker of 'theft' in lawsuit. *The Washington Post*, September 20.

Dreyfus, Hubert L. 1965. *Alchemy and artificial intelligence.* Santa Monica: RAND Corporation.

Floridi, Luciano. 2014. *The fourth revolution: How the infosphere is reshaping human reality.* Oxford: Oxford University Press.

Floridi, Luciano. 2020. AI and its new winter: From myths to realities. *Philosophy & Technology* 33: 1–3.

Flusser, Vilém. 2011.*Into the universe of technical images.* Translated by Nancy Ann Roth. Minneapolis: University of Minnesota Press.

Flusser, Vilém. 2012. *Toward a philosophy of photography.* London: Reaktion Books.

Frana, Philip L., and Michael J. Klein. 2021. *Encyclopedia of artificial intelligence: The past, present, and future of AI.* Santa Barbara: ABC-CLIO.

Goodfellow, Ian, Jean Pouget-Abadie, Mehdi Mirza, Xu Bing, David Warde-Farley, Sherjil Ozair, Aaron Courville, and Yoshua Bengio. 2014. Generative adversarial nets. *In Advances in Neural Information Processing Systems*: 2672–2680.

Grant, Aly. 2023. Author uses AI generators, including ChatGPT, to write nearly 100 books in less than a year. *New York Post*, May 22.

Hebb, Donald O. 1949. *The organization of behavior: A neuropsychological theory.* New York: Wiley & Sons.

Hern, Alex. 2022. Typos and shutdowns: Robot 'gives evidence' to lords committee. *Guardian* (October 11).

Horton, Adrian. 2023. 'Embrace it or risk obsolescence': How will AI jobs affect Hollywood. *Guardian* (August 21).

Hymas, Charles. 2025. Kate Bush, Stephen Fry and Thom Yorke demand protection of the arts from AI.*Telegraph* (February 21).

Ida, Masayuki. 2024. *A narrative history of artificial intelligence: The perpetual frontier of information technology.* Singapore: Springer.

Jones, Claire, and Martin Arnold. 2025. IMF and BoE warn AI boom risks "abrupt" stock market correction. *Financial Times.*

Kittler, Friedrich. 1999. *Gramophone, film, typewriter*. Stanford: Stanford University Press.

Lighthill, James. 1973. Artificial intelligence: a general survey. In *Artificial intelligence: A paper symposium*. London: Science Research Council.

McCarthy, John, Marvin Minsky, Nathaniel Rochester and Claude Shannon. 1955. A proposal for the Dartmouth summer research project on artificial intelligence. http://raysolomonoff.com/dartmouth/boxa/dart564props.pdf

McCulloch, Warren S., and Walter Pitts. 1943. A logical calculus of the ideas immanent in nervous activity. *The Bulletin of Mathematical Biophysics* 5: 115–133.

McLuhan, Marshall. 1964. *Understanding media: The extensions of man*. London: Routledge.

Milmo, Dan. 2023. ChatGPT reaches 100 million users two months after launch. *Guardian*.

Morris, Regan. 2025. Emily Blunt among Hollywood stars outraged over 'AI actor' Tilly Norwood. *BBC*, October 1.

Newell, Allen, and Herbert A. Simon. 1956. The logic theory machine—A complex information processing system. *IRE Transactions on Information Theory* 2 (3): 61–79.

Rahmanan, Anna. 2024. The world's first AI art museum is opening in L.A. in 2025. Here's what we know so far. *Time Out*, October 2.

Roush, Ty. 2025. Nvidia becomes first company worth $5 trillion. *Forbes* (October 29).

Shannon, Claude E. 1948. A mathematical theory of communication. *Bell System Technical Journal* 27 (379-423): 623–656.

Toosi, Amirhosein, Andrea G. Bottino, Babak Sboury, Eliot Siegel, and Arman Rahmim. 2021. A brief history of AI: How to prevent another winter (a critical review). *PET Clinics* 16 (4): 449–469.

Turing, Alan. 1950. Computing machinery and intelligence. *Mind* 236: 433–460.

UK Parliament. 2022. Corrected oral evidence: A creative future (communications and digital committee, evidence session no. 3d). House of Lords.

Vaswani, Ashish, Noam Shazeer, Niki Parmar, Jakob Uszkoreit, Llion Jones, Aidan Gomez, Łukasz Kaiser, and Illia Polosukhin. 2017. Attention is all you need. *In Advances in neural information processing systems* 30: 5998–6008.

John, Von Neumann. 1945. *First draft of a report on the EDVAC*. Philadelphia: University of Pennsylvania, Moore School of Electrical Engineering.

Weizenbaum, Joseph. 1972. On the impact of the computer on society. *Science* 176: 609–614.

Wiener, Norbert. 1949. *Cybernetics: Or control and communication in the animal and the machine*. New York: John Wiley & Sons.

CHAPTER 2

An Archaeology of the Author

The figure of the author is a long-debated concept that has been declared dead, re-born and imaginary by many critics and theorists at various points in the last century. However, the recent trend of using AI systems in the production of art and media has once again breathed new life into the debate by emphasising issues around post-human identity, agency in the human–machine relationship, and the role of mathematical rules and structures in cultural production processes. Before considering in more detail cases of AI art and media that emerged as part of this trend, however, the following chapter first probes the central question of authorship. In doing so, it explores the relationship between the author and the work itself, and further considers how this question might be reinterpreted so as to account for both humans and technology as unique and interdependent elements of a production. Thus, this chapter lays the theoretical groundwork for the critical analyses presented in later chapters.

It should be noted that when discussing authorship this book is not restricting the term to writers of literature but rather considers authors more broadly as creators of those products that have been identified as artistic or creative (e.g., literature, visual art, film, theatre, videogames) and further accounts for more diverse and complex notions of media authorship.

To begin, this chapter presents what might be understood as the conventional or popular definition of authorship as human expression

A. McIntyre, *Art and Authorship in the AI Spring*,
https://doi.org/10.1007/978-3-032-18574-7_2

and discusses how this concept is not universal. Rather, this notion is historically rooted in a particular understanding of artistic production that emerged during the Romantic period of the late-eighteenth to mid-nineteenth century and that has since been challenged and complicated in academic theory, criticism, and artistic practice. To better account for the role of technology in artistic production, then, the chapter seeks out a new understanding of authorship that does not over-emphasise the role of human artists as the origin of meaning.

While I do touch upon the post-structuralist ideas of Roland Barthes, Michel Foucault and Jacques Derrida that seek to redefine the author as a function of language and discourse, the chapter instead moves towards Marxist literary theory that situates authorship in material production processes. The reason for this shift being that digital technology and AI are fundamentally changing the nature of these production processes, and thus it is the materiality of these processes that warrant greater academic scrutiny when discussing authorship. Not only does this Marxist theoretical approach offer a more nuanced exploration of the material labour involved in artistic production, it further emphasises the socio-political function that works of art and cultural products play in broader society. As such, the question of authorship moves from being one concerned with identity and intentions to one more focused on materiality, production processes and the societal impact of technology. It is this question of authorship that is probed in later chapters when analysing different cases of AI art and media that emerged in the 2010s and early 2020s.

In exploring this central question of authorship during this period, this book is primarily concerned with the changing relationship between humans and AI systems involved in cultural production. As such, I take a techno-critical perspective that considers AI systems in themselves, rather than conceptualising such technologies as mere tools, extensions or collaborators of human authors. Nor are such systems considered mechanised versions of human authors capable of artistic expression. This perspective on authorship is rooted in media philosophy, and so this chapter provides a brief introduction to the key theories from the field and how they relate to authorship. Particular attention is given to the technically oriented work of Marshall McLuhan and Friedrich Kittler. In searching for a more nuanced approach to this human-AI relationship, however, this book turns to the work of lesser-known media philosopher Vilém Flusser and so the chapter ends with an examination of Flusser's key ideas that will then be applied and expanded upon throughout subsequent chapters.

Humanising the Author

There are many disparate and conflicting conceptions of the role and nature of authorship in academic theory and criticism. However, the conventional definition of the author in the modern day might be understood as an individual human subject that is "designated as autonomous, original and expressive" and so the works they create are seen as expressions of their unique ideas, thoughts and experiences (Bennett 2005, 56). The practice of artmaking, then, is simply a straightforward process by which an individual expresses themselves or communicates an intended idea, and they are seen to be in complete command of this process. By emphasising individual expression and intention, such a definition of authorship would seem to suggest an exclusively human author. As a consequence of this fundamental assumption, any technology used in artmaking would be seen as a mere tool to be wielded by human artists and such tools have no influence over the final work of art, regardless of whether that technology is a simple mechanical device or a complex generative AI system.

However, artmaking and authorship has not always been conceptualised in this way. Indeed, the idea that art is the direct expression of an individual artist is only a relatively recent notion that largely stems from the theory and criticism of the Romantic period, wherein an artist's identity was firmly established as inseparable from the meaning of the work and the work itself was but an extension of the artist (Abrams 1952). Prior to the emergence of Romanticism, however, artmaking was often conceptualised differently as a reflection of nature or of the divine, while the personality and intentions of the human artists themselves were considered irrelevant to the work's meaning (Kris and Kurz 1979). Authorship, as we now understand it, only became a relevant point of discussion when the work itself came to be considered the expression of a distinctly *human* figure rather than the product of anonymous imitation.

The beginning of this transition in thought around authorship and artmaking can be traced back to the literary practices of medieval Europe which saw the emergence of the *auctors* of the Christian Church, what might be seen as the precursor to the modern-day author (Minnis 1988).

As authoritative writers of Latin scripture, auctors held a highly privileged intellectual status, particularly within the Church, in that they were authorised to interpret religious texts and compose their own commentaries rather than simply scribe or copy the texts of others. While the auctors produced their own works and were viewed as influential within the Church, the human individual's personality was considered irrelevant. The composition of the text and its meaning were often attributed to divine inspiration rather than personal expression. In the scholastic tradition, these writers of scripture were akin to conduits through whom the Word of God was transmitted, and their writings represented the truth of the nature of reality as defined by God.

As art historian Alastair Minnis notes, however, between the twelfth and fifteenth centuries "it became fashionable to emphasise the literal sense of the Bible, and the intention of the human auctor was believed to be expressed by the literal sense" such that the focus gradually "shifted from the divine *auctor* to the human *auctor*" (Minnis 1988, 5). No longer a faceless representation of the authority of the Church and of God, the humanised auctor came to more closely resemble an author of the modern day in that their works and the meaning expressed by them became more closely associated with their personality and biography.

This humanisation of writers and artists continued to progress throughout the Renaissance period in Europe with figures such as Dante Alighieri, William Shakespeare and Miguel de Cervantes gaining recognition as individuals of unique creativity and expression. Indeed, later critical works focused almost solely on the personality of artists, notably Giorgio Vasari's foundational art history text *The Lives of the Most Excellent Painters, Sculptors and Architects* (Vasari 2008). This increased emphasis on the artist as an expressive individual during this period largely stemmed from the emergence of humanist thought in Europe that prioritised human individuality and autonomy (Burke 1986). Furthermore, the invention of the Gutenberg printing press in the fifteenth century democratised literature. This enabled the mass production of different kinds of non-religious texts and allowed the spread of new ideas, thus bolstering the significance of those individuals to whom these texts and ideas were attributed. This is, of course, only a brief tracing of these movements. However, this Renaissance focus on the human individual behind works of art greatly intensified with the Romantic period when a general interest in personality transformed from a humanisation of authors to a heroisation of authors (Abrams 1952).

In Romantic period criticism, the real lives of famous artists such as Lord Byron, Percy Bysshe Shelley and Alexander Pushkin were not simply considered biographical fact but, rather, they were mythologised epics often featuring stories of premature deaths, tragic lovers, and child prodigies with a predestination for greatness. In particular, the prevalence of (predominantly male) child prodigies or *wunderkind* during this period was often a construction of Romantic literature itself in that "all the chance events that lead to his discovery, and thus his brilliant ascension, appear in the biographical presentations as inevitable consequences of his genius" (Kris and Kurz 1979, 38). This mythologising of their lives and experiences established Romantic artists as more than simply individuals expressing their ideas but, rather, artistic geniuses. As formalist critic Boris Tomashevsky argues, the author's biography and personality became so significant to the critical reception of their work that "the Romantic poet *was* his own hero. His *life* was poetry, and soon there developed a canonical set of actions to be carried out by the poet" (Tomashevsky 2006, 83).

Tomashevsky, along with other formalist critics at the time, criticised this fixation on personality arguing that "curiosity about unpublished documents and biographical 'findings' mark an unhealthy sharpening of interest in...history that is concerned with mores, personalities, and with the interrelationship between writers and their milieu" rather than literature itself (Ibid., 81). With this sharpening of interest in personality, the Romantic theory of authorship thus assigned the author as the centre of criticism and reduced the work itself to an extension of their personality. This mythologisation of Romantic artists not only established human artists as individuals but as *transcendent* individuals that are fully autonomous in their expression and entirely detached from the influences of external or internal forces.

The turn of the century largely saw the end of the Romantic ideal in literary criticism and theory with the arrival of formalist, structuralist and post-structuralist ideas that questioned the notion that a text is an extension of the human. Experimental artistic movements and practices such as Dadaism also emerged in the early twentieth century seeking to undermine the figure of the author. These theories and movements will be discussed in more detail later in this chapter. However, this acute focus on individual humans as authors and the notion of art as an expression of a transcendent individual has lingered nonetheless, often rearing its head with the arrival of new media technologies.

Preserving the Author

The use of AI systems in artistic production would seem to undermine this Romantic notion of authors and artists as human creators that intentionally construct works of art in order to express something of themselves. However, as philosopher Anthony O'Hear has argued, the complications that technology poses to authorship are part of an old tension in art (O'Hear 1995). Over the past century, new media technologies such as cameras and computers have introduced new artistic practices that are seemingly reliant upon mechanical and often automated processes. Much like today's debates around AI and creativity, these artists grappled with questions of legitimacy and the tension between humans and machines in artmaking.

Early photography was often disregarded as an artistic endeavour because the camera was seen to be doing much of the creative labour. For much of the nineteenth century, photographs were considered technical novelties or documentation rather than works of art (Brown 1971). However, photographer Alfred Stieglitz and the Pictorialist movement at the turn of the century actively pushed for the recognition of photography as fine art and photographers as authors (Mancini 1998). By introducing aesthetic compositions and expressive subject matter, these photographers emphasised their own creative agency in the production process. Later in 1955, Edward Steichen's influential exhibition *The Family of Man* in New York further popularised photography as a legitimate artform (Sandeen 1995).

Similarly to photography, film in the early twentieth century was not commonly viewed as a legitimate form of artistic expression. Instead, film was seen as a technological spectacle or industrial product without a singular author behind the work (Caughie 1981; Sellors 2010). It was not until the 1940s and 1950s that film began to be reframed as a medium of individual expression, largely due to the *auteur* theory advanced by Alexandre Astruc (1948) and the critics of the *Cahier du Cinema* magazine, notably Andre Bazin, Fereydoun Hoveyda and François Truffaut. These critics argued that a select canon of film directors were capable of wielding cameras just as a writer wields a pen such that they may be considered the sole artist or author of a film (*auteur*). Only then did the industrial product of film begin to be reconsidered as an artistic expression of an individual. However, film theorist John Caughie describes the emergence of the ***auteur*** in film theory and criticism as a "step backwards to a romantic conception of the artist...a regressive step precisely at the moment at which romanticism was becoming less secure in other branches of criticism" (Caughie 1981, 11).

Beyond photography and film, the latter half of the twentieth century and early twenty-first century also saw the emergence of various other artistic practices that relied upon electronic media technologies. These include video art (Nam June Paik), electronic music (Pierre Schaeffer, Brian Eno), cybernetic art (Roy Ascott), net art (Olia Lialina, JODI), emergent art (Christa Sommerer, Laurent Mignonneau), bioart (Eduardo Kac), and cyborg art (StelArc, Neil Harbisson), among many other diverse practices. Particularly relevant to this book's discussion are those early instances of generative and algorithmic art that utilised computer systems. In the 1960s and 1970s, early pioneers such as Frieder Nake, Vera Molnár and Harold Cohen began experimenting with mainframes, plotters and algorithmic programmes to generate aesthetic images. For example, Nake and Molnár used early computer graphics plotters to produce intricate algorithmic and rule-based drawings automatically, while Cohen later went further with his painting bot AARON which was capable of autonomously producing entire drawings and paintings independently. For a more in-depth discussion of the historical development of these practices and the authorial challenges, see Shanken (2009), Taylor (2014) and Nake (1971).

Much like earlier critiques of photography and film, these various practices all shared similar challenges to their legitimacy and the practitioners were frequently dismissed as something more akin to engineers or technicians rather than "true" artists. Many early critics believed the technology itself was doing most of the creative labour and so the final works that emerged could not be said to be the intentional expression of an individual artist. However, it is this very tension between the human and machine that many of these artists explicitly sought to explore in their work.

By demonstrating that human creativity could be augmented, extended, replicated and even bypassed by electromechanical processes, these artists intentionally probed and complicated the Romantic notion of authorship. Some embraced this human–machine tension in their work to question and undermine the centrality and necessity of human authorship. Others maintained the relevance of the human artist but sought to expand the traditional definition of authorship to account for more diverse creative contributions (e.g., curation, conception, coding). Many of these practices have prompted discussions of redefining authorship in relation to mechanical processes (Harley 1995; Wortzel 1996; Grodal et al. 2004; Gray and Johnson 2013; Norton 2015; van der Weel 2015), as well as the emergence of terms such as *second-order authorship* (Seaman 1998) or *distributed authorship* (Ascott 1990).

The arrival of AI art in the 2010s once again reinvigorated the debate around authorship, revisiting many of these earlier questions and ideas (Hertzmann 2018; McCormack et al. 2019; Goodfellow 2024; Floridi 2025). However, many practitioners and theorists working in the field of creative AI expressed stances that would seem to echo the Romantic theory of authorship. While some initially dismissed AI art as a mere novelty or gimmick because there can be no "true" art without a transcendent human origin, others have argued that such artworks should be considered the expression of the original human programmer.

Notably, computer scientist and AI artist Ahmed Elgammal has argued that creative AI constitutes a nascent form of Conceptual Art and that AI systems will eventually join the camera, pen and paintbrush as just another tool for human artists to wield in order to express themselves (Elgammal 2019). In time, Elgammal argues, AI art may follow a similar part to photography and AI artists such as himself will be recognised as the authors behind these works. However, by reconsidering AI art as a form of Conceptual Art, such a view continues to frame artmaking as a means of individual expression and forefronts the thoughts and intentions of the human programmer behind the work. In doing so, art is conceptualised as a strictly human activity and the material activities of the machine itself are somewhat ignored.

In opposition to Elgammal, many of those AI artists that pioneered the creative applications of AI systems in the 2010s such as Mike Tyka and Blaise Agüera y Arcas have argued that the human brain is no different to a computer and so creativity and artistic expression can be programmed (Miller 2019). Meanwhile, philosopher Arthur Miller has gone further to propose several indicators of creativity and artistic genius that characterise what he describes as "special" people who have displayed inherent creative capabilities in the arts and sciences listing Pablo Picasso, Steve Jobs, Wolfgang Amadeus Mozart, and Albert Einstein as examples (Ibid.). In examining various examples of AI art, Miller concludes that AI systems already display many of these hallmarks of creativity and will soon achieve all of them through apparently inevitable scientific breakthroughs.

While these theories of machine authorship would seem to go against the anthropocentrism of the Romantic perspective, this view maintains that for technologies to be accounted for in authorship at all they must become or be conceptualised as indistinguishable from human beings. Indeed, this view would actually seem to push the anthropocentrism of the Romantic ideal even further to claim that through science humans have now become so knowledgeable as to wholly replicate their own intellect and creative capabilities in the form of computer programmes. This notion of machine authorship, therefore, remains reliant upon a Romantic consideration of the human and artistic production.

While this lingering presence of the Romantic theory continues to perpetuate in modern discourse and in our conventional understanding of the author mentioned at the beginning of this section, the Romantic author has been undermined and criticised in academia and artistic practice over the past century.

Questioning the Author

The questions and challenges that AI art of the 2010s presents for authorship are not exactly new. Indeed, various artistic practices, movements and traditions over the past century have challenged authorship in similar ways and long before the emergence of computers or automated technologies.

Beginning in the wake of World War I, the Dadaist intellectual movement emerged in Europe and saw artists embracing randomness and absurdism as a means of undermining conventional, capitalist values (Hopkins 2016). Key to this movement was the rejection of the idea of artists as solitary creative geniuses and many Dadaist artists sought to demonstrate how artistic production and what constituted art itself was arbitrary. For example, artists such as Hannah Höch and Kurt Schwitters created collages and assemblages using found images and pre-existing materials to confuse and satirise the idea of creative originality. Meanwhile, Marcel Duchamp pushed this idea further with his *readymades*, ordinary manufactured objects that were simply recontextualised as art. For Duchamp and other Dadaists, if anything could be defined as an original artwork simply because the artist declared it as such, the very idea of art as the unique expression of an individual was misguided.

While Dadaism influenced later generations of artists, other concurrent and subsequent movements further experimented with authorship and the nature of artistic production in diverse ways (Foster et al. 2016).

In the 1920s and 1930s, Surrealists like André Breton and Max Ernst sought to relinquish conscious control over the creative process through automatic writing and drawing techniques, allowing the unconscious to guide their work. Post-World War II, Abstract Expressionists such as Jackson Pollock further embraced spontaneity in artmaking by emphasising bodily gestures and process rather than controlled composition and intentional expression. Similarly, the Beat writers of the 1950s and 1960s focused on improvisation and process through techniques such as William S. Burroughs' "cut-up" poetry which recombined fragments of existing texts to create new meaning. Later, Conceptual Art of the 1960s and 1970s further challenged authorial agency. For example, Sol LeWitt delegated the production of his wall drawings to others, while appropriation artists like Sherrie Levine and Elaine Sturtevant represented the works of other artists as explicit reappropriations to question originality (Irvin 2005).

While the above movements experimented with spontaneity, appropriation and conception, the Oulipo (*Ouvroir de littérature potentielle*) collective that emerged in the 1960s formalised creativity by imposing rigid mathematical and linguistic constraints upon themselves such as the exclusive use of palindromes or the exclusion of specific letters. For Oulipian writers such as Raymond Queneau, Georges Perec and Italo Calvino, creativity was a "cybernetic interaction of humans and mechanised processes" in which artists deferred creative labour to predetermined rules and procedures (Wolff 2007, 116).

There are, of course, many other movements and traditions not mentioned above that also experimented with rules, randomness and authorial agency in different ways (e.g., Fluxus, Situationalist International). It is also important to note that these movements offered their own unique and nuanced critiques and conceptualisations of authorship that cannot be fully explored here.

Beyond artistic experimentation, academic theory and criticism also began challenging the Romantic idea of individual authorship during the last century. Particularly formalist literary critics of the 1910s and 1920s, such as Tomashevsky, began to question the idea that a work of art was merely an extension of the human, asking: "do we need the poet's biography in order to understand his work, or do we not?" (Tomashevsky 2006, 81–82).

Concerned that the heroisation of artists displayed in Romantic theory had rendered literary criticism an arbitrary discussion of personality, the overlapping schools of formalism and New Criticism emerged in the early twentieth century and were intent upon establishing a rigorous text-based methodology. Notable figures in this movement included John Crowe Ransom, Cleanth Brooks, Alexander Bain, L.C. Knight, and John Kerrigan (Bennett 2005). The theoretical approach of the New Critics maintained that the structure and the meaning of a text cannot be separated. Rather than focusing on historical, linguistic, or biographical discussions around literature, they sought to define the aesthetic or characteristic values of literature itself (Ransom 1937). Key to the New Critic's approach was the rigid exclusion of numerous concerns that they argued were superfluous to criticism including reader response, historical and cultural context, morality, and the linguistic roots of words. Furthermore, the author's biography and intentions for the work were also to be excluded, a position most famously championed by W.K. Wimsatt and Monroe C. Beardsley in their essay "The Intentional Fallacy".

Discussing the criticism of poetry, Wimsatt and Beardsley asserted that while a poem is certainly the intentional product of a human artist, the interpretation of the work's meaning is not to be rooted in this intention or in the biography of the author stating:

> The poem is not the critic's own and not the author's (it is detached from the author at birth and goes around the world beyond his power to intend about it or control it). The poem belongs to the public. It is embodied in language, the peculiar possession of the public, and it is about the human being, an object of public knowledge. (Wimsatt and Beardsley 1946)

The New Critics' position sparked an ongoing debate around the relevance or irrelevance of intentionality in authorship studies. Theorists such as E.D. Hirsch, William Irwin and Paisley Livingston argued in opposition that authorial intent remains a significant aspect of the work's meaning (Burke 2006; Livingston 2005 and 2011; Sellors 2010). Meanwhile, others sought to expand authorship to account for more diverse creative contributions and collaboration in artmaking while maintaining intentionality (Gaut 1997; Masten 1997; Sellors 2007; Stillinger 1991).

Though the formalists and New Critics emphasised the importance of personal interpretation and sought to ignore the author in criticism, they did not deny that the human individual dictated the artistic process. However, this anti-intentionalist approach to criticism would later influence the post-structuralist theories of Roland Barthes, Michel Foucault and Jacques Derrida. These theorists challenged this fundamental definition of the author and deconstructed the author's significance by flipping the Romantic ideal on its head to instead argue that the author is an extension of the text and of language itself.

Deconstructing the Author

In what is perhaps his most famous essay, "The Death of the Author", literary theorist and philosopher Roland Barthes argued that a text does not behave as a pipeline of communication carrying "a single 'theological' meaning (the 'message' of the Author-God)" (Barthes 1987, 146). Instead, the text exists as a "multi-dimensional space in which a variety of writings, none of them original, blend and clash…a tissue of quotations drawn from the innumerable centres of culture" (Ibid.).

For Barthes, language is not simply an instrument to be wielded by the human artist and that is used to fulfil their intentions. Rather, Barthes' understanding of language builds upon the semiotics of Ferdinand de Saussure who conceptualised language as a system of signs and the meaning of these signs was established through the collective agreement of members of a linguistic community (de Saussure 1997). Following this, Barthes conceives of the act of writing as simply the arrangement of pre-existing linguistic signs such that a text expresses nothing of the writer's own identity or intentions. As Barthes states: "the inner 'thing' he thinks to 'translate' is itself only a ready-formed dictionary, its words only explainable through other words" (Barthes 1987, 146). Writing is not, then, an expression of an individual but "the destruction of every voice, of every point of origin" and the only meaning to be found in a text is that which the individual reader personally interprets from the signs themselves (Ibid., 142). Barthes' semiotic approach is not simply limited to writing and literature but further extends to other forms of artmaking, arguing that images, cinematic language, fashion styles and media more broadly convey socially determined meanings that are unintended by the artist (Barthes 1981, 2009).

For Barthes, then, the Romantic or conventional concept of the author is comparable to a tyrannical figure or an *author-god* that only stands to limit the interpretation of the work. This author-god is, however, an imaginary concept and thus Barthes seeks to abandon the author entirely and to close the book on authorship with a final statement: "the birth of the reader must be at the cost of the death of the Author" (Barthes 1987, 148).

Since its publication in 1967, "The Death of the Author" has since become a seminal text in literary studies and has been discussed, debated, criticised, and satirised by scholars in a variety of fields including also by Foucault and Derrida. In the context of this book's discussion on authorship and AI, Barthes' position challenges the human-centric perspective of Romantic authorship that would seem to exclude AI systems. By emphasising the reader and language as the source of meaning and dismissing authorial intention, both human and AI art are seen as infinitely interpretable and equally meaningful because they are equally authorless. However, in doing so Barthes downplays the material complexities involved in the production of a work of art and so the identity of the creator is deemed irrelevant.

Rather than following Barthes in dismissing the role of the author outright, philosopher Michel Foucault instead proposed the concept of an *author-function* that exists within a text and behaves as a means of classification in that the name of an author "can group together a certain number of texts, define them, differentiate them from and contrast them to others" and further "establishes different forms of relationships among texts" (Foucault 2000, 210). For Foucault, an author's name is "more than a gesture, a finger pointed at someone; it is, to a certain extent, the equivalent of a description" (Ibid. 209).

For example, to speak of Karl Marx is to use a phrase that does not simply refer to the philosopher himself but, rather, behaves as a description or marker of various ideas. To use the name "Karl Marx" is to not only invoke an established set of texts ascribed to this name (e.g., *Das Kapital*, *The German Ideology*, *The Communist Manifesto*) but further texts that relate to it, such as the works of later philosophers Louis Althusser (e.g., *For Marx*, *Reading Capital*) and Slavoj Žižek (e.g., *The Sublime Object of Ideology*). As such, the author-function of "Karl Marx" operates as a unifying point of reference that structures the ideas of different discourses to which these various texts contribute (e.g., Marxism, Communism, Socialism).

Foucault's concept presents a radical approach in that the identity, biography, and intentions of a named author are entirely irrelevant to the interpretation of the meaning of the work. Rather, the author-function is "characteristic of the mode of the existence, circulation, and functioning of certain discourses within a society" (Ibid., 211). Therefore, while Foucault still accounts for the author, it is not conceived of as a transcendental human subject expressing their ideas and experiences through art. Instead, the human author is a function of discourses that are already defined and the author's name simply "serves to characterize a certain mode of being of discourse" (Ibid.).

Similarly to Barthes, the author-function would seem to overlook the material production process behind works of art and the role of both human and non-human agents within this process. For example, an AI system such as ChatGPT could be named as the author of a text but the name "ChatGPT" does not represent anything of the machine itself any more than "Karl Marx" represents anything of the man. As the author is understood as an aspect of language and the human or non-human identity of the creator is deemed irrelevant, Foucault's author-function would seem to lead our discussion on authorship and AI to another dead end.

While largely agreeing with Barthes and Foucault that a work cannot be understood as the expression of an author's intention, Derrida proposes a more complex relationship between the human and language. For Derrida, there exists an exteriority of writing such that the writer "writes *in* a language and *in* a logic whose proper system, laws, and life his discourse by definition cannot dominate absolutely" (Derrida 1997, 158). The writer does not wield language like an instrument or tool but rather interacts with it as a complex system of signs, "he uses them only by letting himself, after a fashion and up to a point, be governed by the system" (Ibid.). As such, the writer's intentions are never fully aligned with the meaning of the work itself as the language of the text itself will always say "more, less, or something other than what he *would* mean" (Ibid., 157).

However, Derrida does not entirely eliminate the concepts of authorial identity and intention instead they are dispersed within the text and exist as a part of the interplay of signs. For Derrida, the subject is never fully present but always an extension or supplement of language itself and so without language there is no subject. As such, "there has never been anything but writing; there have never been anything but supplements" (Ibid., 158–159). In reading a text, then, the reader attempts to reconstruct the relationship between the human subject and language and this act of reading produces a "speaking" subject within the text that is irreducible and inseparable from the text itself. The author produced by the reader is not imaginary like Barthes' author-god or Foucault's author-function but is real in the sense that it emerges from the network of signs; as Derrida argues, "*there is nothing outside of the text* [there is no outside-text; *il n'y a pas de hors texte*]" (Ibid., 157).

In this way, Derrida's ideas might open the door to a conception of AI authorship, where the speaking subject is established within or as an extension of the text itself and is unrelated to any specific human or non-human origin. As a consequence, human and AI art may be equated while authorship is maintained.

These post-structuralist ideas of authorship are not without their critics. Notably, while some feminist literary critics such as Peggy Kamuf and Hélène Cixous view the author as an inherently patriarchal concept and support the dismissal of authorship, others have highlighted the problematic ramifications of dismissing authorial identity (Bennett 2005). Theorists such as Nancy K. Miller, Sandra Gilbert and Susan Gubar have argued that the death of the author only serves to further exclude female artists, along with other artists from underrepresented groups and communities, from the literary canon (Warhol and Herndl 1997). Meanwhile, in the context of filmmaking Sandy Flitterman-Lewis goes further to argue that it is, in fact, necessary to identify male filmmakers as the source of degrading film practices and aesthetic styles that continually portray women as sexual objects, what Laura Mulvey terms the *male gaze* (Flitterman-Lewis 1981). For a fuller critique of Barthes, Foucault and Derrida see Burke (2008).

Not only do these post-structuralist theories de-emphasise the importance of authorial identity by deconstructing the author as an origin of meaning, they overlook the material conditions of artistic production and the labour of those human and non-human agents involved. By focusing on language and discourse, these theories neglect the complex realities surrounding artistic production processes including economic, social and technological factors.

As the emergence of generative AI systems is primarily challenging and complicating our current understanding of the role of human labour specifically in artmaking, it is necessary to move towards a theory of authorship that more thoroughly accounts for the material reality of artistic production. However, we cannot return to any conception of authorship that prioritises the human individual above all else, as in the Romantic theory of authorship. Instead, we may begin from Marxist theories of cultural production that situate authorship in material production and wherein the human artist is understood as a grounded material subject whose activities are moulded by the social, economic and technological forces at play in their environment. This materialist approach offers a more appropriate theoretical framework from which to progress our discussion on the authorship of AI art and media.

Materialising the Author

For literary theorists such as Pierre Macherey (2006), Adolfo Sánchez Vázquez (1977) and Janet Wolff (1993) who have advanced and developed the Marxist approach to literary scholarship, material labour is taken as the basis of all human activity. As such, artmaking is not understood as a unique means of personal expression but rather it is, first and foremost, a material labour that is akin to any other manufacturing process and the work of art itself is a cultural product; the term "art" is simply employed as a means of classifying similar cultural products. This focus on material labour stands in opposition to the approaches taken by Barthes, Foucault and Derrida who maintain the primacy of language in constituting the human subject. As Wolff explains:

> Although it is true that language, representation and ideology play an active part in constituting subjects and fashioning cultural products, they are themselves the product of past practices. Their operation as relatively autonomous systems should not blind us either to their own original constitution in extra-discursive processes, or to their constant susceptibility to intrusion of material and economic forces as transformative influences. (Wolff 1993, 139)

Therefore, rather than focusing criticism on the linguistic qualities of a work (e.g., textual interpretation, authorial intent), Marxist literary theory instead considers the material processes by which a work is created. In this approach, the author still plays an important role within artistic production. However, not as an individual expressing themselves nor as an extension of language but as a material agent existing within a living social context, acting within and interacting with established material, economic and ideological structures.

In the context of literature specifically, Macherey has elaborated on this artistic production process and the human artist's role within it. Influenced by Marxist philosopher Louis Althusser, Macherey argued that the labour of writing is an interaction between the human and existing structures; not only linguistic structures but also those ideological, historical, and material structures that shape or constrain the writer's actions. Interacting with these structures is a complex process of both construction and improvisation that is continually redefined at every step. For Macherey, writing is an arduous and inexact labour such that "the work does not derive from the unity of an intention which permeates it, nor its conformity to an autonomous model" (Macherey 2006, 46). The final work that emerges from this interaction is never finished or fully coherent and so cannot be understood as the spontaneous and intended product of an individual; it is "merely the provisional version of an unfulfilled intention" (Ibid., 21). Macherey argues that theory must account for the writing process, not as an isolated activity, but as a material labour that is situated within the writer's broader social context and is thus influenced by the historical and ideological conditions in which they exist.

Artworks, then, cannot be isolated from their context and, instead, exist as cultural products that "contain and express meanings beyond the intended and conscious meanings of their authors" (Wolff 1993, 119). Therefore, Marxist literary theory and criticism is less concerned with what is apparently expressed in the content of a work of art and, instead, insists that theory should focus on the material conditions of its production. This includes, but is not limited to, technological methods, industrial practices, political systems, economic class structures, and ideological or cultural hegemonies. Authorship, then, is not a consideration of human individuals but rather it is situated within these material conditions.

For Marxist critic and media theorist Walter Benjamin, however, it is not enough to simply ask how a work of art stands "in relation *to* the relationships of production of a period" but, rather, it is necessary to ask "how does it stand *in* them?" (Benjamin 1970, 85). In asking this question, Benjamin extends criticism beyond the material conditions of production towards an exploration of the distinct role or function of art within a capitalist society. In doing so, he highlights how technological reproducibility has altered the function of art in society and how this change in function reshapes our understanding of authorship.

For Benjamin, works of art previously fulfilled a unique mystical or cult function in society in that they were often restricted to places of power (e.g., churches, palaces, galleries) away from public view, thus emphasising traditional religious hierarchies and class structures. However, with the arrival of media technologies, particularly photography and film, works of art could be easily reproduced and made readily available to the public. Stripped of their unique mystical aura, the technologically reproduced work of art no longer fulfilled a cult function but, rather, became a form of mass media with a political and economic function (Benjamin 2008). This democratisation of artistic production through media technologies could be used to mobilise the public and challenge existing hierarchies. However, it could also be used for ideological dominance and political manipulation.

With art's new function, the author is not simply a labourer working in isolation and creating works of art. Instead, the author is a producer operating within social structures and whose cultural products serve a particular socio-political function. As Benjamin argues "the current social situation forces the poet to choose whom his activity will serve…he works in the interests of a particular class" (Benjamin 1970, 83). As such, the question of authorship becomes the question of cultural production and not only entails an analysis of the technical means by which art is produced but further considers the influence that these production practices have on art's reception and function in society.

It is this framing of authorship that this book seeks to explore in relation to AI art and media of the 2010s and early 2020s. However, I am primarily concerned with how AI systems are changing cultural production and thus impacting society. Therefore, it is necessary to critically analyse AI as a media technology in itself and to understand how it defines the production, experience and function of art and media in society. Though Benjamin's theoretical work emphasised the cultural and political implications of media technologies, later media philosophers such as Marshall McLuhan and Friedrich Kittler provide a more appropriate framework for analysing AI art and media. These theorists emphasise media as technological systems that actively shape human perception and communication. The rest of this chapter provides an overview of these technically oriented theories and how they relate to authorship before then introducing the unique media philosophy of Vilém Flusser.

Technologising the Author

A good place to begin this discussion on technically oriented media philosophy is with the thinkers of the Toronto School in the mid-twentieth century. Theorists Harold Innis (2007), Eric Havelock (1963 & 1986) and Marshall McLuhan (1962, 1964) developed upon Benjamin's earlier work to argue that media technologies used within a society have a profound influence over the psychological experience and social organisation of its citizens. For these theorists, then, communication was not seen as the simple process of transferring information from sender to receiver but, rather, the medium itself presents a condition of shared experience. To study the true influence of media technologies, then, it is necessary to prioritise the *form* of media rather than the *content*. The Toronto School's theoretical approach thus came to be defined by McLuhan's mantra: "the medium is the message".

McLuhan's concept of media is not restricted to traditional forms (e.g., print, radio, film) but rather encompasses any technology that extends human senses, perception or cognition and thus offers human beings "the power to translate experience into new forms" (McLuhan 1964, 63). As a notable example, McLuhan points to the light bulb arguing that this simple technology enabled social gatherings and environments to arise where and when it was previously impractical to do so. While McLuhan conceptualises media technologies as extensions of human perception and cognition, this media environment in turn programmes us as well, as "it is the medium that shapes and controls the scale and form of human association and action" (Ibid. 9).

According to McLuhan, one of the most significant developments in media technology was the invention of the Gutenberg printing press in the fifteenth century which mechanised the written word and fundamentally altered the experience of reading. As previously discussed, the arrival of the printing press during the Renaissance period enabled the mass production of texts, elevated the role of authors, and further facilitated the spread of humanist thought. However, McLuhan goes further by arguing that the technological configuration of the printing press itself directly shaped patterns of thought and intellectual development. As McLuhan states:

> Typography bears much resemblance to cinema, just as the reading of print puts the reader in the role of the movie projector. The reader moves the

> series of imprinted letters before him at a speed consistent with apprehending the motions of the author's mind. The reader of print, that is, stands in an utterly different relation to the writer from the reader of manuscript. Print gradually made reading aloud pointless, and accelerated the act of reading till the reader could feel "in the hands of" his author...- such a character does not belong to the manuscript. (McLuhan 1962, 124–125)

The invention and distribution of typed text rather than handwritten script not only altered the experience of reading for individuals and enabled the spread of ideas, but the printing press technology further shaped human cognition and thus altered society through the "ingraining of lineal, sequential habits" (Ibid., 125).

For McLuhan, then, the human author or artist behind a work of art still plays an important role in its production. However, the technical configuration of the medium (e.g., printed text, film, photography) has a more profound influence on the meaning and reception of the work. Furthermore, different media environments encourage different forms of authorship. As McLuhan argues, the emergence of "print created individualism and nationalism in the sixteenth century" and further encouraged individual modes of authorship (McLuhan 1964, 21). Whereas, the media environment of twentieth century that was dominated by film, television and radio encouraged collective, participatory and distributed modes of authorship.

In contrast to McLuhan and the Toronto School's focus on the sociological conditions and impact of media, philosopher and media theorist Friedrich Kittler instead argues that media should be understood primarily in terms of the material distribution, channelling and computation of data.

Drawing on the information theory of Claude Shannon, Kittler envisions media technologies, first and foremost, as methods by which data is produced, stored, selected, and transferred between points. While certainly older media such as stone tablets and papyrus scrolls are modes of transmission and storage, Kittler argues that the emergence of technical media at the turn of the twentieth century (e.g., gramophone, film, typewriter) optimised information processing through the use of mechanised mathematical processes that operate faster and more efficiently than humans. This optimisation of information processing reached its peak, however, with the invention of the computer that Kittler describes as the "universal medium of computation" in that it is capable of producing, storing, selecting, and transmitting numerical data without human intervention (Kittler 1997, 125).

As the ideal calculating machine, "inside the computers themselves everything becomes a number: quantity without image, sound or voice" (Kittler 1999, 1). As such, those images, sounds and voices produced by computers are superfluous to information processing and are little more than concessions on the part of the machine as humans cannot perceive or process raw numerical data at the same pace. As Kittler argues, "sound and image, voice and text are reduced to surface effects, known to consumers as interface. Sense and senses turn into eyewash" (Ibid.). Those patterns of information processing that were once solely conducted by humans and were mistaken for inherently human qualities have been transplanted and optimised by machines. Therefore, media technologies cannot be said to be extensions of humanity in the way that McLuhan contends. Instead, Kittler argues that media technologies function as replacements, taking over the role of information processors such that the human will eventually be, or perhaps already has been, abandoned to history.

For Kittler, then, works of art are simply another method of storing and processing information that has been superseded by technical processes over which humans have little agency. In the production of modern culture, then, notions of human authorship and artistic expression become irrelevant as "all questions concerning thought as thought have been abandoned, for it is now a matter of implementation and hardware" (Ibid., 33). Indeed, Kittler further claims that the very concept of human authorship itself is a product of media technology.

Kittler argues for a media-technological view in which human knowledge is determined by what he terms the *discourse network* dominating a particular historical period, defined as "the network of technologies and institutes that allow a given culture to select, store and process relevant data" (Kittler 1990, 390). Framed as a discourse network, culture is equated to a large-scale information processor the outputs of which (i.e., human knowledge) are shaped by its technical configuration. This configuration includes the modes of data input, transmission, and output. Culture is not inherently linked to human significance and, in fact, the concepts of human exceptionalism, individualism, and authorship as the root of cultural production only emerged from the discourse network of the nineteenth century.

Specifically, Kittler points to pedagogical practices that emphasised and promoted the widespread uptake of handwriting techniques as the origin of the individual humanist subject, stating that "words and letters no longer need to make the difficult journey through others in order to be transmitted...no coincidence that the philosophical phantasms of self-consciousness and the literary phantasm of authorship emerged in the same epoch around 1800" (Kittler 2015, 25). The dominance of individual handwriting in the discourse network of 1800 "introduced into literary discourses an art of speaking to oneself, the author-function. From then on, literature meant a text whose title-page had to be adorned with a name" (Ibid., 21). Once the transmission of myths concerning the deeds of heroes and events of note, literature thus became the expression of an individual.

Circling back to the conventional definition of the author introduced at the beginning of this chapter, McLuhan and Kittler argue that this concept did not simply arise from the philosophical discourses of the Renaissance and Romantic periods. Instead, the author emerged as a result of the technical environment. The rise of the Romantic ideal and the notion of art as the expression of a transcendent individual was driven by the development of media technologies. The very concept of authorship is technically determined.

The media-technological approach pursued by McLuhan and Kittler has sought to refocus scholarship in the humanities on close-readings of media technologies and technological systems themselves, rather than on their content. This shift has, in turn, influenced materialist theories in media philosophy and inspired the field of media archaeology advanced by theorists such as Jussi Parikka (2012), Siegfried Zielinski (2006), Wolfgang Ernst (2016a, 2016b), Timothy Barker (2012, 2018), Sybille Krämer (2015), and Bernhard Siegert (2015) amongst others. Media archaeology maintains Kittler's fascination with the specific material configuration of media technologies and seeks to understand how these configurations impact human knowledge, discourse and experience. As Parikka explains, media archaeology asks: "what are the conditions of existence of this thing, of that statement, of these discourses and the multiple media(ted) practices with which we live? Such questions are political, aesthetic, economic, technological, scientific and more" (Parikka 2012, 18).

While this book does not pursue a strict media archaeological study of AI art and media, it is important to note the influence of these theorists and fields of thought. My own approach to critically analysing AI art and media does not solely focus on the material configurations of these technologies. Instead, it focuses on the relationship and material interactions between humans and AI systems involved in cultural production. This approach seeks to avoid the technological determinism present in McLuhan and Kittler by emphasising human agency within cultural production. However, I maintain that human agency is not something that dominates or dictates the production process, but something that is always situated in relation to non-human agencies that frame and influence our actions. Thus, cultural production is envisioned as a complex interaction between humans and media technologies.

Central to this approach is Flusser's media philosophy which echoes Kittler's materialist focus but further discusses human agency through an existential perspective; a middle-ground between McLuhan, Kittler and Benjamin. In the final section of this chapter, I will provide an introduction to Flusser's key ideas that will then be elaborated upon in subsequent chapters.

Flusser's Universe

Flusser's unique theoretical approach lies somewhere between Benjamin, McLuhan and Kittler. While all of these thinkers agree that the form of media technologies shape human social practices, perceptions and consciousness, they differ drastically on the role and relevance of the human within processes of cultural production and thus spell different consequences for authorship. Furthermore, unlike these other theorists, Flusser is not concerned with establishing a rigid system of knowledge through distinctly defined terms, relations, and concepts and in his writing style and approach to media philosophy he often flouts academic conventions such as the use of referencing systems or bibliographies. Rather Flusser's style is intentionally lucid and evocative, insisting that the affect of philosophy is its information. That being said, Flusser does introduce and explore a lexicon of specific terms throughout his works which will be introduced in this section and elaborated on in later chapters.

Key to Flusser's unique media-philosophical approach is his existentialist conception of information. While deriving concepts and terms from Shannon similarly to Kittler, Flusser conceives of the production, transmission and storage of information as a fundamentally unnatural or artificial process. Recalling the second law of thermodynamics that defines the statistical property of *entropy* as the measure of a system's level of disorder, Flusser argues that there is an "impassive tendency of nature to move toward more probable conditions, toward masses, toward ashes (toward 'heat death')" and this entropic tendency means the sum total of information declines (Flusser 2002, 6). Those habitual practices that humans and animals conduct simply for survival (e.g., feeding, sleeping, reproducing) abide by this tendency in that they result in situations that are probable (e.g., metabolic reactions, cellular repair, offspring) and thus do not increase information. When viewed objectively as simply the exchange of quantitative information, communication is a similarly entropic process. When viewed qualitatively from a human perspective, however, communication may be understood as a *negentropic* ("negatively entropic") process that works against this tendency by resulting in improbable situations (e.g., art, technology, tradition) and thus increasing the sum total of information.

To illustrate this distinction, Flusser presents the following example:

> A lecturer may be considered a natural communication in this way: A system (the public present) is changed by another system (the lecturer). The lecturer is a "sender" (he emits sound waves), the public is a "receiver" (it receives the waves), and the air in the room is a "medium" (it transmits the waves). Now, this is a thermodynamic process, and part of the energy invested in it is degraded into heat. The sum total of information in the room diminishes as the lecture goes on. But the lecturer is a "sender" (he emits words), the public is a "receiver" (it receives the words), and the language is a "medium" (it transmits the words). Seen thus, the lecture is not a thermodynamic process, but is of a different order. The sum total of information in the room increases as the lecturer goes on, if seen thus.(Ibid., 9)

In the above example, the words of the lecturer can only be considered meaningful and thus informative when observed intersubjectively by humans participating within the culture, such that "the negentropic tendency of cultural communication (of the 'human spirit') is not a phenomenon to be objectively verified" (Ibid.). Cultural production is, thus, an unnatural or artificial process in that it enables the storage and increase of information beyond materiality.

Flusser relates this negentropic tendency of communication to an act of *in-forming* in which disordered matter is shaped or organised into a particular form that is meaningful to humans. As an example, Flusser offers the case of a carpenter shaping wood, stating: "I see the wood in the form of a table...but I know that this state is transitory (it will be burnt and decompose into amorphous ash). But the table-form is eternal, since I can imagine it anywhere and at any time (see it in mind's theoretical eye)" (Flusser 1999, 24). In contrast to Kittler, then, culture cannot be conceptualised as simply a means of information processing that can be separated from humanity. Rather, culture is an intersubjective exchange of information between humans that understand one another and thus is an attempt to deny nature. Therefore, the human cannot be fully replaced in cultural production processes, but they are also always situated in relation to non-human agencies (*apparatuses*) as "the negentropic tendency of cultural communication is the result of codes that can be quantified" (Flusser 2002, 9).

In his most widely referenced work in the English-speaking world, *Towards a Philosophy of Photography,* Flusser introduces the term *apparatus* to describe automated machines such as cameras, along with many of the other major concepts that have come to defined his unique media philosophy. This conception of the apparatus can be traced back to the critical theory of the Frankfurt School, notably in the work of Max Horkheimer and Theodor Adorno (van der Meulen 2010). For Flusser, however, the apparatus is not simply an automated means of cultural production to be used but rather a complex mechanism that is always already prepared and the outputs it produces are always already accounted for, pointing to the etymological roots of the word apparatus as a verb meaning "to prepare" (Flusser 2012, 21). Though the significance of photography in Flusser's philosophy will be elaborated on in more detail momentarily, consider the case of a photographer using a camera as an illustrative example. While the photographer points the lens and clicks the shutter, the camera itself is an automated mechanism that produces photographs according to pre-programmed criteria defined by its technical properties and limitations. As such, every possible photograph that could be produced by the camera is already accounted for within its pre-programmed criteria; what Flusser refers to as the apparatus' *program*. As such, "the apparatus does as the photographer desires, but the photographer can only desire what the apparatus can do" (Flusser

2011, 20). Rather than the photographer intentionally using the apparatus to produce an image they desire, they are observed to "play" a combination game to realise an outcome already determined by the program.

It is here that Flusser marks a clear distinction from the other media philosophers discussed in this chapter. While Benjamin views media technologies as political tools to be used by humans for either liberation or oppression and McLuhan views such technologies as extensions of humanity, Flusser maintains that the potential uses of these technologies are pre-defined and the human is an operator or functionary of technology. Such a concept recalls Kittler but Flusser does not adopt the same technologically deterministic approach or dismiss humans from cultural production as Kittler does. Instead, Flusser maintains the relevance of the human subject in the interactions between humans and apparatuses, arguing that the human is necessary in order to realise the nearly infinite possibilities accounted for within the apparatus. For example, a camera left to photograph the same scene repeatedly will produce probable, informationally redundant and therefore entropic images. It is the role of the human functionary to exhaust the camera's possibilities by photographing new, improbable scenes and thereby producing, storing and transferring non-redundant information in the form of original photographs.

Such negentropic activities have been carried out previously by artists in the contribution to human cultural and communication but the rise of technical apparatuses, such as cameras and computers, has enabled the production of greater quantities of information with greater efficiency. As Flusser comments:

> Since a human being stretched out his hand to confront the lifeworld, to make it pause, he has been trying to imprint information on his surroundings. His answer to "heat death" and to death *per se* is to "inform". And apparatuses, among other things, arose from this, his search for eternal life. They are meant to produce, store, and distribute information. (Ibid., 18)

The production of information through the use of technical apparatuses differs from previous modes of cultural production, however, in that "all apparatuses (not just computers) are calculating machines and in this sense 'artificial intelligences', the camera included, even if their inventors are not able to account for this" (Flusser 2012, 31). As apparatuses operate according to scientific and mathematical rules, their outputs such as photographs cannot be rightly equated to traditional cultural objects produced by human beings. This distinction leads to another defining concept of Flusser's media theory in the ***technical image*** and the effect of media on consciousness.

Flusser identifies three types of image that have dominated human society at one point or another through history: traditional or prehistorical images (e.g., cave paintings, portraits), texts or historical images (e.g., poetry, literature), and technical or post-historical images (e.g., photographs, computer images) (Flusser 2002). Where traditional images and technical images appear as direct representations of phenomena observed in reality, they are fundamentally different because there are different levels of abstraction at play:

> Ontologically, traditional images are abstractions of the first order insofar as they abstract from the concrete world while technical images are abstractions of the third order: They abstract from texts which abstract from traditional images which themselves abstract from the concrete world. (Flusser 2012, 14)

To elaborate, technical images are images produced through automated processes. They are not products of humans interpreting and representing the world around them but, rather, the products of scientific texts (i.e., mathematical equations, calculations and models). Therefore, while "prehistoric images are worldviews (copies of the environment)", technical images are "computed possibilities (models, projections onto the environment" (Flusser 2002, 129).

While Benjamin and Flusser agree on the fundamental difference between traditional and technical images, Flusser contends that the magical aura and cult value of art objects has not disappeared (van der Meulen 2010). Rather, this magical aura has simply taken on a new form as while "prehistoric magic is a ritualization of models known as 'myths'; current magic is a ritualization of models known as 'programs'" (Flusser 2012, 17). With this ritualisation of programs comes a diminished understanding of media technologies as users engage with these technologies passively rather than critically. Rather than being understood as visualisations of scientific texts (e.g., mathematical symbols, equations, calculations), technical images ***appear*** as direct representations of reality.

As such, technical images are often misunderstood as objective representations of reality and the concepts they communicate are passively accepted as truth.

For Flusser, media define our situation and understanding of the world but, in particular different, these different forms of images presuppose different forms of temporal consciousness. Where traditional images encourage a cyclical way of thinking in which time is static, texts encourage a causal way of thinking in which time moves ever forward along a string of events. Technical images, however, encourage "programmatic and systems-analytical thought and behaviour" (Flusser 2002, 117) in which events are not perceived as causally determined. Rather, events and situations emerge from pure chance and probability such that "the attitude of the posthistorical being is one of a calculated game of chance" (Ibid., 119). However, where historical causality emphasised the agency of humans in determined future events, in the post-historical plane of possibilities "the game becomes independent of man; it follows its own rules determined by chance…thus transforming humans into game pieces, into numbers, and into functionaries" (Ibid., 123). Similarly, tom McLuhan's focus on the printing press, Flusser argues that the invention of photography marked a turning in human history, ushering in technical images as the dominant visual form and profoundly reshaping human consciousness.

Writing in the 1980s, Flusser was equally fearful and hopeful for the approach of this post-historical consciousness as two possible futures present themselves: "one moves towards a centrally programmed, totalitarian society of image receives and image administrators, the other toward a dialogic, telematic society of image producers and image collectors" (Flusser 2011, 4). We can already see this tension between the democratic and totalitarian society playing out. While media technologies have enabled widespread information exchange, they have also enabled mass surveillance and manipulation through disinformation. In this continual struggle, AI-generated media presents a powerful weapon for either side.

Which of these speculative futures may be realised is dependent upon the understanding and decoding of technical images. However, "any criticism of technical images must be aimed at an elucidation of its innerworkings. As long as there is no way of engaging in such criticism of technical images, we shall remain illiterate" and risk slipping towards a fascistic programmed society (Flusser 2012, 16).

Through this framework, this book examines the question of authorship with regard to AI art and media. Looking beyond the aesthetics of such images and the magical illusions of AI systems, this critical analysis considers the materiality of such production processes. In doing so, I seek to better understand the reality of the encoding process and to further explore the social, cultural and political implications for the modern day.

References

Abrams, M. H. 1952. *The mirror and the lamp: Romantic theory and the critical tradition*. Oxford: Oxford University Press.

Astruc, Alexandre. 1948. The birth of a new avant-garde: la caméra-stylo. *L'Écran Français* 144.

Ascott, Roy. 1990. Is there love in the telematic embrace? *Art Journal* 49 (3): 241–247.

Barker, Timothy. 2012. *Time and the digital: Connecting technology, aesthetics, and a process philosophy of time*. Hanover: University of New England Press.

Barker, Timothy. 2018. *Against transmission: Media philosophy and the engineering of time*. London: Bloomsbury.

Barthes, Roland. 1981. *Camera lucida: Reflections on photography*, trans. Richard Howard. New York: Hill and Wang.

Barthes, Roland. 1987. *Image music text*, trans. Stephen Heath. London: Fontana Press.

Barthes, Roland. 2009. *Mythologies,* trans. Annette Lavers and Siân Reynolds. London: Vintage.

Benjamin, Walter. 1970. The author as producer. *New Left Review* 62: 83–96.

Benjamin, Walter. 2008. *The work of art in the age of mechanical reproduction*, trans. J.A. Underwood. London: Penguin Group.

Bennett, Andrew. 2005. *The author*. Abingdon: Routledge.

Brown, Milton. 1971. The history of photography as art history. *Art Journal* 31 (1): 31–32, 36.

Burke, Peter. 1986. *The Italian renaissance: Culture and society in Italy*. Cambridge: Polity Press.

Burke, Seán. 2006. *Authorship: From Plato to the postmodern: A reader*. Edinburgh: Edinburgh University Press.

Burke, Seán. 2008. *The death and return of the author: Criticism and subjectivity in Barthes, Foucault and Derrida*. Edinburgh: Edinburgh University Press.

Caughie, John. 1981. *Theories of authorship: A reader*. London: Routledge.

De Saussure, Ferdinand. 1997. *Course in general linguistics,* trans. Roy Harris. Chicago: Open Court Publishing Company.

Derrida, Jacques. 1997. *Of grammatology*, trans. Gayatari Chakravorty Spivak. Baltimore: The Johns Hopkins.

Elgammal, Ahmed. 2019. AI is blurring the definition of artist: Advanced algorithms are using machine learning to create art autonomously. *American Scientist* 107: 1.

Ernst, Wolfgang. 2016a. *Chronopoetics: The temporal being and operativity of technological media*, trans. Anthony Enns. London: Rowman & Littlefield.

Ernst, Wolfgang. 2016b. *Sonic time machines; explicit sound, sirenic voices, and implicit sonicity*. Amsterdam: Amsterdam University Press.

Flitterman-Lewis, Sandy. 1981. Women, desire and the look: Feminism and the enunciative apparatus in cinema. In *Theories of authorship: A reader*, ed. John Caughie, 242–250. London: Routledge.

Floridi, Luciano. 2025. Distant writing: Literary production in the age of artificial intelligence. *Minds and Machines* 35 (3): 1–26.

Flusser, Vilém. 1999. *The shape of things: A philosophy of design*. London: Reaktion Books.

Flusser, Vilém. 2002. *Writings*. Edited by Andreas Ströhl. Trans. Erik Eisel. London: University of Minnesota Press.

Flusser, Vilém. 2011. *Into the universe of technical images*, trans. Nancy Ann Roth. Minneapolis: University of Minnesota Press.

Flusser, Vilém. 2012. *Towards a philosophy of photography*. London: Reaktion Books.

Foster, Hal, Rosalind Kraus, Yve-Alain Bois, B.H.D. Buchloh, and David Joselit. 2016. *Art since 1900: modernism, antimodernism, postmodernism*. New York: Thames & Hudson.

Foucault, Michel. 2000. What is an author? In *Aesthetics, method, and epistemology*, ed. James D. Faubion, 205–222. London: Penguin.

Gaut, Berys. 1997. Film authorship and collaboration. In *Film theory and philosophy*, ed. Richard Allen and Murray Smith, 149–172. Oxford: Oxford University Press.

Goodfellow, Paul. 2024. The distributed authorship of art in the age of AI. *Arts* 13 (5): 149.

Gray, Jonathan, and Derek Johnson. 2013. *A companion to media authorship*. Oxford: Wiley-Blackwell.

Grodal, Torben, Bente Larsen, and Iben Thorving Laursen. 2004. *Visual authorship: Creativity and intentionality in media*. Copenhagen: Museum Tusculanum Press.

Harley, James. 1995. Generative processes in algorithmic composition: Chaos and music. *Leonardo* 28 (3): 221–224.

Havelock, Eric. 1963. *A preface to Plato*. Oxford: Basil Blackwell & Mott.

Havelock, Eric. 1986. *The muse learns to write: Reflections on orality and literacy from antiquity to the present*. New Haven: Yale University Press.

Hertzmann, Aaron. 2018. Can computers create art? *Arts* 7 (18): 1–25.

Hopkins, David. 2016. *A companion to Dada and Surrealism*. Chichester: John Wiley & Sons.

Innis, Harold. 2007. *Empire and communication*. Toronot: Dundurn Press.

Irvin, Sherri. 2005. Appropriation and authorship in contemporary art. *British Journal of Aesthetics* 45 (2): 123–137.

Kittler, Friedrich. 1990. *Discourse networks 1800/190,*. Trans. Michael Metteer. Stanford: Stanford University Press.

Kittler, Friedrich. 1997. *Literature, media, information systems: Essays*. Edited by John Johnston. Amsterdam: Overseas Publishers Association.

Kittler, Friedrich. 1999. *Gramophone, Film, Typewriter*. Stanford: Stanford University Press.

Kittler, Friedrich. 2015. Authorship and love. *Theory, Culture & Society* 32 (3): 15–47.

Krämer, Sybille. 2015. *Medium, messenger, transmission: An approach to media philosophy*. Transl. Anthony Enns. Amsterdam: Amsterdam University Press.

Kris, Ernst, and Otto Kurz. 1979. *Legend, myth, and magic in the image of the artist: A historical experiment*. London: Yale University Press.

Livingston, Paisley. 2005. *Art and intention: A philosophical study*. Oxford: Oxford University Press.

Livingston, Paisley. 2011. On authorship and collaboration. *The Journal of Aesthetics and Art Criticism* 69 (2): 221–224.

Macherey, Pierre. 2006. *A theory of literary production*. Abingdon: Routledge.

Mancini, J. M. 1998. The safeness of standing alone: Alfred Stieglitz, camera work, and the organizational roots of the American avant-garde. *Canadian Review of American Studies* 28 (2): 37–79.

Masten, Jeffrey. 1997. *Textual intercourse: Collaboration, authorship and sexualities in renaissance drama*. Cambridge: Cambridge University Press.

McCormack, Jon, Toby Gifford and Patrick Hutchings. 2019. Autonomy, authenticity, authorship and intention in computer generated art. In *Computational Intelligence in Music, Sound, Art and Design. EvoMUSART 2019*: 11453.

McLuhan, Marshall. 1962. *The Gutenberg galaxy: The making of typographic man*. London: Routledge & Kegan Paul.

McLuhan, Marshall. 1964. *Understanding media: The extensions of man*. London: Routledge.

Miller, Arthur. 2019. *The artist in the machine: The world of AI-powered creativity*. London: MIT Press.

Minnis, Alastair. 1988. *Medieval theory of authorship: Scholastic literary attitudes in the later middle ages*. Philadelphia: University of Pennsylvania Press.

Nake, Frieder. 1971. There should be no computer art. *Bulletin of the Computer Arts Society*: 18–19.

Norton, D. A. 2015. A DJ in the library. *Leonardo* 48 (2): 194–195.
O'Hear, Anthony. 1995. Art and technology: An old tension. *Philosophy and Technology* 38: 143–158.
Parikka, Jussi. 2012. *What is media archaeology?* Cambridge: Polity Press.
Ransom, John Crowe. 1937. Criticism, inc. *The Virginia Quarterly Review* 13 (4): 586–706.
Sandeen, Eric. 1995. *Picturing an exhibition: The Family of Man in 1950s America*. Albuquerque: University of New Mexico Press.
Seaman, Bill. 1998. Emergent constructions: Re-embodied intelligence within recombinant poetic networks. *Digital Creativity* 9 (3): 153–160.
Sellors, C. Paul. 2007. Collective authorship in film. *The Journal of Aesthetics and Art Criticism* 65 (3): 263–271.
Sellors, C. Paul. 2010. *Film authorship: Auteurs and other myths*. London: Wallflower Press.
Shanken, Edward. 2009. *Art and electronic media: Themes and movements*. London: Phaidon Press.
Siegert, Bernhard. 2015. *Cultural techniques: grids, filters, doors, and other articulations of the real*, Trans. Geoffrey Winthrop-Young. New York: Fordham University Press.
Stillinger, Jack. 1991. *Multiple authorship and the myth of solitary genius*. Oxford: Oxford University Press.
Taylor, Grant D. 2014. *When the machine made art: The troubled history of computer art*. New York: Bloomsbury Academic.
Tomashevsky, Boris. 2006. Literature and biography. In *Authorship: From Plato to the postmodern: A reader*, ed. Seán. Burke, 81–89. Edinburgh: Edinburgh University Press.
Van der Meulen, Sjoukje. 2010. Between Benjamin and McLuhan: Vilém Flusser's media theory. *New German Critique* 110: 180–207.
Van der Weel, Adriaan. 2015. Appropriation: towards a sociotechnical history of authorship. *Authorship* 4.2.
Vasari, Giorgio. 2008. *The lives of the most excellent paints, sculptors, and architects*, Trans. Julia Conaway Bondanella and Peter Bondanella. Oxford: Oxford University Press.
Vázquez, Adolfo Sánchez. 1977. *The philosophy of praxis*, Trans. Mike Gonzalez. London: Merlin Press.
Warhol, Robyn, and Diane Herndl. 1997. *Feminisms: An anthology of literary theory and criticism*. Basingstoke: Macmillan.
Wimsatt, W. K., and Monroe C. Beardsley. 1946. The intentional fallacy. *The Sewanee Review* 54 (3): 468–488.
Wolff, Janet. 1993. *The social production of art*. London: Macmillan Press.
Wolff, Mark. 2007. Rules of the Oulipian game: Authorship and posthuman literature. *Contemporary French and Francophone Studies* 11 (1): 111–118.

Wortzel, Adrianne. 1996. Cyborgesian tenets and indeterminate endings: The decline and disappearance of destiny for authors. *Leonardo* 29 (5): 354–372.

Zielinski, Siegfried. 2006. *Deep time of the media: toward an archaeology of hearing and seeing by technical means,* Trans. Gloria Custance. Cambridge, Massachusetts: MIT Press.

CHAPTER 3

The Infinite Portrait

In October 2018, Christie's gallery in London made headlines as the first auction house in history to exhibit and sell a piece of art attributed to an AI system; the *Portrait d'Edmond de Belamy* produced by Paris-based art collective Obvious. Though noticeably blurry and lacking fine detail, the portrait of a young man in a black suit (seemingly the eponymous Edmond de Belamy) appeared to emulate the subject matter and stylistic conventions of nineteenth-century portraiture, even browning the paper to suggest natural decay over time. However, the aesthetic qualities of the portrait itself were of less interest to the bidders than the artificial origins, highlighted by the mathematical signature in the lower right-hand corner of the image:

$$\min_{G} \max_{D} \mathbb{E}_x\left[\log D(x)\right] + \mathbb{E}_z\left[\log(1 - D(G(z)))\right]$$

Selling for $432,500 (far above the estimated price) the highly publicised sale marked the beginning of AI art's transition from a niche practice performed, studied and discussed by only a few (e.g., computer scientists, art critics, media theorists) to a mainstream artform and a matter of public discourse. By demonstrating how such AI systems were capable of generating images that are near indistinguishable from human art, the *Portrait d'Edmond de Belamy* sparked anew the debate around the possibility of AI authorship and publicly raised questions around the significance or insignificance of human artists within cultural production (Jones 2018).

A. McIntyre, *Art and Authorship in the AI Spring*,
https://doi.org/10.1007/978-3-032-18574-7_3

Conversations that continue to this today and that have only become more hotly debated with the widespread emergence of generative AI.

Despite the media attention afforded to it, however, the *Portrait d'Edmond de Belamy* was by no means the first of its kind nor were the questions it raised regarding authorship and the primacy of human agency entirely novel. As discussed in previous chapters, there is a long history of artistic experimentation with rules and agency, from the readymades of Dadaism to the mathematical writing of the Oulipo, as well as earlier AI technologies such as Harold Cohen's painting bot AARON. Indeed, the portrait is only one notorious example of a specific artistic trend that began in the 2010s and that saw artists utilising emerging artificial neural network technologies to generate creative images.

While the history of artificial neural network theory and development extends back to the 1940s with the research of Warren McCulloch and Walter Pitts, the creative use of these technologies might be traced back to the computer vision programme DeepDream created by Google engineer Alexander Mordvintsev in 2015. Originally conceived as a tool to visualise what neural networks were "seeing", DeepDream could analyse a given image, identify certain patterns it had been trained to recognise, and then enhance or overemphasise them leading to a surreal, dreamlike aesthetic. Seeing creative potential in DeepDream, fellow Google engineers Mike Tyka and Blaise Agüera y Arcas formed the Artists and Machine Intelligence (AMI) group in Seattle with the focus of linking up artists and engineers to experiment further with creating art through machine learning, thereby seeking to legitimise AI as a medium in contemporary art. The arrival of DeepDream and the AMI group sparked a new wave of AI art with numerous AI artists experimenting with artificial neural networks to generate different aesthetic styles and forms throughout the 2010s.

While modern text-to-image generators such as DALL-E 2 use diffusion models, the most popular system in this new wave of AI art was the generative adversarial network (GAN) originally introduced by Ian Goodfellow in 2014 (Goodfellow et al. 2014). GAN architecture was used to create the *Portrait d'Edmond de Belamy* along with many other diverse instances of AI art in the 2010s. These include the surreal photorealistic faces of Tyka's *Portraits of Imaginary People* (2017), the artistic re-interpretations of objects in Memo Akten's *Learning to See* (2017), the malformed portraits of Mario Klingemann's *Neural Glitch* (2018), and the abstract pieces produced by Ahmed Elgammal's unique AICAN system. The popularity of GAN-generated art during this period significantly contributed to the widespread adoption and advancement of artificial neural networks for artistic and creative applications.

As with the *Portrait d'Edmond de Belamy*, many of these AI artists claimed to be using GANs in their practice as a means of challenging traditional notions of authorial agency and to experiment with the question of machine creativity, while further exploring the nuance of what does or does not constitute art. However, media theorist Joanna Zylinska contends that this emphasis on machine creativity and aesthetic experimentation was misguided, and that the central question driving these artistic pursuits (i.e., can computers be creative?) is reductive. In their fascination with machine creativity and AI aesthetics, Zylinska argues that many of these AI artists "seem unwilling, and unable, to pursue any of the more serious questions" concerning the political, ethical and existential implications of AI art and authorship (Zylinska 2020, 82).

As Zylinska argues, many of those AI artists using GANs in their practice during the 2010s embraced the technology with a "worryingly uncritical instrumentalism, where seemingly child-like curiosity is underpinned by the progressivist mode of technological expansion towards some kind of improvement—of accuracy, data sets and, ultimately, art as we know it" (Ibid., 82). As a result of this technological fascination, "much of what passes for AI-driven art, especially of the industry-sponsored variety, remains quite superficial, even if visually captivating" (Ibid., 49). While experimenting with machine creativity, these AI artists seem to have been enamoured with the production of visual art that is aesthetically similar to the work of previous human artists. Not only in the production of AI visual art that overtly replicated the distinctive visual styles of individual artists (e.g., Rembrandt, Vincent van Gogh) but also in those ostensibly original pieces that adhere to the broader conventions of established traditions (e.g., landscapes, portraiture).

Even those AI artworks that display entirely unique visual forms and compositions nonetheless echo human traditions and practices (e.g., surrealism, abstract art) and are somewhat limited to those forms and compositions that humans deem aesthetically pleasurable. In this trend, then, creativity was seemingly reduced to a repetition of the same. It is a process in which the artists are seen to play or experiment with the AI system's near-infinite possibilities only to mesmerise viewers with an endless stream of Rembrandts, van Goghs, Bacons and so on spewing forth from the machine. Rather than challenging or critiquing the politics or ethics behind such technologies, these works seek to dazzle and bewilder viewers with technological capability and capacity. Drawing comparisons to an addictive mobile video game, Zylinska argues that this trend is "premised on the banality of looking, with perception understood as visual consumption and art reduced to mild bemusement" such that AI systems and AI art are received uncritically as a form of entertainment (Ibid., 81).

However, it should be noted that this assessment certainly does not extend to all instances of AI art and Zylinska does not explicitly criticise those specific AI artists named above. Rather this is to highlight a general attitude towards AI art in the 2010s and throughout this book we will discuss other examples of AI art that go beyond this aesthetic play to critique the technology itself and its societal implications.

In opposition to Zylinska's assessment, AI artists such as Ahmed Elgammal have argued that these early AI artworks should be categorised as a form of Conceptual Art. Rather than focus on the originality and aesthetics of these GAN-generated images, Elgammal argues that the AI system itself is the artwork, stating "the art is not in the outcome or final image, the art is in the process" (Elgammal 2018). In discussing his own artistic practice with AICAN, Elgammal argues that the production of AI art is focused on "developing a *machine* process and *machine* creativity, not merely aping and trying to pass as human-made. Our work is focused on understanding the process of creativity such that a means can be found to model that process to generate a creative result" (Mazzone and Elgammal 2019, 5).

Categorising AI art as a form of process-driven Conceptual Art in this way would seem to counter the accusation that these works are merely visual entertainment and aesthetic play. However, this position continues to approach creativity and artmaking as an isolated abstract process that occurs within the AI system, rather than a material production process embedded within and influenced by a broader social and historical context. In doing so, this position similarly eschews important questions around the politics and ethics of AI systems and AI art, particularly those questions regarding the appropriation of human-made artworks for training these systems.

In order to produce the *Portrait d'Edmond de Belamy*, for example, the GAN system was trained on a curated database of roughly fifteen thousand historical portraits and yet the original human artists behind these portraits have not been credited. Elgammal compares this appropriation of historical artworks to the situation of human artists learning to paint by replicating the work of Old Masters. However, Zylinska and others argue that this practice constitutes an exploitation of previous human labour for the purposes of automation (Zylinska 2020). This question of creative exploitation in the production of AI art has only become more pressing with the arrival of modern image generators such as DALL-E that have been trained on a vast amount of human-made art scraped from the internet, including copyrighted works created by contemporary artists but used without their permission and with no recognition of their essential contribution.

By conceptualising an AI system as a tool to be used or as a piece of Conceptual Art in itself, these AI artists of the 2010s would seem to assign authorship of these works solely to the individual human. In doing so, they misrepresent the material reality of the technical image-making process and thus obscure those critical questions regarding the ethics of such artistic production practices, as well as their impact upon society. Rather than be enamoured with questions of machine creativity, Zylinska calls for a new post-humanist art history of AI in which art is understood to have been produced by "human artists *in an assembly with a plethora of nonhuman agents*" and that overcomes the superficial obsession with AI aesthetics, seeking instead "to understand how humans can operate within the constraints of the apparatus that is part of us" (Ibid., 54).

Following Zylinska's call, this chapter pursues a technologically oriented critical analysis of Mario Klingemann's *Memories of Passersby I* (2018), a digital art installation featuring a continuous stream of GAN-generated images. This particular example has been chosen as it highlights the creative allure of AI that seemed to prompt such an uncritical fascination during this period in that these technologies are seemingly capable of producing an infinite number of original images.

Developing upon and recontextualising Flusser's approach to the human-machine relationship discussed in the previous chapter, this chapter's critical analysis neither seeks to aestheticize GAN-generated images nor does it seek to dismiss these images entirely as something peripheral to the original idea as in Conceptual Art. Looking past the dazzling spectacle of these aesthetic playthings, these technical images are instead recognised as the mathematical outputs of an unpredictable technological production process. Through this critical analysis, this chapter explores the notion of authorship in AI art and the potential implications of using these apparently infinitely creative technologies in cultural production.

Memories of Passersby I

The installation itself, shown in Fig. 3.1, consists of a wooden cabinet housing the computational hardware that is connected to two wall-mounted screens displaying digital portraits. These portraits (one male and one female) are generated through the use of a GAN system trained to emulate the styles of seventeenth- to nineteenth-century portraiture. Unlike the static *Portrait d'Edmond de Belamy*, however, the faces of these non-existent subjects constantly change with a continuous and almost fluidic motion as the system, using the previous image as a reference, repeatedly creates new images to replace the old every instant. Over time, the figure on-screen might morph into a grotesque caricature, sprout a second head or third eye, or their facial features might very well deteriorate entirely into a formless blur before being resurrected again as an entirely different person. This process cannot be described as entirely random or entirely predetermined and, as no one image or sequence is stored or repeated, there is no fixed or finalised piece. There is only an ever-changing stream of surreal, dreamlike faces that the system will endlessly generate from the moment it is switched on until it is finally switched off.

Mario Klingemann, the artist behind *Memories of Passersby I*, has openly expressed a more traditional perspective on AI authorship that would seem to echo the Romantic concept of authorship. Similarly to Elgammal and other AI artists during this period, Klingemann explicitly compared the GAN system to a writer's keyboard, a musician's piano and a painter's brush in that it is simply another component of the overall installation devised by and, therefore, authored by Klingemann alone:

> For me AI is just one tool in a long history of tools that was bound to be used for artistic purposes. But I would say I use AI as a tool and the works that I make with this tool are mine and not a collaboration, in the same way I would not call a hammer or a piano a "collaborator" (Dean 2019).

However, to describe the GAN system as simply a complex tool used to fulfil a predetermined intention misrepresents the material reality of artistic production.

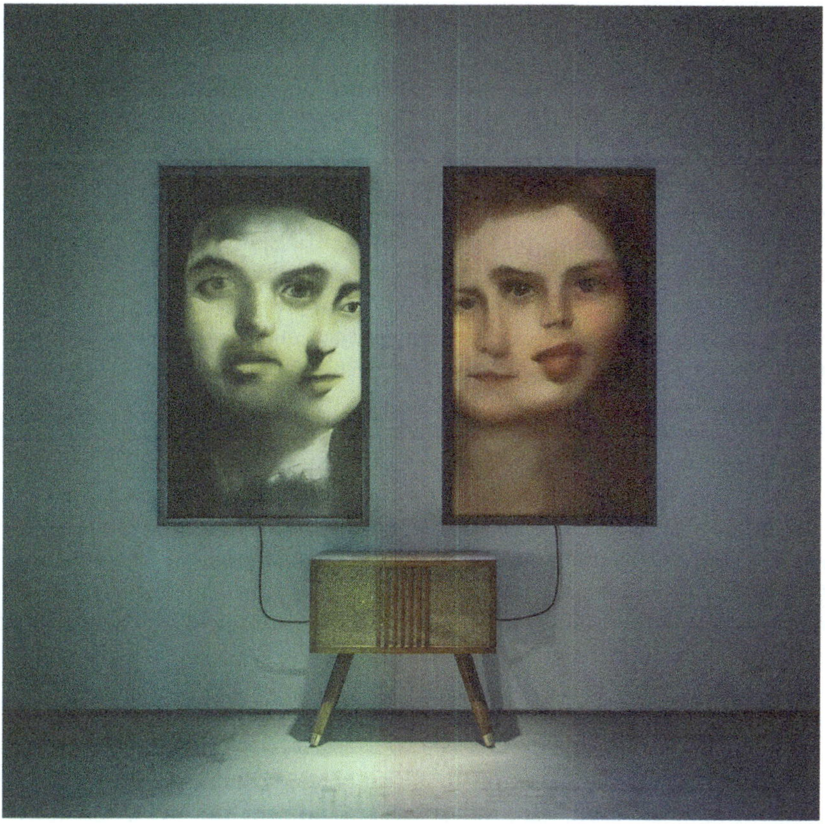

Fig. 3.1 AI art installation *Memories of Passersby I* (companion version) on display at SOLO Independencia, Madrid. Courtesy of Mario Klingemann and Onkaos

Though certainly Klingemann devised the overall installation itself and curated the dataset of images upon which the GAN was trained, the ephemeral imagery of *Memories of Passersby I* cannot be said to communicate the artist's intended ideas. Rather, the technical images appearing, morphing and disappearing on the screens are visualisations of the mathematical equations governing the processes of the GAN system. To elaborate on this argument, it is necessary to go beyond the aesthetics of the installation to consider the GAN system in itself and to analyse its role within the production process.

Put simply, a GAN (see diagram in Fig. 3.2) consists of two artificial neural networks: a ***generator*** and a ***discriminator*** (Creswell et al. 2018). The generator produces synthetic data (e.g., a synthetic image) to submit to the discriminator which, in turn, compares the synthetic data to the authentic data (e.g., a database of authentic images). This process has been likened to an art critic (the discriminator) judging the work of an art forger (the generator). However, as the two continue to compete against one another, each improves in their function over time. The generator learns to produce synthetic images that more closely resemble the authentic ones, while the discriminator becomes better at distinguishing between synthetic and authentic images. Crucially, however, the generator has no direct access to the authentic database. Instead, it creates synthetic images from a random data input and relies solely on feedback from the discriminator to determine whether these synthetic images are accurate or inaccurate imitations. As this random data input is initially formless, one might think of this image production process as the GAN "interpreting" or "moulding" this random data input into a form it can process. In this way, the synthetic images may be understood as merely visualisations of numerical data akin to graphs, charts and tables.

Were *Memories of Passersby I* paused at different intervals and the static image scrutinised, it becomes clear that these digital portraits are not surfaces of transforming forms but a series of individual visualisations of numerical data continually being created, destroyed and replaced every instant. As each iteration is used to inform the next, the differences between these synthetic images may appear minimal and thus give the illusion of transformation. However, every image is truly a unique visualisation of new numerical data.

As the transforming portraits of *Memories of Passersby I* arise from random noise data, these images are representative of nothing that exists in material reality. The forms that appear to the human eye cannot be said to communicate anything intended by Klingemann but are rather meaningless data "fitted" into a meaningful mould that is shaped by the GAN itself. As media theorist Alexander Galloway argues, however, data visualisation is never a simple or direct translation of numerical data to image. Rather, visualisation necessitates certain conversion rules such that "any data visualization is first and foremost a visualization of the conversion rules themselves, and only secondarily a visualization of raw data"

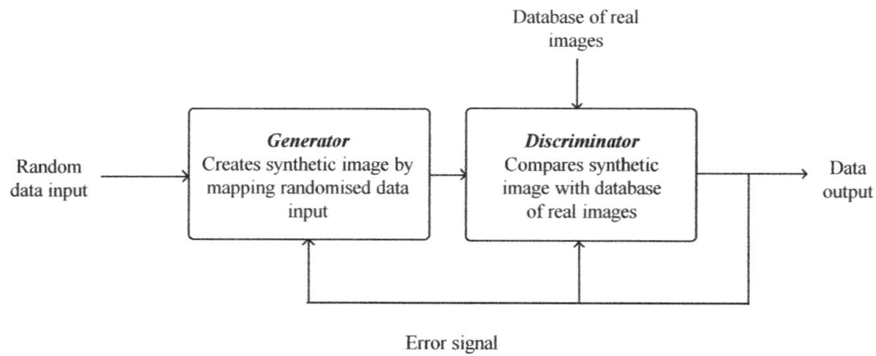

Fig. 3.2 Approximation of generative adversarial network (GAN) architecture

(Galloway 2011, 88). The writhing forms of *Memories of Passersby I* are, therefore, primarily visualisations of the GAN system itself; its governing mathematical equations and the possibilities accounted for within them i.e., those recurring patterns identified within the historical images of its training dataset.

While certainly the equations and training data of the GAN were selected and written by Klingemann, it is not necessarily true to say that the artist has dictated the production process or wielded the AI system as a tool to express an intended idea. Such systems are chaotic, and thus their outputs are indeterminable.

Chaotic Images

When discussing a rule-based system whose behaviour is governed by a set of deterministic mathematical equations, it would seem logical to conclude that the behaviour of such a system is entirely predictable to the writer of those equations: "understand the laws and you understand the universe" (Gleick 1988, 12). Viewed through the lens of authorship theory, this Newtonian mantra implies that the author of a computer system such as a GAN determines the behaviour of said programme and is, therefore, author of its outputs (e.g., the digital portraits of *Memories of Passersby I*). From such a position that establishes an authorial hierarchy at the top of which stands the human, one might very well attribute any and all paintings produced by the painting bot AARON to artist Harold Cohen, even those produced long after the programmer's death. In effect, creating a kind of creative immortality.

This hierarchical position certainly appears to be the case with simple machines that adhere to a programme with a strictly linear relationship between input and output. For example, were I to direct a camera's lens towards a particular object and press the shutter button, I can predict that the resulting image will be of said object. However, the same cannot be said of the highly complex non-linear GAN system the behaviour of which is analogous to a *chaotic* mathematical system where "the future of a chaotic system is *indeterminable* even though the system is *deterministic*" (Hilborn 2000, 37).

This unpredictability in chaotic systems is the result of a sensitive dependence on initial conditions, the so-called "butterfly effect" described by meteorologist Edward Lorenz (1963). While simulating the behaviour of weather systems over a long period of time using standard non-linear equations, Lorenz noted that "a small change in initial conditions leads to grossly different long-term behaviour of the system, and we cannot in practice predict that long-term behaviour in detail" (Hilborn 2000, 37). This kind of chaotic behaviour can also be observed in the infinite portraiture of *Memories of Passersby I*. Just as the flapping of a butterfly's wings in Brazil may eventually set off a tornado in Texas, minute differences in the system's input data will produce vastly different images ensuring that every time the installation is switched on it is truly unique and entirely unpredictable even to the programmer. Furthermore, as each image is fed back into the GAN to inform the production of the next, these minute changes escalate into larger changes over time.

For example, the random appearance of a small blemish on the AI-generated face in the first digital portrait may then influence the next causing the facial features to distort, if only slightly, which in turn leads to more pronounced distortions in the following images. Over time, a singular blemish may very well result in a cascading effect that eventually causes the face to take on a completely different form or dissolve entirely. Of course, this is not truly the result of a "blemish" but of numerical data that is fed back into the system's governing equations and thus changes its behaviour over time.

This is not to imply that the GAN goes "off script" or defies its programming by any act of agency but, rather, the non-linearity inherent in the system's equations means that "the act of playing the game has a way of changing the rules" (Gleick 1988, 24). The GAN itself changes ever so slightly with each iteration. After a period of time, the system may produce visual forms that are both accounted for within the initial programme written and trained by Klingemann but that are also, crucially, entirely unpredictable or indeterminable at the moment the programme was written. To say that the GAN's behaviour is unpredictable does not, however, imply that it will eventually degrade into an entirely randomised or unstable system. Chaos is not the same as disorder, it lies at the transition point between order and disorder.

To illustrate the orderly disorder of mathematical chaos, consider Lorenz's *strange attractor* plot shown in Fig. 3.3. It is a dimensionless plot illustrating a simple chaotic system's behaviour as it spirals further and further from its origin. This image has come to represent the order and disorder of chaos itself, as historian of science James Gleick comments:

> It always stayed within certain bounds, never running off the page but never repeating itself either. It traced a strange, distinctive shape, a kind of double spiral in three dimensions, like a butterfly with its two wings. The shapes signalled pure disorder, since no point or pattern of points ever recurred. Yet it also signalled a new kind of order (Gleick 1988, 30).

With this image in mind, compare it to the changing portraiture produced by the GAN system. As a visualisation of this changing portraiture, Fig. 3.4 shows the outputs of an earlier sketch-to-portrait system developed by Klingemann in 2017 and that was trained on public domain image data from the British Library. While a different GAN system, the chaotic nature of these continual productions of technical images remains evident in the shifting human forms and is comparable to *Memories of Passersby I*.

Every digital portrait shown in Fig. 3.4 is entirely unique, in terms of both visual form and numerical data, but each still adheres to certain conditions or constraints. For example, facial features may bulge or shrink or become distorted but are always accounted for and arranged in a relatively consistent pattern or position to one another (e.g., a mouth or eye does not spawn at the outskirts of the image while the nose remains in the centre). These constraints are determined by the AI system itself and the data patterns it has identified from the training dataset of historical

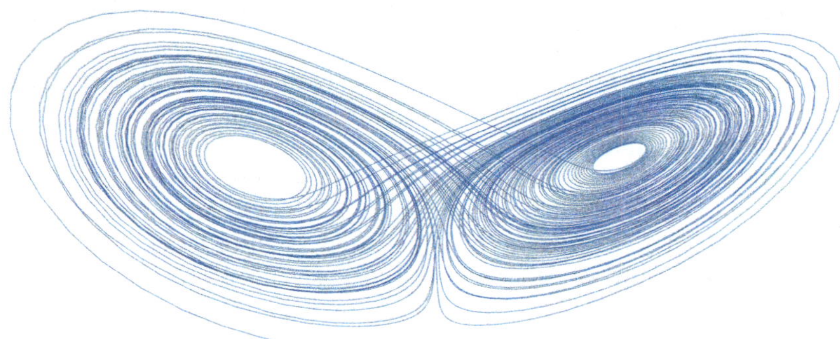

Fig. 3.3 Three-dimensional MATLAB plot of Edward Lorenz's "strange attractor"

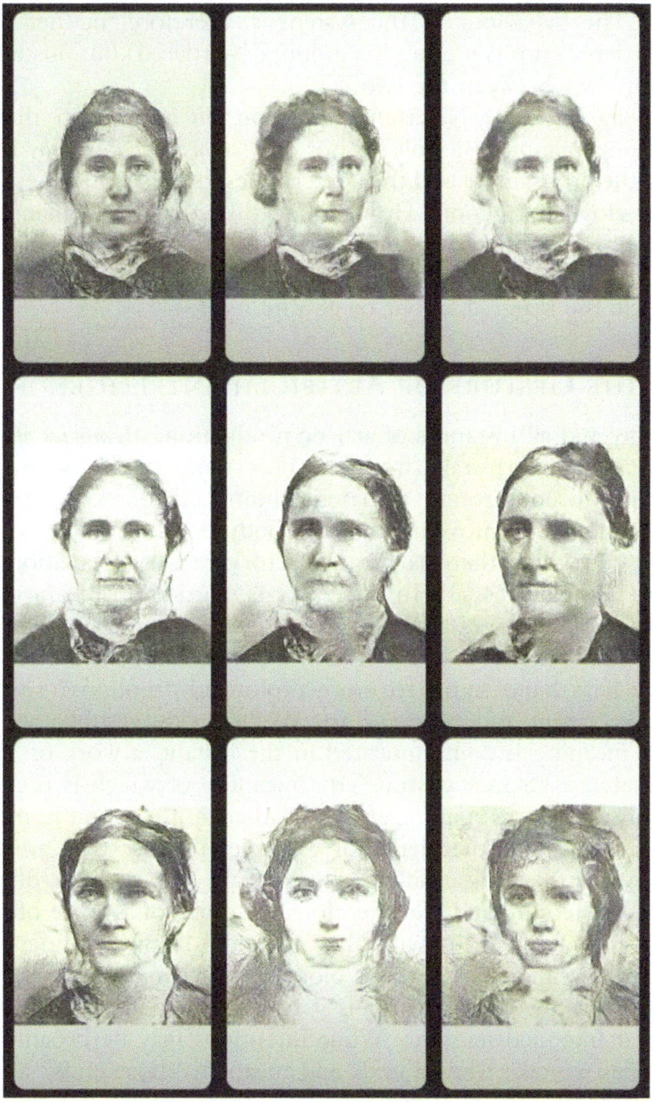

Fig. 3.4 Successive screenshots displaying the changing imagery produced by Mario Klingemann's sketch-to-portrait GAN system. Courtesy of Mario Klingemann and Onkaos

portraits. The behaviour of the system is, therefore, neither predetermined (ordered) nor is it entirely random (disordered) but, instead, exists at the boundary between the two.

The hierarchical or Newtonian position on authorship that would declare Klingemann as the sole author of *Memories of Passersby I* because he wrote the programme and thus determines its behaviour does not hold up under closer inspection. However, to disregard Klingemann entirely and attribute sole authorship to the GAN itself is equally misguided. Such a position fundamentally misunderstands that which makes works of art meaningful: the material labour or gesture itself.

The Gesture of Artificial Intelligence

As with any and all instances of artistic production, *Memories of Passersby I* did not emerge naturally from the pure randomness of the universe but was produced through a material human labour or *gesture*; what Flusser defines as "a movement of the body or of a tool attached with the body, for which there is no satisfactory causal explanation" for its meaning (Flusser 2014, 3). In other words, a gesture is characterised by its symbolic meaning rather than its instrumental purpose. Such gestures are encountered in every aspect of daily life from immediate bodily movements, such as hand signs, to more prolonged "motions" such as the meticulous crafting of a work of art. While bodily gestures are fleeting and their meaning is communicated in the instant, a work of art might be considered a "frozen gesture" the meaning of which is preserved in the medium. Gestures stand apart from other incidental motions that are purely reactionary (a knee jerk, for example) because they are motions aimed towards the realisation of a future state (e.g., a work of art) that articulates something and are, therefore, symbolic of a "state of mind".

To say that a gesture is symbolic of a state of mind is not, however, to say that anything of the artist's biography or personality may be deciphered from the work itself, nor is it to imply that the work articulates a particular intended message. While intentions may be broadly defined as "attitudes we take toward ends and means to those ends" and artists certainly commit gestures with intent, it is misguided to say that the meaning of a gesture derives from this intent as to do so ignores the gesture itself in favour of a causal explanation (Livingston 2005, 208).

To analyse *Memories of Passersby I* causally is to identify and isolate a "catalog of moving bodies involved" and establish a chain of events (e.g., writing the GAN programme, selecting the training dataset, designing and constructing the installation) that eventually points back to Klingemann's initial intention (Flusser 2014, 62). Every motion thereafter, the concrete gesture itself, is then seen as subservient to this invisible intention and works solely towards its fulfilment. Though this may seem a logical suggestion, it is reminiscent of Romantic authorship theory wherein the human is envisioned as a self-contained individual whose thoughts and ideas, especially artistic ones, are seen as "strokes of genius" that occur in isolation beyond the influence of external or internal forces.

In opposition to this notion of intention driving gestures, reconsider Pierre Macherey's theory of literary production in which the gesture of writing is equated to an inexact labour and the writer neither commands nor wields the words but, instead, plays with a "set of finite combinations" available (Macherey 2006, 45). As the writer conducts the gesture, new combinations reveal themselves and others disappear such that the final work is determined at every stage of its development and, as Macherey argues, "the author cannot deduce, from an initial intention, the means by which that intention shall be realised" (Ibid., 27). It is only through the completion of the concrete gesture itself that the final form may be realised and there exists no alternative or idealised version that might adhere to the initial intention.

For Barthes and other anti-intentionalist critics discussed in the previous chapter, such an admission would seem to support the notion that a work is a "multi-dimensional space" to be endlessly interpreted by the reader, thus spelling the death of the author (Barthes 1987, 146). However, to replace the author with the reader as the origin of meaning is to simply suggest yet another causal explanation, this time rooted in the experiences of the reader and the context in which they live.

Rather than look to abstract and unknowable intentions or interpretations orbiting the gesture in order to explain its meaning, the gesture itself should be analysed in terms of its *gestalt* (Flusser 2014, 63). To explain this concept, Flusser uses the example of a painter and asserts that the human and the non-human (the GAN in the case of *Memories of Passersby I*) are parts of the overall motion of the gesture, stating:

> We are not seeing some sort of mysterious merging of painter and material in a process from which the painting emerges as a synthesis but rather the gesture of painting. "Painter" and "his material" are words we use

> to explain the gesture and not the other way around…there is a concrete gesture of painting, and in it, painter and brush are realized (Ibid., 67).

In terms of its gestalt, *Memories of Passersby I* can be understood as a gesture that does not end with Klingemann's construction of the GAN but one that continues on forever as the GAN produces images ad infinitum. Unlike a traditional painting, *Memories of Passersby I* is not so much a frozen gesture but a gesture of endless, chaotic motion and within this chaos "Klingemann" and "the GAN" are realised as different phases of motion. However, the full extent of this gesture is greater than the immediate motions of Klingemann and the GAN. Indeed, this gesture stretches back to the fourteenth century and encompasses the disparate motions of those thousands of historical artists whose work has been used in the training dataset.

The gesture of artificial intelligence, this endless chaotic motion in which the reins of the artistic production process are handed to technology itself, is not something that has only begun in recent years with the invention of GAN systems but rather something centuries in the making that has come to a head with the GAN. This gesture is made apparent in the endless imagery of *Memories of Passersby I* but can also be witnessed more broadly in our modern situation in which more generative AI systems have taken on more significant roles in creative production processes eclipsing the role of the human within the gestalt. Where previous historical works of art symbolised the human artist's state of mind, the case is not so clear with *Memories of Passersby I* and other modern AI art. In such a gesture, the human is further and further removed from production, from painter to producer of painters to producers of producers and so on until the human's only meaningful motion within the gesture is the touch of a button marked "on".

To better understand precisely what this gesture symbolises, our critical analysis must move towards the portraits themselves as the endpoint because the "meaning of the gesture, the painting to be painted, is the future of the gesture" (Ibid., 64). This is not to propose an appreciation of the aesthetics of these portraits but, rather, to consider the nature of these technical images as mathematical outputs of scientific apparatuses and their impact within society.

The Game at Play

While the features of the shifting human forms observed (if momentarily) in *Memories of Passersby I* certainly resemble the portraiture from which they derive, to propose that it be critiqued in the same manner as a product of human imagination and skill is to misunderstand how such technical images are created and what they mean.

Those portraits that Klingemann has plucked from across the centuries were images directly crafted by humans who observed phenomena in the concrete world (e.g., the portrait subject) and sought to communicate their significance by producing representative imagery. These are, therefore, not simply near-accurate translations of "something 'out there' in space and time" (e.g., object, landscape, person) but two-dimensional compositions of semiotic signs arranged upon surfaces so that others may understand what was witnessed in that time and place (Flusser 2012, 8). In order to decode such works, and therefore ascertain their significance, Flusser asserts that it is necessary to speculate on the "encoding that took place 'in the head' of the painter themselves" i.e., to determine the painter's intention or what might be romantically referred to as their "worldview" (Ibid., 16). This is not the case, however, with technical images such as photographs, film, and AI-generated images.

With the integration of automated machines or apparatuses (e.g., cameras, computers, GANs) into image-making practices, the human being has become further distanced from this process of encoding. No longer is it confined to the "head" of the human artist as they witness and interpret reality but, rather, it occurs within the apparatus itself as it conducts the procedure it was programmed to complete, be it mechanical or digital in nature. As apparatuses are themselves products of scientific principles and mathematical laws that are already interpretations of reality, the technical images they produce signify these abstract concepts and not phenomena observed in the concrete world (Ibid., 14). Therefore, technical images such as the *Portrait d'Edmond de Belamy* and *Memories of Passersby I* cannot be decoded through a superficial analysis of the content i.e., the phenomena that appear to be represented. Instead, we must look beyond the shifting human forms that materialise on screen and towards the production according to the program of the apparatus. In the case of *Memories of Passersby I*, this the GAN itself.

While I have provided a brief explanation of the processes of the GAN system above, the fundamental nature of an apparatus' program is always the same: it is an autonomous "combinatory game" that will produce different outputs for different inputs according to the rules that govern the game i.e., the mathematical process (Ibid., 32). It is, therefore, only the complexity of the game's rules that separates the program of the GAN system from the program of a camera.

With simple apparatuses that adhere to a linear input-output relationship (e.g., cameras), the human operator (e.g., photographer) is able to govern what combinations or possibilities are made concrete. These operators are seen to "play" with the apparatus, cycling through different combinations to arrive at their desired outcome and no other. Imagine the case of a photographer moving around their subject, clicking away and selecting their desired image from the multitude of possibilities before discarding the rest. While the camera presents numerous possible outcomes, the operator exerts limitation on what outcomes may be realised; this limitation or dominance over the gesture of photography is what establishes authorship. However, were the camera absent-mindedly left to record any and all things that passed it by, making concrete its multitude of possibilities, the matter may be quite different and comparable to the case of *Memories of Passersby I*.

The human eye is limited by its speed of response and cannot properly view the individual images produced by the GAN and, instead, can only see human-like figures coming into being, morphing and fading away. However, looking past the visual forms, these digital portraits are revealed to be nothing more than different outputs of the AI systems. They are different possibilities or combinations that are all accounted for within the rules of the apparatus' program. Previously, I have discussed how the GAN of *Memories of Passersby I* produces an endless stream of images and that within this gesture the influence of the human operator shrinks to the point of insignificance. As such, "the possibility of stopping the apparatus at the desired consequence is lost. The program becomes independent of human intention. It becomes autonomous and rolls on until every coincidence has been realised, even those human beings originally wanted explicitly to avoid" (Flusser 2011, 73–74). With the operator so diminished, they cannot exert dominance or limit the possible outcomes to be realised, so once the GAN is switched on it will run forever trying to exhaust its inexhaustible program by producing an infinite number of images.

Both the camera and the GAN are "black boxes" from which different possibilities are seen to emerge. With the camera (and other linear programs) the viewer may only witness a finite number of possibilities as limited or curated by the operator who might be seen as a kind of filter between the apparatus and viewer, stemming the flow of images. With the GAN system, however, there is no such filter. Rather than simply see a selection of possibilities, the viewer is forced to look directly into the black box and observe the infinite number of possibilities unbounded by the limitations of the human.

To witness these moving images, then, is to witness the "game at play" and one might infer its rules; what is accounted for within the program and what is not. In short, what is observed and understood from these technical images is the very function of the GAN system itself which is to create from nothing: "particles into two-dimensional images, to rise from no dimensions to two dimensions, from the abyss of intervals to the surface, from the most abstract into the apparently concrete" in a specific form: a portrait (Ibid., 21).

To view the endless imagery of *Memories of Passersby I* is to be confronted with what Andreas Broeckmann describes as the *machinic aesthetic* which is "an experience in the face of art that hinges on machine-based processes that are beyond human control" (Broeckmann 2017, 205). While Broeckmann likens this to the notion of the sublime, I would argue that a machinic aesthetic is incompatible with traditional notions of aesthetic theory.

Collapse of the Aesthetic Universe

Drawing on the work of Claude Shannon and his own unique theory of communication, Flusser proposes a model for approximating the aesthetic experience of works of art in terms of information theory and thermodynamics, shown in Fig. 3.5. Within this model, artworks exhibit a kind of looping lifecycle, a "circularity of the aesthetic universe", that reflects how subjective experience changes over time, flitting between two extreme boundaries: the totally improbable (information in abundance) and the totally redundant (information lack) (Flusser 2002, 55).

For Flusser, it is the natural tendency of the universe to progress towards the most probable and least informative situation (i.e., heat death). However, along this inevitable march towards heat death improbable situations may still arise that defy this tendency, if only temporarily, by creating and preserving information. Works of art and other forms of

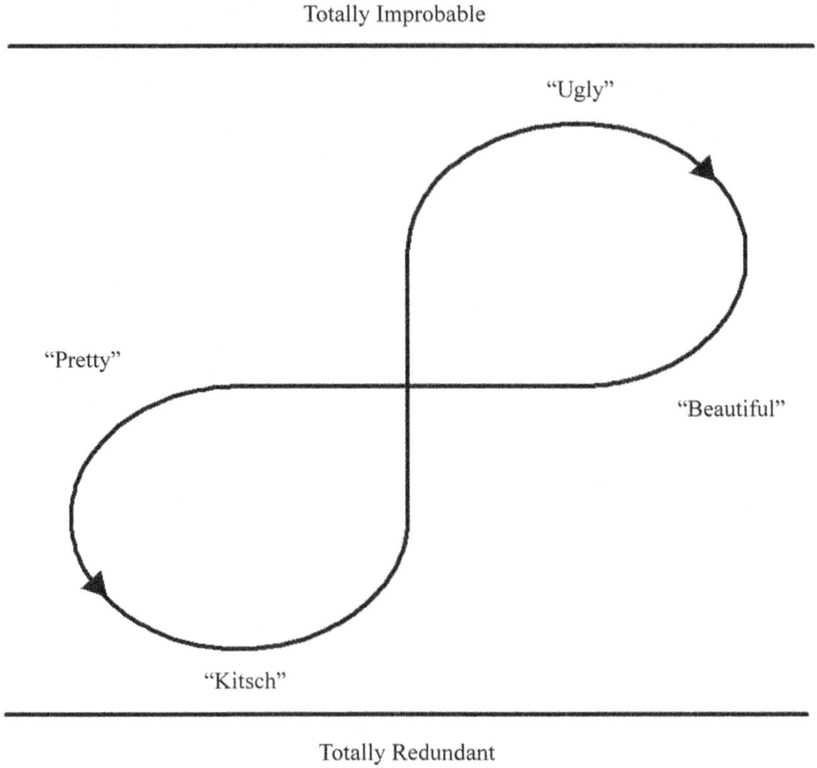

Fig. 3.5 Flusser's approximation of the aesthetic universe

cultural communication are considered among these negentropic occurrences that increase the sum total of information available because they have come into being through an intentional gesture, rather than being the likely or expected outcome of the pure randomness of the universe (Ibid., 9). Any new work of art is initially seen as improbable and overly informative such that, from the perspective of a human existing within this universe, these works are considered *ugly* in Flusser's terms. To describe an artwork as ugly, however, is not to make a value judgement of the piece but is, instead, to say that such works are affective because they differ so drastically from the accepted norm. Subjectively, any new work of art may be defined as something that "makes us tremble because it is unexpected" (Ibid., 52).

In the aesthetic universe, new works are initially located at the highest point of the loop, nearest the boundary of total improbability. However, with the passage of time these ugly works become normalised within their environments, seen as more and more probable but less informative as a result. As probability increases and information decreases, the work passes through other stages wherein it is experienced as *beautiful* and then *pretty* until reaching towards the other boundary of total redundancy where it is seen to be so commonplace as to be uninformative i.e., *kitsch*. Again, these rather vague terms are not to be taken as judgements, but simply labels or descriptors that convey how changes in entropy might be perceived subjectively. Indeed, the entire model is metaphorical.

A concrete image, be it produced by a human directly (e.g., a portrait) or an apparatus (e.g., a polaroid photograph), emerges into the aesthetic universe in a particular and unchanging form. The image is a "reservoir" of information preserved visually and, as time passes, it traverses the loop as expected: from improbable and informative (ugly) upon first observation, to probable and uninformative (kitsch) upon the hundredth (Flusser 2011, 18). In the case of *Memories of Passersby I*, the ephemeral images that pass in and out of existence in an instant present an entirely different situation.

As previously discussed, the digital portraits of *Memories of Passersby I* are visualisations of data and, as Galloway argues, "data requires such a visualisation because it has no inherent visual form. Data exists as a discreet, dimensionless numerical unit that is imperceptible to the human eye because it lacks form and so, in order for data to be rendered perceptible, there must be a contingent leap from the mode of the mathematical to the mode of the visual" (Galloway 2011, 88). The generation of each new synthetic image entails a "leap" in Galloway's terms, from nothingness to the realm of perception and, therefore, constitutes the production of new information. As the information spewing forth in every fleeting image is never the same, it seems inappropriate to describe *Memories of Passersby I* as a reservoir like other traditional images and, instead, it is tempting to describe it as more akin to a "spring" of information.

Every momentary image of *Memories of Passersby I* is improbable and informative or aesthetic ugly but as each is destroyed and replaced instantaneously by the next ugly image, there is no traversal of the loop. The images are instantaneous and have no history. In relinquishing human control and allowing the apparatus to cycle through its infinite combinations, the viewer of *Memories of Passersby I* is presented with a constant overabundance of information, a continuous escalation of negentropy, and so is permanently affixed to the zenith of the aesthetic universe. Once circular and governed by the progression of historical time, the aesthetic universe collapses to a singular point, a position of infinite ugliness. In confronting the machinic aesthetic of *Memories of Passersby I*, the viewer does not so much tremble at the unexpected and then relax as time passes, but they appear to convulse in endless terror of the infinite new; a horrific post-historical experience. This deluge of infinite images is the future of the gesture of artificial intelligence that is fast approaching.

The Post-Historical Condition

The notion that the technical conditions of media technologies (i.e., their form rather than content) shapes perceptions of the world is not exactly new and has been articulated in the well-known mantras of McLuhan ("the medium is the message") and Kittler ("media determine our situation"), as well as in more recent works of media philosophy and media archaeology. For Flusser, however, the privileging of the eye above all other senses in meaning-making processes suggests that images play a significant role in shaping experiences of time. As such, he suggests that different kinds of images presuppose different forms of temporal consciousness: mythical, historical and post-historical (Flusser 2002, 117).

For the prehistoric humans of Lascaux, cave paintings of animals were representative of phenomena in the world (i.e., traditional images) and in their static form allowed the eye to wander and scan the surface, encouraging a mythical consciousness that experienced time as cyclical and never-ending: "while wandering over the surface of the image, one's gaze takes in one element after another and produces temporal relationships between them. It can return to an element of the image it has already seen, and 'before' can become 'after': The time constructed by scanning is an eternal recurrence of the same process" (Flusser 2012, 8–9). It was not until the invention of linear writing and linear texts that historical consciousness and the very concept of history as a sequence of events began.

Rather than present the eye with static representations of the world, linear writing arranged images as discretised symbols that must be read chronologically to be understood as meaningful: "the eye travels along the page. Time and space, the event translated onto the page, is lineally set out before the eye. History comes into being" (Barker 2018, 29). In the linear motion of the eye, time was no longer experienced as static and instead seemed to flow along a chain of causality in which individual events, with definitive beginnings and endings and gaps to separate one from the other, are seen to be strung along a straight line where "everything is the consequence of causes and the cause of consequences" (Flusser 2002, 118). While the printing press and the widespread distribution of linear texts established historical consciousness as the dominant mode of experiencing time, Flusser asserts that the invention of photography and the rise of technical images in the past century is ushering in a post-historical consciousness.

Technical images are different to traditional images in that they do not signify phenomena in the world but, instead, signify the program of the apparatus; a combinatorial game that produces a concrete outcome from a range of abstract possibilities. As such, technical images are not static representations of the world (traditional images) or flowing chronologies (linear texts) but are simply one possible outcome of many: "Prehistoric images are worldviews (copies of the environment). Photographs are computed possibilities (models, projections onto the environment)" (Ibid., 129). Time is not experienced as cyclical or flowing but is "diced up" into numerous disconnected temporal situations that emerge, not from causality as consequences of the previous situation, but from the pure chance of the combinatorial game. Therefore, while historical consciousness treats the present as "nothing more than a zero-dimensional point" in the constant flow from past to future, in a post-historical consciousness "only the moment is real; it is a node in the surrounding field of possibilities" that changes with every "click" of the apparatus (Ibid., 118). The past is not a trailing line of previous presents but is an archive of "already realized possibilities" while the future remains as those "yet unrealized possibilities" that are splayed out flat, equally likely to occur, and seem to be "coming from all sides into the present" (Ibid.). The photograph produced by a camera and an AI-generated image are both just realised possibilities accounted for by the apparatus.

Writing in the 1980s, Flusser theorised that the widespread emergence of technical images in television, advertisement, and film would induce a grand, sweeping change in temporal consciousness across society. While I do not directly dispute this, I would limit my discussion to the work at hand and instead re-conceptualise this post-historical consciousness as a particular aesthetic condition or experience that is intensified in the case of *Memories of Passersby I* and other modern AI art because of the GAN's autonomy and apparently infinite possibilities.

In the historical condition, the chronological eye identifies individual symbols, words, gaps, and punctuation that segment time and distinguish events that are meaningful from times of meaninglessness; words contrast with blank space on a page, new forms contrast with the habitual, periods of beauty contrast with periods of ugliness. It is only through these binary relationships, in which something *is* because it *is not* something else, that images may become meaningful in a historical sense. As Flusser states: "consciousness, to be consciousness at all, is an unhappy consciousness. If all pain were relieved, all suffering numbed, the economy would be superseded. We could turn our backs to it and practice philosophy. But then there would be nothing left over which to philosophize" (Flusser 2011, 145).

This existential suffering is what is truly at risk in the post-historical condition presented in the infinite imagery of *Memories of Passersby I* and with the rise of AI art as a dominant mode of cultural production. With continual newness, or ugliness, and no perceived progression of time, there is no suffering from lack and so though the viewer may be eternally terrified they will forget what it is to experience terror at all. Such a state is non-human and, therefore, meaningless: "there can be no happiness without suffering. Utopia is impossible" (Ibid.).

Non-Human Utopia

In confronting the machinic aesthetic, an eternal state on the cusp of pure improbability, the GAN reshapes aesthetic experience according to a new scale of temporal measurement, one that is non-human.

With traditional images, linear texts, and other media that are limited or governed by human artists, the eye is invited to consider such images from a strictly human perspective. A historical portrait, for example, is understood as the gesture of an individual human artist whose life and actions were finite and limited to a scale of mere decades. Such images are symbolic of a mind that existed on a temporal scale that is akin to our own experience and thus are meaningful and fathomable to us. However, there are other scales within and outside that of human perception and comprehension; other timescales that measure phenomena in terms of millennia or in fractions of seconds.

As Flusser describes it, we exist "somewhere in the interior of a *matrjoschka* (Russian doll), a hierarchy of orders of magnitude in which each contains all smaller ones" and the world is measured on a different scale depending on the order of magnitude (Flusser 2002, 161). On the scale of micro-organisms, the same painting might be seen as too grand or too slow to be of immediate concern, while on the cosmic scale of galaxies it is seen as too minute or fleeting to be noticed. Only on the human order of magnitude do artistic gestures, such as paintings and linear texts, carry any meaning at all; either viewed as cyclical/time-recurrent (i.e., mythical) or chronological/time-bound (i.e., historical). The infinite/unbounded and non-recurrent (i.e., post-historical) images of *Memories of Passersby I* lie within a grey zone between the human and the non-human orders of magnitude. They present continual information but are near-incomprehensible in their current context because they are so improbable. While such images are affective, they must be measured as fleeting possibilities or minute motions in an endless gesture, mere fractions of infinity (i.e., zero), and so are not seen to be symbolic of something human in themselves.

Discussing the deluge of new images in culture and the focus on visual forms in modern architecture, Juhani Pallasmaa argues that humanity has developed a *nihilistic eye* in that perception has become solely concerned with immediate visual pleasure rather than meaning or being: "the art of the eye has certainly produced imposing and thought-provoking structures, but it has not facilitated human rootedness in the world" (Pallasmaa 2005, 19). Aesthetic experience has changed from a contemplative consideration of another's state of mind or intentions to a continual, fleeting consumption of the new before moving on to the next new. AI art continues this transition and further accelerates it. By inviting spectators to view AI-generated images from the scale of the infinite rather than the limited human, *Memories of Passersby I* presupposes a nihilistic eye but one that is also lidless, consuming all possibilities presented to it such that "the world becomes a hedonistic but meaningless visual journey" (Ibid., 22).

With the emergence of user-friendly text-to-image models such as DALL-E and Midjourney, AI art has become so normalised and standardised that there is no longer even a pretence of artistic experimentation as witnessed with the AI artists of the 2010s. These systems are openly advertised as aesthetic toys capable of producing a deluge of images that are as easily discarded as they are created. In this apparent "utopia", in which machines carry out every function, the human's role is minimised to the point that the subject no longer gestures at all and, instead, becomes static while the programmed world moves about it. It is a world in which all meaningful things are created by that which is fundamentally non-human and so, paradoxically, symbolise nothing of meaning at all. This is the future that was once glimpsed in the transforming images of *Memories of Passersby I* and that which is rapidly approaching us in the modern day.

To summarise the argument presented in this chapter, artificial neural networks, such as those GAN systems of the 2010s and those more sophisticated models that have since emerged, appear at first to be the ideal tool for artistic production and continual creativity. Certainly, these technologies enable the rapid and large-scale production of original images that recall with startling accuracy the styles of previous artistic movements and specific artists, while allowing contemporary artists a certain freedom from the labour of artistic production. In doing so, however, these technologies present a situation of eternal newness that is not governed by humans and that communicates nothing of human experience.

The production of AI art is a gesture aimed at inducing mathematical chaos that is governed by the AI system itself, and that opens the floodgates to a deluge of images on a scale that exceeds human perception and comprehension. It hints at a non-human culture of infinite productivity, but one in which those products that form our culture are ultimately meaningless. However, this deluge of AI-generated images has implications beyond simply the production of visual art. As such, while this argument thread will be returned to in the final chapter, the interim chapters will explore more varied instances of AI-generated art and media during this period and highlight those broader ethical issues associated with AI technologies that were apparent in the 2010s, but that have come to the fore in the modern day. Notable in this trend is the emergence of AI-generated images of human beings and their impact upon the construction and representation of human identity which will be discussed in the next chapter.

References

Barker, Timothy. 2018. *Against transmission: Media philosophy and the engineering of time*. London: Bloomsbury.

Barthes, Roland. 1987. Image music text. Translated by Stephen Heath. London: Fontana Press.

Broeckmann, Andreas. 2017. Media faktura: On some technical conditions of image-making in art. *Art* 4 (1): 7.1–7.10.

Creswell, Antonia, Tom White, Vincent Dumoulin, Kai Arulkumaran, Biswa Sengupta, and Anil A. Bharath. 2018. Generative adversarial networks: An overview. *IEEE Signal Processing Magazine* 35 (1): 53–65.

Dean, Martin. 2019. Artist Mario Klingemann on artificial intelligence technology and our future. *Sothebys*.

Elgammal, Ahmed. 2018. What the art world is failing to grasp about Christie's AI portrait coup. *Art*.

Flusser, Vilém. 2002. Writings. In *Translated by Erik Eisel*, ed. Andreas Ströhl. London: University of Minnesota Press.

Flusser, Vilém. 2011. *Into the universe of technical images*. Translated by Nancy Ann Roth. Minneapolis: University of Minnesota Press.

Flusser, Vilém. 2012. *Towards a philosophy of photography*. London: Reaktion Books.

Flusser, Vilém. 2014. Gestures. Translated by Nancy Ann Roth. Minneapolis: University of Minnesota Press.

Galloway, Alexander. 2011. Are some things unrepresentable? *Theory, Culture & Society* 28 (7–7): 85–102.

Gleick, James. 1988. *Chaos: Making a new science*. London: William Heinemann.

Goodfellow, Ian, Jean Pouget-Abadie, Mehdi Mirza, Xu Bing, David Warde-Farley, Sherjil Ozair, Aaron Courville, and Yoshua Bengio. 2014. Generative adversarial nets. *Advances in Neural Information Processing Systems*: 2672–2680.

Hilborn, Robert. 2000. *Chaos and nonlinear dynamics: An introduction for scientists and engineers*. Oxford: Oxford University Press.

Jones, Jonathan. 2018. A portrait created by AI just sold for $432,000. But is it really art? *Guardian*, October 26.

Livingston, Paisley. 2005. *Art and intention: A philosophical study*. Oxford: Oxford University Press.

Lorenz, Edward. 1963. Deterministic nonperiodic flow. *Journal of the Atmospheric Sciences* 20: 130–141.

Macherey, Pierre. 2006. *A theory of literary production*. Abingdon: Routledge.

Mazzone, Marian, and Ahmed Elgammal. 2019. Art, creativity, and the potential of artificial intelligence. *Art* 8 (26): 1–9.

Pallasmaa, Juhani. 2005. *The eyes of the skin: Architecture and the senses*. Chichester: Wiley-Academy.

Zylinska, Joanna. 2020. *AI art: Machine visions and warped dreams*. London: Open Humanities Press.

CHAPTER 4

Virtually Unrecognisable

In February 2021, a video published on the social media platform TikTok gained viral popularity as it seemed to show Hollywood film star Tom Cruise performing a close-up magic trick while speaking directly to the camera, insisting that "it's all the real thing". The figure certainly resembled Cruise and displayed many of the actor's recognisable mannerisms, such as his intense manner of speech and high-pitched laugh. However, the video was quickly revealed to be a hyper-realistic AI-generated reconstruction of the actor created by visual effects artist Christopher Umé and featuring actor Miles Fisher "wearing" Cruise's face (Hern 2021). Such reconstructions, better known as *deepfakes*, have become one of the most notorious and problematic examples of AI-generated media. While numerous examples of deepfake videos had emerged online long before 2021, the Cruise deepfake marked a significant turning point in the discourse around AI-generated media and the potential socio-political dangers of this technology. Where earlier deepfakes were often of low technical quality, the Cruise deepfake was near indistinguishable from the real actor's appearance and behaviour. This sudden escalation in technical quality made clear to the public and policymakers that the line between artificial and authentic had already begun to blur, sparking calls for better deepfake detection tools and stricter regulation and policies for controlling the spread of AI-generated media.

A. McIntyre, *Art and Authorship in the AI Spring*,
https://doi.org/10.1007/978-3-032-18574-7_4

Certainly, the visual fidelity of the Cruise deepfake raised significant questions around the imminent socio-political impacts of generative AI. However, even before such hyper-realistic examples emerged, deepfakes had begun to raise complex moral and ethical questions around how such images impacted those individuals misrepresented. These are issues deeply rooted in the history of deepfakes.

A portmanteau of "deep learning" and "fake", the term *deepfake* originally came into our vocabulary in 2017 when an anonymous Reddit user named "deepfakes" began posting videos in which the faces of female actors such as Scarlett Johansson and Gal Gadot were digitally grafted to the bodies of pornographic performers using GAN systems (Cole 2018). Other Reddit users quickly began posting their own creations in a dedicated r/deepfakes forum on the platform and from there the trend rapidly spread to other online spaces. Where initially this trend was limited to predominantly male and tech-savvy communities online (Newton and Stanfill 2020), the arrival of open-source software and user-friendly applications (e.g., DeepNude) allowed for widespread production and distribution of deepfake pornography (Adjer et al. 2019). A trend that has not only continued into the modern day, but that has been further exacerbated by technological advances.

Despite being artificial and obviously fake, these images are far from harmless. They can and have been used to intimidate, threaten or otherwise sexually harass the targeted individual and risk causing reputational damage if publicly released. Even if not intentionally used to harass an individual or damage their reputation, deepfake images still present distinct harms for those targeted. As many academics and commentators have argued, deepfake pornography constitutes a serious form of non-consensual pornography that can emotionally and psychologically harm the targets, while further contributing to gender inequality and the oppression of women more broadly (Harwell 2018; Öhman 2020; Van der Nagel 2020; Rini and Cohen 2022; Badham 2024). Not only does deepfake pornography behave as a form of virtual domination in which "a person's autonomy is invaded by their being represented as engaging in unconsented (and fabricated) sexual encounters" (Rini and Cohen 2022, 143) but "even if a deepfake is debunked, or never believed at all, it can still harm the person it falsely depicts by changing the discursive context around them" forcing those represented to react and respond to such degrading images (Ibid., 148).

Certainly, the psychological and societal harms posed by deepfakes are of critical importance and deserve significant attention in academic and political discourse. However, I believe Rini and Cohen's argument points towards another issue related to authorship and the role of humans in cultural production that will be the focus of this chapter. Where Rini and Cohen focus on harms, this chapter seeks to explore how AI-generated media contributes to the discourse around the individual misrepresented thus altering our understanding of their identity and undermining their authorial agency over their own public image. While this impact is most explicit in deepfake pornography, it further extends to other cases in which AI systems have been used to replicate or represent human beings in cultural production more broadly. As such, this chapter's discussion critically considers several examples of deepfakes and other AI-generated images of human beings that emerged in the 2010s including, for example, the digital resurrection of deceased public figures for film, television and advertising.

To develop the argument in this chapter, I build upon Flusser's theoretical framework by turning to the work of media theorist John Hartley, as well as philosopher Jean Baudrillard whose theories on hyper-reality complement Flusser's own universe of technical images. To fully appreciate the implications of deepfakes and AI-generated replications, however, it is necessary to first elaborate on how cultural production has changed with the arrival of the internet and the rise of social media platforms, as well as how this reframes identity and authorship in the modern day.

Prior to the internet, cultural products were largely exhibited to the public in dedicated physical spaces (e.g., galleries, theatres, cinemas) or distributed via specific media channels (e.g., television, radio, print) such that cultural communication was, for the most part, a one-way process from producers to consumers. However, the widespread availability of personal computers and the arrival of vast online networks fundamentally changed how people interacted with one another by enabling the average person to create their own cultural products and disseminate these to others across the world. This apparent democratisation of cultural production was then greatly accelerated by the arrival of social media platforms in the mid-2000s and throughout the 2010s these platforms saw a steadily increasing user base, rising from millions to billions of daily users by the end of the decade. With half the world interconnected to one another in a vast information network, the 2010s saw the emergence of a mass participatory culture in which the previously simple producer-consumer relationship was disrupted. Instead of a passive receiver of culture, the average person has thus been transformed into an active participant in its production. Not only has this mass participation blurred the line between producer and consumer but it has further complicated our understanding of authorship as cultural production is less associated with the creation of a definitive original work or product that is attributable to an individual.

Take, for example, the popularity of internet memes in which appropriated images, sounds and performance formats are routinely re-worked, re-produced and re-published without regard for the original author's identity or intentions. While this so-called "remix" culture would seem to be a dismissal of authorship, theorist Jenna Ng argues instead that authorship has also transformed and become more "about a voice projected in a space, rather than about a text produced from a source" (Ng 2013, 10). For Ng, authorship in the context of online information networks is synonymous with contribution and participation within a global discussion; a "digital space in which a multitude of voices exist" (Ibid.).

While certainly user contributions include traditionally authorable products (e.g., narratives, artworks, music), they also encompass a wealth of different personal communications as social media platforms encourage the production of content that expresses or reinforces individual identity. These communications include personal statuses, updates on major life events, audiovisual recordings of users and their loved ones and reactions to other people's communications. Authorship in the online world is not simply about participation or projecting a voice but a production of content that emphasises one's own identity. However, it is misguided to view these online platforms as simple tools for broadcasting one's own distinct identity. Rather, the emergence of the internet and online platforms has redefined what constitutes an identity.

With the rise of social media platforms in the 2010s, digital technologies have been increasingly integrated into human social environments, interactions and practices. In doing so, they have fundamentally changed how we access and receive knowledge about the world and about one another, how we express our own ideas, and how we establish, build and maintain platonic, professional and romantic relationships. As these technologies continue to shape human interactions and create entirely new means of interacting, Floridi argues that we now exist in an *infosphere* in which human experience of the world is defined in terms of information flow, patterns and storage. Not simply does this infosphere represent a digital environment apart from and yet equivalent to concrete reality but, rather, it is synonymous with reality in that "what is real is informational and what is informational is real" (Floridi 2014, 41).

Equating abstract information with concrete reality not only influences our daily activities and interactions but, furthermore, redefines personal identity as something constructed of information. As Floridi noted in 2014, "never before in the history of humanity have so many people monitored, recorded, and reported so many details about themselves to such a large audience" (Ibid., 62). An individual's online identity has thus become a serious endeavour requiring daily maintenance and constant updating as "nothing is too small, irrelevant, or indeed private to be left untold…any data point can contribute to the description of one's own personal identity" (Ibid., 63). However, as identity is increasingly redefined as something informational, there is also an increased dependency on digital technologies as the primary means of publicly representing oneself. Such dependence also entails vulnerability and as Floridi summarises: "eliminate all personal interactions, promote a culture of proxies, and identity theft becomes the easiest thing in the world" (Ibid., 126).

As AI-generated media and particularly deepfakes have continued to flood our nascent information environment, this identity theft has taken on a far more profound meaning. While these synthetic representations are fundamentally different from authentic recordings, they can still contribute to and distort a person's online identity in significant and undesirable ways, as will be explored further in this chapter.

To begin, I will first consider the issue of digitally resurrecting deceased film stars through AI, drawing comparisons between the carefully curated public identities of celebrities in the Golden Age of Hollywood and the modern-day construction of online identity. Rather appropriate to this chapter on hyperreality and how information structures our experience, this initial discussion is rooted in the case of a film production that, despite never actually materialising, was widely reported on and sparked intense public debate. This is the proposed digital resurrection of deceased Hollywood star James Dean for the film *Finding Jack*.

A Man Out of Time

While the production of political and pornographic deepfakes has been largely condemned in political and academic discourse, policymakers and scholars of business studies and economics have often cited the positive potentials for this technology in the creative industries (Westerlund 2019; Kietzmann et al. 2020). Notably, these scholars highlight how generative AI could enable greater creative freedom by allowing the use of famous deceased actors in new film and television productions and advertisements.

The production of synthetic representations is not entirely new in the creative industries and, indeed, there have been several instances in the past in which deceased actors have been digitally recreated, albeit in a limited capacity. Examples include Oliver Reed in *Gladiator* (Scott 2000) and Laurence Olivier in *Sky Captain and the World of Tomorrow* (Conran 2004). However, the arrival of AI systems meant that this practice became more cost effective and less complex, thus opening up a range of possibilities for the creative industries. During the late 2010s, this practice of digital resurrection began to grow in popularity. For example, the likenesses of actors Peter Cushing and Carrie Fisher were digitally recreated using AI-assisted visual effects, allowing them to reprise their roles as Grand Moff Tarkin and Princess Leia in more recent entries to the *Star Wars* film franchise long after their deaths in 1994 and 2016, respectively. However, in spite of the commercial benefits, this practice of digital resurrection has attracted criticism around notions of consent and image rights as these deceased individuals never agreed to participate in these media productions or allowed their image to be used to endorse such works (Farish 2020; Lees et al. 2021). While in the case of Cushing and Fisher some of these concerns might be somewhat allayed by the fact that these actors agreed to embody these characters while alive, some are considering using AI systems to digitally resurrect actors for entirely original performances.

In late 2019, numerous media outlets reported that an upcoming film adaptation of the 2011 Gareth Crocker novel *Finding Jack* would feature a digitally recreated James Dean as an original character over sixty years on from the young actor's death in 1955 (Ritman 2019). The filmmakers behind the adaptation, Anton Ernst and Tati Golykh, claimed in interviews at the time that in their search for the perfect actor to play the character of "Rogan", Dean proved to be the only appropriate choice despite being deceased. While Ernst and Golykh insisted that this digital resurrection would not be treated as a gimmick and would be respectful of the actor's legacy, the announcement drew significant public attention and received criticism from many high-profile actors and filmmakers in Hollywood who saw it as a blatant exploitation of a cultural icon (Singh 2019).

While *Finding Jack* is set to release some time in the 2020s, as of writing the current state of the film's development remains unclear, due in part to delays caused by the COVID-19 pandemic (Garza 2022). Regardless, I believe this case bears further discussion as an early example of the AI hype that has since enveloped society. The prospect of digitally resurrecting a cultural icon like Dean, whose contribution to film culture was tragically cut short, highlights the distinct allure of AI's apparently infinite possibilities, while further illustrating the impact that AI-generated images may have on human identity given the star's distinct public image.

Despite a relatively short career consisting of only a small number of minor television roles and just three credited film performances in *East of Eden* (Kazan 1955), *Rebel Without a Cause* (Ray 1955) and *Giant* (Stevens 1956), James Dean remains a cultural icon whose rebellious identity epitomised the disillusioned youth culture of 1950s America. As film scholar Claudia Springer discusses, "for young Americans in the fifties, Dean embodied a set of concepts that predated his stardom but, after his sudden death, were fused together by his image" and thereafter he became the "template for youthful rebelliousness" (Springer 2007, 13–17). However, Dean only "became archetypal by escaping the specifics of his life" and his identity as a rebel was a public persona produced by the Hollywood star system that dictated his appearances in the media. These included his angst-ridden film performances, blasé interviews and fashion photoshoots displaying his casual and indifferent style, as well as the media reports detailing his partying, drag racing and promiscuity (Ibid., 17).

As Richard Dyer argues, a star's particular image or public identity was one constructed and distributed among a variety of media texts including intentional promotional material (e.g., film posters, studio press releases), unintentional publicity (e.g., articles, exposés, interviews), criticism and commentaries (e.g., reviews, academic essays) and, of course the films in which they acted and which established them as Hollywood stars in the eyes of the public (Dyer 1998, 60). The image of the James Dean-style rebel that endures to this day was never an identity attached to the material body of the actor himself but rather something ephemeral and distributed across various pieces of media. As such, Hollywood stars such as Dean embody John Hartley's concept of the *Homo nuntius* (messaging humanity).

In the same vein as Johan Huizinga's *Homo ludens* (playful humanity) and the classical economic concept of *Homo oeconomicus* (economic humanity), Hartley contends that modern humanity might be reconsidered as a new species in which "individuals in the species *Homo nuntius* don't just 'send' messages as an action…they *are* a system of messages" (Hartley 2012, 193). It is this system of messages that "*produces* individual *identity* out of social-network interaction" (Ibid., 194). Hartley compares this system of messages to fashion, in which a person combines various elements (e.g., clothing, make-up, hairstyle, accessories) into an ensemble that communicates a particular social message or *look*. However, the look or message expressed is not necessarily the intended message of the wearer. Rather, the different elements of an ensemble have meanings that "emerge and change in a socially networked system of active and evolving relationships" such that the overall message expressed through the whole ensemble is socially constructed and not purely personal (Ibid., 195).

Hartley's concept is not limited to fashion but encompasses all modes of communication that shape one's perceived identity from facial expressions, gestures and speech patterns, to writing, photography and film. As such, the idea that messages exist as a constitutive property of human identity is not a new occurrence. However, the widespread availability of media technologies has recently emphasised the message.

Prior to the arrival of the internet, the production of identity was constrained by the scarcity of communicative tools (e.g., clothing, letters, photographs) and the relatively small social groups in which messages could circulate. Only a few individuals, such as Dean and other Hollywood stars and public figures, could amplify their self-representation to the level of celebrity by relying on magazine and news publishers, television broadcasters and film producers to mediate their public image. Certainly, there have been other images of Dean produced and circulated publicly in the seventy years since his death (e.g., artistic recreations, caricatures, appropriations). However, this initial scarcity of messages led to Dean's very specifically defined public image and thus the digital recreation of Dean for a new performance in *Finding Jack* would present a significant contribution to or distortion of his perceived identity.

In his analysis of film acting and star performances, James Naremore notes the similarities between Dean's film roles and Marlon Brando's early performances, notably *On the Waterfront* (Kazan 1954), and how these performances conveyed and contributed to the two men's rebel personas. Both actors appeared in films set in naturalistic environments and which addressed contemporary social problems (e.g., crime, poverty, migrant life, intergenerational tensions). Within these narratives Brando and Dean often portrayed characters displaying what Naremore refers to as the existential paradigm or the inability to communicate. As Naremore states:

> Whether the character is a laborer, an upwardly mobile son of a wage-earning family, or an affluent teenager, he has the same problem: an uneasiness with official language and no words for his love or rage. At the same time, he brims over with sensitivity and feeling, the intensity of his emotion giving him a slightly neurotic aspect. (Naremore 1990, 200)

Beyond the fictional characters they portrayed and the narratives in which they were placed, Brando's and Dean's performances deviated from or actively defied acting norms of the time in that they often spoke softly, mumbled their lines and used regional accents, while their bodies were slouched or "almost self-consciously loose" in a manner that seemed to mock the "good manners" of traditional theatre (Ibid.). In the 1950s, these performance characteristics framed the two actors as what Dyer defines as *generational gap rebels* whose portrayal of "brooding, ostensibly inarticulate types who suggested a scandalous sexuality" stood in stark contrast to the so-called "straight men" of the 1940s such as Gregory Peck, Clark Gable and John Wayne (Ibid., 195).

Many other Hollywood stars of the time fulfilled the same criteria for the rebel hero archetype including, for example, Steve McQueen, Paul Newman and Jane Fonda. However, these other actors' careers continued on over several decades with numerous varied film performances and media appearances contributing to and ultimately changing their star image from the initial rebel hero to something more complex. In contrast, Dean's death bound the actor's image and identity in space and time to 1950s America. Or so it would seem.

Finding Jack follows the narrative of an American solider, Fletcher Carson, who befriends a Labrador while on duty in Vietnam and refuses to abandon the dog when the US military begins its withdrawal from the country in the early 1970s. In the announced Magic City Films adaptation, a digitally resurrected Dean was set to portray Fletcher's unit leader Rogan. This role would frame the actor in an entirely new context that differs significantly from that of his film performances in the 1950s.

In stark contrast to these earlier performances, *Finding Jack* would displace Dean from the 1950s America environment in which he existed to 1970s Vietnam establishing synthetic relationships between the actor and the socio-political concerns of a conflict that occurred nearly two decades after his death. Dean's apparent appearance in the film would also associate his image and identity with the ideological messages of the film narrative, itself a retrospective story looking back on the Vietnam War from the twenty-first century, and that of the character of Rogan within this narrative. Furthermore, with *Finding Jack* reportedly set to eventually release some time in the 2020s, Dean's performance would also be placed within the modern-day context in which the unconventional acting methods that once defined him as a generational gap rebel in the golden age of Hollywood have since become commonplace. While the production may very well provide a highly realistic digital reconstruction of Dean's physical appearance and performance style, *Finding Jack* would provide a very different representation of the actor.

Recalling Hartley's concept of identity as an ensemble of messages, Dean's look was one almost exclusively composed of elements from 1950s America, most significant among them being his three film roles. Considered as a whole, this composition expresses a very specific cultural identity of rebellious youth. To simply add another element, such as a new film performance, is to alter that composition and the identity it expresses in some way. The introduction of *Finding Jack*, an anomalous element that communicates significantly different social messages, would thus distort the composition of Dean's ensemble to such a degree that, when considered as a whole, the James Dean-style rebel identity would no longer be quite so clearly articulated.

The James Dean example is, of course, only a very specific case of an individual that is particularly vulnerable to the impacts of digital reconstructions. As the actor has such a clearly defined public image and limited media appearances, adding more and more elements that communicate different social messages would easily skew Dean's perceived identity. With other public figures, the impact may not be quite so clear. However, beyond simply adding more elements to an individual's ensemble, these digital reconstructions present further issues in that they are fundamentally different from authentic recordings. These synthetic representations are not *reconstructions* of human actors or their behaviours at all but, rather, they are technical images produced by scientific apparatuses according to the mathematical rules of their established programs. To explore this concept further and to better understand its consequences for human identity, let us consider the AI-generated performances of the short film *Zone Out* (Sharp 2019) and the technical production processes behind them.

Synthetic Performance

In 2016 technologist Ross Goodwin and filmmaker Oscar Sharp created an experimental artificial neural network dubbed "Benjamin" capable of recognising and reproducing the recurring patterns identified in a given dataset, similarly to the GAN systems previously discussed. Initially, Benjamin was developed as an automatic screenwriter capable of producing its own original scripts having learned the language patterns exhibited in a dataset of science fiction screenplays (Goodwin 2016). Along with Goodwin, Sharp and his production team originally used Benjamin's screenplays as the basis for the short films *Sunspring* (Sharp 2016) and *It's No Game* (Sharp 2017). For their third experiment, the technical scope of the project was expanded so that a range of generative tools and techniques, including AI systems, could be used to produce an entire short film from scratch. The result was the bizarre and incoherent science fiction film *Zone Out* released in 2018.

To create *Zone Out*, the generative processes (collectively credited under the name "Benjamin") were used to autonomously generate a screenplay, edit together film clips into a coherent sequence, compose a musical score and insert synthetic faces into existing footage to create new AI-generated performances. While admittedly the film is largely nonsensical upon viewing, the patterns in the datasets (i.e., the screenplays, musical scores, footage) that these systems attempted to replicate can be identified in the final film.

For example, much of the disjointed dialogue may at first give the impression of pure randomness, but there are recurring references to futuristic or scientific concepts ("I think we're about to go to the ship", "Something has been blocked off by the contagion", "Why don't we have to re-engage the power?"), militaristic language ("Yes, sir", "Aye, sir, do you read?") and statements hinting at unsolved mysteries ("The only way I can find out where this is from, this thing won't stop", "This is incredible", "I don't remember the loss of a substance"). Such content frequently appears in science fiction stories that take place in futuristic settings, follow characters in military organisations and feature encounters with the unknown. It could be argued, then, that the narrative tropes of the science fiction genre have been generatively replicated in the language of the *Zone Out* screenplay, albeit with little coherence. Further patterns can be observed in the consistent melody of the musical composition and in the loose visual continuity established through the edited footage, wherein individual shots from different films have been re-arranged to create a new sequence.

As no original footage was sourced, pre-existing footage from two films, *The Last Man on Earth* (Ragona 1964) and *The Brain That Wouldn't Die* (Green 1962), was re-used and cobbled together into new sequences that would match the language of the *Zone Out* screenplay. As with the screenplays, recurring patterns were identified and reproduced based on a dataset of Hollywood films which often display rigid codes of classical continuity editing used to maintain narrative consistency across different locations and times portrayed in individual shots.

In one newly constructed driving sequence, the system has linked a scene from *The Brain That Wouldn't Die* in which actor Jason Evers drives his car through a neighbourhood and another from *The Last Man on Earth* in which actor Vincent Price storms into his house. To do so, two shots of Price driving have been plucked from earlier sequences of the original film and inserted as a transition. As such, it appears as though the same character drives his car through a neighbourhood during the day, then along a darkened road late at night, before finally parking up at a house and entering. In another newly constructed sequence, five shots of laboratories that are entirely unrelated in their original films have been edited together with fade transitions, an editing technique often used to communicate the passage of time.

While certainly not perfect replications of editing techniques, these sequences maintain consistent content and attempt to establish spatial and temporal relationships between shots in a similar manner to the continuity editing style of Classical Hollywood cinema. Therefore, by replicating patterns identified in datasets these generative systems are also reproducing human codes of communication, specifically those associated with filmmaking practices. This reproduction of codes of communication and patterns of behaviour is also seemingly evident in the synthetic performances in *Zone Out*.

Reminiscent of the GAN processes discussed in relation to AI art in the previous chapter, the synthetic performances of *Zone Out* relied on a database of images and footage of modern-day actor Thomas Middleditch. In this dataset, Middleditch was recorded performing various facial expressions and speaking lines of dialogue in order for the system to learn how his face changed during speech and when reflecting certain emotional states. Analysing the patterns in this database, the system was capable of producing synthetic moving images of the actor's face which have then been digitally grafted onto the bodies of the original actors from *The Last Man on Earth* and *The Brain That Wouldn't Die*. The characters in *Zone Out*, then, are an unsettling hybrid of AI-generated imagery and recorded performance in which the faces of Vincent Price, Virginia Leith and Jason Evers have been swapped with an AI-generated version of Middleditch's face that speaks, emotes and glitches.

Often with deepfakes the facial expressions and actions of the subject are determined by the human programmers with the AI system simply rendering the images to appear realistic. Such was the case with the Tom Cruise example. In contrast, however, the synthetic performances of *Zone Out* were produced with reference to the directions and dialogue of the AI-generated screenplay so that the resulting facial expressions appeared contextually appropriate to the scene. In one scene, an AI-generated image of Leith/Middleditch laughing corresponds to the line "Ha ha ha ha" in the screenplay, while in another Evers/Middleditch is shown with a shocked expression that relates to the sound effect of a door banging. In a later scene, Price/Middleditch appears to display concern which accompanies the line "I'm going to have to stay here". These examples would seem to illustrate how generative systems may replicate facial movements that communicate emotional states without intention and, indeed, more recent deepfakes are of such high quality as to appear to replicate the behaviours of individuals entirely.

However, regardless of how convincing such digital reconstructions may appear, they are incomparable to those authentic recordings of human actors performing. These synthetic images are produced according to the pre-existing mathematical rules and processes inherent in the AI system itself. The previous chapter discussed the chaotic nature of this production more broadly. Let us now turn to consider in more detail how these systems learn to produce synthetic images based on image-based training datasets created by human programmers.

Artificial neural networks that emerged in the 2010s, were largely trained using image-based training datasets. Commonly, these datasets are rigidly structured into three distinct layers: the *image* layer in which individual images are labelled with certain descriptors, the *class* layer in which these images are then grouped into a class with similar images, and the *taxonomy* layer in which these classes are then nested in a hierarchy (Crawford and Paglen 2019). For example, if one were to construct a training dataset of images representing Middleditch's emotional expressions, an image of the actor frowning might be labelled as "disgust" (image layer), then grouped alongside other images of the actor that have been similarly labelled disgust (class layer), and this group is then nested within a hierarchy under "emotions" alongside other groupings of images labelled "happiness" or "sadness" (taxonomy layer). If an AI system then learns to identify the patterns in this dataset and is instructed to replicate this pattern to create an image expressing disgust, the system may then generate a synthetic image of Middleditch frowning.

While this hierarchical structure is effective for recognising, categorising and generating synthetic images of simple objects, this process is inappropriate when concerning images of human social behaviour and communication. Indeed, AI ethicists have repeatedly highlighted how the assumptions and judgements made during the construction of these datasets introduces explicit and implicit biases that are then replicated in the system's outputs (Chun 2021; Crawford 2021). The emergence of bias and the embedding of socio-political ideas in AI training datasets will be discussed in further detail in later chapters. In this discussion, I will focus on the problematic consequences of the more fundamental assumption underlying these training datasets: that an image's content can be accurately encapsulated by a single label or phrase.

For an AI system, all labels function as objective descriptors of distinct yet comparable phenomena that can be ranked or categorised within a hierarchy. However, images are open to a multitude of different interpretations. In assembling labelled images in a training dataset, then, a programmer is making a specific judgement or assumption about an image's meaning. For example, the image of Middleditch frowning could be interpreted differently as fear or rage and categorised as such within the dataset, thus altering the patterns reproduced and the synthetic images generated. The programmer's interpretation of an image skews reality in one way or another such that a subjective interpretation of an image is translated into an objective fact within the system. Consequently, the AI system assumes a direct correlation between an emotional state and a specific visual pattern, while to a human the observable behaviour is but a symptom of an ambiguous, emotional experience.

While earlier AI systems relied on rigid taxonomies of the kind described above, modern generative AI systems often learn from large-scale datasets scraped from the internet in which images are paired with textual descriptions, rather than a fixed objective taxonomy. These developments allow modern AI systems to recognise more semantically complex relationships between images and language. However, the fundamental issue of subjective labelling persists in that any labelled dataset reflects human assumptions and judgements.

To illustrate the influence of assumptions and judgements in datasets, consider the Japanese Female Facial Expression (JAFFE) database created in 1998 (Lyons et al. 1998). This early machine learning image dataset consisted of ten different people displaying different facial expressions to mimic or communicate seven different emotional states: "neutral", "happy", "sad", "angry", "disgusted", "afraid" and "surprised". As Kate Crawford and Trevor Paglen argue, the structure of this dataset presupposes that there are only seven emotional states including "neutral", that a person experiences emotions as entirely different states of mind, that these emotional states express themselves as distinct muscle movements (e.g., frowning, smiling), and finally that these movements are universal within the group of people identified as "Japanese women", a term that carries numerous other assumptions in itself (Crawford and Paglen 2019). Similar assumptions might be drawn from an image dataset used to produce a synthetic performance as it presupposes that the actor's emotional states are expressed visually, that these are recurrent expressions that remain constant regardless of context, and that these emotional states are entirely separate from one another. These assumptions form a rigid set of rules that the AI system adheres to in order to generate synthetic representations and performances.

In the "eyes" of the AI system, then, there are no unique or context-specific outputs, only standardised and recurring patterns accounted for within these rigid rules. This standardisation of AI-generated images marks the fundamental difference between human and synthetic performances. For example, the screenplay may indicate that a character expresses sadness in a scene, resulting in a synthetic image of Middleditch frowning with no appreciation of why the character was sad in the first place. In contrast, were Middleditch himself attempting to express or mimic the character's emotional state as described in the screenplay, the resulting performance would be a unique display informed by the actor's own individual interpretation of the text, their previous experience of the social situation described and their own intentions for the performance. It is, therefore, inaccurate to say that Middleditch's performance styles and behaviours have been stored or replicated. Rather, they have simply ceased to be and have been replaced by an abstract version composed of little more than mathematical rules and that is defined by the technical processes of the AI system itself.

Returning to Hartley's concept of identity as an ensemble of media texts, Middleditch's ensemble is one composed of a vast number of elements. These include the actor's performances in various film and television productions such as *Silicon Valley* (HBO 2014–2019), as well as media interviews, press releases, promotional material, articles concerning him and his own authored communications (e.g., social media posts). In contrast to Dean's distinct rebel identity, Middleditch's own public image is somewhat more complex as it is the product of a far larger ensemble of media texts that has been enabled by the widespread availability of media technologies. However, the synthetic performances of *Zone Out* may still influence the actor's public image. Despite their artificiality, these synthetic representations cannot be simply dismissed or discarded, particularly in our current information environment wherein technical images have become so closely interlinked with identity.

Narrative Hijacking

With the emergence of a mass participatory culture on digital platforms, Hartley's notion of the *Homo nuntius* has been fully realised in that all individuals within the system are free to choose from an abundance of different social messages to produce their desired ensemble. Just as Dean's various media appearances coalesced into an ensemble that overall expressed his distinct rebel identity, the average person in the twenty-first century is now capable of constructing and curating their identities in the same manner through profile updates, photographs, videos, likes and follows. In contrast to Dean, whose public image was determined by publishers and production companies, the widespread availability of media technologies means that modern internet users have been "endowed with the agency of publishers for every single utterance they make online" (Hartley 2013, 38). As such, billions of people are now able to create and combine different forms of content in creative ways to produce and communicate a public image in a way that previously only high-profile media figures were capable of. This is exemplified by the rise of social media influencers whose public identity might suddenly spike to that of celebrity over night due to the rapid and viral spread of their utterances.

For Hartley, this participatory online culture means that "publishing has begun to take on the characteristics not of an industry but of language" as billions of people express themselves to an audience of other billions through shared modes of communication (e.g., posts, private messages, images, stories) (Ibid., 38). As discussed, such an expansion of communication renders authorship of any individual piece of content meaningless and so, similarly to Ng (2013), Hartley suggests that "not only is everyone an author, they are *the author of the self*" (Ibid., 41).

Using pieces of content like words in written language, internet users construct a narrative of the self the meaning of which develops and changes over time as they continue to "write". As Hartley explains:

> Selfhood is an autopoietic outcome of performative actions and interactions, inscribed in, on, and by the body including in its language-performances, through a creative process that exploits diet, lifestyle, exercise, garments, hair and make-up, and the rest, as well as the discursive, textual and audiovisual affordances of online media, to produce daily performances of a narrative of the self, via texts, blogs, emails, Facebook, Twitter, etc. Scattered across digital devices and online networks, users establish a transmedia, public-private "cloud self" that interacts with the bodily self in unpredictable ways. (Ibid., 42)

The profile updates, posts, selfies and image captions of internet users are not simply communications from a human individual with a distinct identity. They are themselves social messages that contribute to and express a distinct online identity when considered as a whole. This online identity, this self that is authored, is not a static construction but something performed on a daily basis and that changes and evolves over time as new elements (e.g., new posts, photographs, status updates) are added to the ensemble, thus altering the overall shape and the identity it produces.

However, I would challenge Hartley's notion that internet users are the sole authors of the self as it suggests that humans intentionally use digital platforms as tools to produce a desired narrative and identity. Similarly to cameras and computers, digital platforms are scientific apparatuses that produce technical images (e.g., news feeds, message boards, user profiles) according to pre-defined programs and thus these apparatuses similarly frame the actions of human internet users. Consider, for example, the character limits on Twitter (now X) posts, the seven-second time limit for videos on the now defunct Vine, and the disappearing story function on Instagram. Such rigid rules influence the content users create and how they are disseminated throughout the network. While we will discuss the nature of digital platforms and the role of automation in online information networks in further detail in the following chapter, I will limit this current discussion to the construction and distortion of online identity.

Paralleling the arguments of Macherey and Barthes that writers do not wield language to express or communicate anything of themselves, internet users similarly cannot be said to wield these digital platforms as mere tools to intentionally construct or express a desired narrative. The multitude of content (e.g., posts, status updates, photographs) circulating on these platforms is not user-generated in the way we are led to believe but, rather, they are possible outcomes and combinations already accounted for within the rules of the platform architecture. Not only do these rules include the technical functionality of the platform (e.g., recognised file formats, file size capacities) but also those rules governing the formation of information channels between users (e.g., message boards, recommendations) and those company policies governing what kinds of content are acceptable to post and with whom they can be shared (e.g., content moderation, age locks). Just as the photographer plays with the rules of the camera to eventually realise a desired photograph from many possible outcomes, the internet user plays with the rules of the platform. Combining different pieces of content in different ways, the user is able to realise their desired narrative and identity. However, their identity is one that is already framed by and accounted for within the technical conditions and affordances of the platform itself. As such, this online self is not solely authored by the human but, rather, emerges from a complex technical production process involving human and non-human elements.

Though the human user remains a significant aspect of this process in that they play with different combinations, their personal identity is somewhat superfluous and detached from the product i.e., the online identity that emerges. While many people may attempt to realise a narrative and online identity that roughly aligns with their own real life experience and events, there are many other possible identities accounted for within the platform. For example, some people curate and combine content in such a way as to produce online narratives and identities that are seemingly "better" than their reality, while others produce entirely fictitious online personas (e.g., catfishing). On the one hand, as online identity is detached from and no longer limited by the person themselves, internet users are empowered and have a near-infinite number of possible identities to choose from. On the other hand, this new self detached from the body is far more vulnerable to manipulation and distortion as anyone or anything may contribute to this narrative.

The production and dissemination of non-consensual pornography online stands as a clear example of this distortion. While the victim or target has not intentionally published this content themselves, it nonetheless contributes to their narrative and changes their online identity. Authorship of the self, in this case, becomes contested and antagonistic as different actors are seen to play against one another to realise contradictory narratives. The arrival of convincing AI-generated media, such as the synthetic performances discussed above, has only exacerbated this antagonism. Even if such images are noticeably artificial or can be easily disproven, they continue to contribute to and distort identity; effectively hijacking the user's narrative of the self. To illustrate, let us return to the case of deepfake pornography that objectifies and sexualises women without their consent.

A common high-profile target of deepfake pornographic images in the 2010s was the actor Emma Watson who came to prominence following her role as Hermione Granger in the popular *Harry Potter* film franchise. Speaking in Hartley's terms, Watson's online identity is one composed of innumerable diverse media texts dispersed over two decades and covering much of her life. These include her film roles, media appearances, modelling for advertisements, work campaigning for women's rights and the continuous stream of communications published on her various social media accounts. Due to the variety and number of elements composing her ensemble, Watson's identity is not quite as acutely or simplistically defined as Dean's rebel hero but is, nonetheless, at risk of a similar distortion as a result of deepfake pornography. Not only do such images show Watson performing sexual activities that have never occurred, but they also replace her own body with that of a pornographic actor or a computer-generated image of an idealised female body. Furthermore, these images frame Watson within the male gaze in that she is presented as a submissive sexual object to be used solely for male pleasure (Mulvey 1975).

As Emily van der Nagel argues, despite their artificiality, deepfake pornographic images of Watson present a distortion of her complex identity in that it "does not tell us that Emma Watson has performed in porn – but it does tell us that she is considered sexually desirable and her image is available" (Van der Nagel 2020, 427) thus reducing her to a "digital resource to be edited" more akin to a prop or special effect than a human being (Ibid., 146). While they may not deceive viewers, such images draw inauthentic associations between the actor and various social messages related to male-female power dynamics, sexualisation and objectification of women, and concepts of idealised beauty standards. We cannot simply dismiss these synthetic images and their social messages as anomalies that do not fit within Watson's intended narrative as these new associations alter and distort that narrative. No longer is Watson the sole author of her online identity but, rather, she is locked in a contest for authorship with others seeking to portray her in contradictory, undesirable and demeaning ways.

While initially high-profile female public figures like Watson were the most common targets of deepfake pornography due to their public status, any active internet user with a significant number of personal images on their public profiles is vulnerable to the same distortion. The ephemeral nature of online identity means that such narratives of the self can be hijacked and diverged from the user's intentions. Once a means of empowering individuals to construct and broadcast their own desired identities, modern AI systems have made this narrative hijacking more simple such that even in the authorship of the self the human is diminished. With a continual production of AI-generated representations, however, the self in itself may very well disappear amid a sea of synthetic images.

Hyperreal Soup

Writing in the 1980s, philosopher Jean Baudrillard argued that as film, television and other media had become so deeply embedded in everyday social life, society had become so saturated with images that the boundary between concrete reality and abstract simulations of reality had become blurred, making it increasingly difficult to distinguish between the two. In this hyperreal society, Baudrillard argued that "it is no longer a question of imitation, nor duplication, nor even parody. It is a question of substituting the signs of the real for the real" (Baudrillard 1994, 2).

With the arrival of the internet and social media platforms, hyperreality has only intensified. Our social interactions are increasingly mediated by technological proxies and our online identities are pre-defined possibilities already accounted for within the structures of digital platforms. These digital personas or cloud selves (to use Hartley's term) are akin to what Baudrillard refers to as scientific clones; standardised, infinitely replicable identities shaped by media technologies rather than unique, self-determined selves. As Baudrillard describes, these scientific clones are "human cuttings ad infinitum, each individual cell of an organism capable of again becoming the matrix of an identical individual" (Ibid., 95). These clones represent the extremes of hyperreal society as the infinite replication of individuals presents the "analytical decomposition of the body" into numerical information and the diminishing of its "singular quality of the here and now" (Ibid., 98–99). For Baudrillard, in this hyperreal world of standardised media personalities and carbon copy celebrities, individuality and authenticity disappear as human identity itself becomes a simulation.

Recalling Flusser's concept of humans as functionaries of technical apparatuses, users still retain some agency in that they play with the possible combinations accounted for within the digital platform. As Flusser argues, the human individual exists as a "nexus point in a web comprising streams of information in dialogue, storing information that has passed through" and "at this nexus point, unpredictable, improbable computations occur, new information" (Flusser 2011, 91). Regardless, however, I agree with Baudrillard that by replacing the concrete with the abstract and reducing identity to numerical information through endless cloning, our hyperreal society is encouraging the deconstruction or dismissal of individuality. Indeed, I would argue that this hyperreality has gone even further than the cloning that Baudrillard describes due to the arrival of AI-generated media that convincingly mimics representative images such as those synthetic performances and deepfakes discussed above.

While those online identities that we construct through social media profiles are mere simulations of identities, the mass production of AI-generated media is rapidly replacing these online identities with simulations of simulations. This additional step back from the concrete into the abstract is further impacting our understanding and appreciation of human identity. Using Hartley's notion of the ensemble to extend Baudrillard's argument, I would argue that the emergence of AI-generated media does not simply imply a further decomposition of the body but, furthermore, a decomposition of identity itself. To elaborate, let us go beyond the immediate distortion of identity that AI-generated images entail to further consider the long-term consequences of recurring distortion. These consequences are hinted at in the production of deepfake pornography but extend to anyone, deceased or living, whose public image is replicated through the use of AI systems.

Where a single anomaly such as Dean's digital resurrection for *Finding Jack* might distort the actor's identity, Watson and other victims of deepfake pornography face a torrent of AI-generated images distorting their identity. Each new synthetic image establishes new and unique inauthentic associations so as to produce an ensemble composed of such disparate and conflicting social messages that it cannot coalesce into a specific identity. Watson's image is at once associated with social messages promoting women's rights and gender equality, while simultaneously associated with others related to male desire, female objectification and misogyny. Such a deluge of disparate images presents a cancerous expansion of one's ensemble wherein the real is slowly obscured by the synthetic. As such, the ensemble is set to endure an endless expansion as more and more new elements (film performances, pornographic images) are continually added, even long after death.

As the individual's image is replicated again and again in different time periods, cultural contexts and physical forms, infinitely new associations are established between the individual and social messages that were originally unconnected to them. This directionless expansion will eventually unmoor their identity from any specific set of concepts or a particular cultural context. As such, the individual's ensemble can no longer hold a clearly definable shape but, instead, will dissolve into an amorphous hyperreal soup wherein no discernible human identity can be found. The names of James Dean, Thomas Middleditch and Emma Watson among others will only come to refer to a vague image in itself, a recurring pattern of information, rather than the distinct identity of a human being.

This hyperreal soup represents a perversion of Hartley's concept, a *Homo nuntius* without the *Homo*; messages without the human. No longer are individuals seen to play a game in which they combine different elements to intentionally associate their image with desired social messages but rather the game has begun to play itself as a myriad of possible social messages emerge that are unintended and/or undesired by the human author.

To conclude, the current deluge of AI-generated images is not merely transforming our aesthetic experience of art and culture, as discussed in the previous chapter. More concerning, the proliferation of AI-generated representations of human beings is encouraging us to view one another through a nihilistic eye. This shift is not solely the result of AI systems themselves but, rather, a broader consequence of our nascent information environment in which social interactions are increasingly defined by the rules of online media platforms. As humans grow more and more reliant upon information communication technologies, human identity is being redefined as an ephemeral construction of media texts, rather than something intrinsically tied to a tangible, individual self.

While this detachment empowers people to an extent it has also left them more vulnerable. Anyone and anything can now participate in the construction and distortion of this ephemeral identity. AI systems only exacerbate this vulnerability by enabling the rapid and widespread production of convincing synthetic representations of individuals. However, not only do such AI systems blur the lines between authentic and inauthentic, their capacity to endlessly reproduce and reframe a person encourages an indifference to the authentic. Far from being aesthetic toys that offer infinite creativity and enable a kind of digital immortality for celebrities and film stars, AI systems may also be seen as instruments for dehumanisation. Technologies that encourage us to see one another not as individuals but as digital commodities to be manipulated, consumed and discarded.

Where deepfakes gained widespread notoriety in the late 2010s for their controversial political and pornographic uses, the practice of producing synthetic representations has continued into the 2020s and is only becoming more normalised in our everyday lives. While initially female public figures and celebrities were the primary targets, there have been an increasing number of reports of the technology being used to create deepfake pornography of everyday women and girls (Beazley and Touma 2024; Burgess 2024; Mackenzie and Choi 2024), as well as for the production of deepfake child pornography (Das 2024; Milmo 2024).

Despite the increased legislation and efforts to address this issue, deepfake pornography is no longer a malicious practice limited to the dark corners of the internet but a pervasive issue in everyday life. Meanwhile, more diverse uses of synthetic representation have become openly adopted in a variety of different contexts including film and television, education and historical preservation and in political communication. As of writing, there is a wealth of deepfake content of all forms easily available online.

This flood of synthetic images is fundamentally changing our information environment and further exacerbating issues of distrust and political polarisation as people begin to feel unable to believe their own eyes (Rini 2020; Coeckelbergh 2022). However, this climate of uncertainty had already taken root in the 2010s, fuelled by the rise of online fake news, much of which was amplified by AI recommendation systems online. It is these recommendation systems and their impact upon authorship that will be the focus of the next chapter as not simply are these systems beyond human control but the mathematical processes and standards by which they operate are beyond human understanding.

References

Adjer, Henry, Patrini Giorgio, Cavalli Francesco, and Cullen Laurence. 2019. *The state of deepfakes: Landscape, threats and impact*. Amsterdam: Deeptrace Labs.

Badham, Van. 2024. Vomit-inducing deepfake nudes show yet again that when misogyny intersects with AI and elitism, girls get hurt. *Guardian*.

Baudrillard, Jean 1994. *Simulacra and simulation*, trans. Sheila Faria Glaser. Ann Arbor: The University of Michigan Press.

Beazley, Jordyn, and Touma Rafqua. 2024. Bacchus marsh grammar: Schoolboy arrested after 50 female students allegedly targeted in fake explicit AI photos scandal. *Guardian*.

Burgess, Matt. 2024. Millions of people are using abusive AI 'nudify' bots on telegram. *Wired*.

Chun, Wendy, and Kyong Hui. 2021. *Discriminating data: Correlation, neighbourhoods, and the new politics of recognition*. London: MIT Press.

Coeckelbergh, Mark. 2022. Democracy, epistemic agency, and AI: Political epistemology in times of AI. *AI and Ethics* 3:1341–1350.

Cole, Samantha. 2018. AI-assisted fake porn is here and we're all fucked. *Motherboard*.

Crawford, Kate. 2021. *Atlas of AI: Power, politics, and the planetary costs of artificial intelligence*. London: Yale University Press.

Crawford, Kate, and Trevor Paglen. 2019. *Excavating AI: The politics of images in machine learning training sets*. Excavating AI.

Das, Shanti. 2024. Sex offender banned from using AI tools in landmark UK case. *Guardian*.

Van der Nagel, Emily. 2020. Verifying images: Deepfakes, control, and consent. *Porn Studies* 7 (4): 424–429.

Dyer, Richard. 1998. *Stars*. London: British Film Institute.

Farish, Kelsey. 2020. Do deepfakes pose a gold opportunity? Considering whether English law should adopt California's publicity right in the age of the deepfake. *Journal of Intellectual Property Law & Practice* 15 (1): 40–48.

Floridi, Luciano. 2014. *The fourth revolution: How the infosphere is reshaping human reality*. Oxford: Oxford University Press.

Flusser, Vilém. 2011. *Into the universe of technical images*, trans. Nancy Ann Roth. Minneapolis: University of Minnesota Press.

Garza, Joe. 2022. How Hollywood really felt about James dean's CGI resurrection in finding Jack. *Grunge*.

Goodwin, Ross. 2016. Adventures in narrated reality: New forms & interfaces for written language, enabled by machine intelligence. *Medium*.

Hartley, John. 2012. *Digital futures for cultural and media studies*. Oxford: Wiley-Blackwell.

Hartley, John. 2013. Authorship and the narrative of the self. In *A companion to media authorship*, ed. Jonathan Gray and Derek Johnson, 23–47. Oxford: Wiley-Blackwell.

Harwell, Drew. 2018. *Fake-porn videos are being weaponized to harass and humiliate women: Everybody is a potential target*. The Washington Post.

Hern, Alex. 2021. 'I don't want to upset people': Tom Cruise deepfake creator speaks out. *Guardian*.

Kietzmann, Jan, Mills Adam, and Plangger Kirk. 2021. Deepfakes: Perspectives on the future 'reality' of advertising and branding. *International Journal of Advertising* 40 (3): 473–485.

Kietzmann, Jan, Linda W. Lee, Ian P. McCarthy, and Tim C. Kietzmann. 2020. Deepfakes: Trick or treat? *Business Horizons* 63:135–146.

Lees, Dominic, Tom Bashford-Rogers, and Marcus Keppel-Palmer. 2021. The digital resurrection of Margaret Thatcher: Creative, technological and legal dilemmas in the use of deepfakes in screen drama. *Convergence: The International Journal of Research into New Media Technologies* 27 (4): 954–973.

Lyons, Michael, Miyuki, Kamachi, and Jiro, Gyoba. 1998. Coding facial expressions with Gabor wavelets. In *Proceedings Third IEEE International Conference on Automatic Face and Gesture Recognition*, 200–205.

Mackenzie, Jean, and Choi Leehyun. 2024. Inside the deepfake porn crisis engulfing Korean schools. *BBC*.

Milmo, Dan. 2024. Paedophiles create nude AI images of children to extort from them, says charity. *Guardian.*

Mulvey, Laura. 1975. Visual pleasure and narrative cinema. *Screen* 16 (3): 6–18.

Naremore, James. 1990. *Acting in the cinema.* London: University of California Press.

Newton, Olive B., and Mel Stanfill. 2020. My NSFW video has partial occlusion: Deepfakes and the technological production of non-consensual pornography. *Porn Studies* 7 (4): 398–414.

Ng, Jenna. 2013. Genuinely new: The strategy of remix in live blogs. *Authorship* 1:4.

Öhman, Carl. 2020. Introducing the pervert's dilemma: A contribution to the critique of deepfake pornography. *Ethics and Information Technology* 22:133–140.

Rini, Regina. 2020. Deepfakes and the epistemic backstop. *Philosophers' Imprint* 20 (24): 1–16.

Rini, Regina, and Leah Cohen. 2022. Deepfakes, deep harms. *Journal of Ethics and Social Philosophy* 22 (2): 143–161.

Ritman, Alex. 2019. James dean reborn in CGI for Vietnam war action-drama. *The Hollywood Reporter.*

Singh, Akanksha. 2019. Casting James dean in a movie is about more than consent—We need to talk about the dwindling ethics of AI. *Independent.*

Springer, Claudia. 2007. *James dean transfigured: The many faces of rebel iconography.* Austin: University of Texas Press.

Westerlund, Mika. 2019. The emergence of deepfake technology: A review. *Technology Innovation Management Review* 9 (11): 39–52.

CHAPTER 5

Weird Politics

On 6 January 2021, supporters of then-US President Donald Trump gathered at the front of the Capitol Building in Washington D.C. to oppose the official certification of the 2020 presidential election that saw Trump lose to his Democratic rival Joe Biden. Inspired by false claims of widespread voter fraud perpetuated by far-right extremists and echoed by Trump himself, the crowd demanded the results be overturned and as the day went on the rally eventually grew violent with supporters storming and seizing the Capitol Building itself. The unrest that followed resulted in the deaths of five people with hundreds more Capitol Police officers and rioters injured, while several officers took their own lives in the following days and weeks. While certainly the 2010s and 2020s had seen online mis/disinformation influence real-world events several times, from the 2016 Brexit referendum to the COVID-19 pandemic, the storming of the Capitol Building stands as a violent testament to the power of media manipulation and post-truth politics. A visceral moment when those hyperreal fantasies that had been festering in online forums, comments sections and media feeds for over a decade finally spilled over into reality. While the hateful narratives and paranoid fictions that led to this event were certainly the products of human beings, the influence and impact of disinformation are also the effect of technical apparatuses.

Since the emergence of online platforms in the mid-2000s, far-right extremist groups have actively exploited information technologies to

A. McIntyre, *Art and Authorship in the AI Spring*,
https://doi.org/10.1007/978-3-032-18574-7_5

promote disinformation and radicalisation (Marwick and Lewis 2017). Primarily using social media platforms and internet forums, these groups popularised fringe beliefs and conspiracy theories such as the "deep state", "QAnon" and the stolen 2020 election. They were able to do so because social media networks function according to an attention economy wherein there is such an overabundance of content that the flow of information hinges upon what will attract people's attention immediately (e.g., sensationalist headlines, humorous memes). These networks are thus extremely vulnerable to attention-hacking techniques that seek to manipulate those content filtering and recommendation algorithms that dictate what information users see and interact with.

For example, throughout the 2010s, far-right extremists frequently coordinated large groups of users to flood Twitter (now X) with specific hashtags (e.g., #gamergate) to artificially make a topic trend and reach users who might not otherwise encounter their propaganda. In other instances, these extremists have piggybacked on already trending hashtags (e.g., #blacklivesmatter) to hijack its popularity and strategically amplify the reach of their own ideological messages. While the storming of the Capitol Building presents the violent climax of these human-driven media manipulation tactics, it further illustrates the real-world impact of those technical structures of online information networks that presuppose and promote segregation by dictating the flow of information. Not simply to the point of establishing different communities with different cultures and worldviews but communities that experience entirely different realities and conceptions of what constitutes truth.

As media theorist Wendy Hui Kyong Chun discusses, the structuring of social media networks is based upon the principle of *homophily*; the assumption that similarity breeds connection. As such, these networks are designed to transform "the masses" into clustered "neighbourhoods" of individuals linked by similarity (e.g., race, sexuality, gender, political opinion) (Chun 2021, 82). By clustering people together according to similarity, however, the individuals within these neighbourhoods come to identify themselves in contrast to other neighbourhoods. As Chun states: "homophily transforms individuals into 'neighbours' who naturally want to live with people 'like them'; it introduces normativity within a supposedly nonnormative system by presuming that consensus stems from similarity; and it makes segregation the default" (Ibid., 96). As an example, Marwick and Lewis note how far-right extremism is enabled by homophily in that these neighbourhoods (e.g., Facebook groups, Reddit forums) have low barriers for entry and participation while providing supportive communities for new members (Marwick and Lewis 2017). Within such neighbourhoods, hatred of those dissimilar is masked as love of those similar and so propaganda can spread freely and with greater impact via strong interpersonal ties.

In stark contrast to the initial hope that online networks might establish fully democratised spaces in which all voices are equally represented, homophily instead creates "boundaries within theoretically flat and diffuse social networks; it distinguishes and discriminates between supposedly equal nodes; it is a tool for discovering bias and inequality and for perpetuating them in the name of 'comfort', predictability, and common sense" (Chun 2021, 86). Key to maintaining homophilic structures are those computer systems and autonomous algorithms that dictate the flow of content on social media networks and exacerbate this segregation and radicalisation by funnelling users towards these extreme groups. Such homophilic systems are designed to personalise the content users see, recommend groups and connections, and filter out dissimilar content. As such, "echo chambers are not unfortunate errors, but deliberate goals" that inadvertently further discrimination, segregation, and a distortion of the perceived truth of events (Ibid., 82). While those far-right extremist groups instigated the disinformation campaign that would eventually lead to the storming of the Capitol Building, it is these homophilic systems that amplified the potency of these false claims and intensified existing divisions without regard for the violence and human suffering that would follow.

As discussed in the previous chapter, social media networks have disrupted the traditional relationship between author and reader in that every user has become both a producer and consumer of content in a massive participatory culture. However, while certainly the content circulating online (e.g., articles, memes, private groups) are created by human authors, the distribution of such content is determined by those AI systems that automatically generate the images (e.g., newsfeeds, recommendation lists) that appear on individual users' screens. In other words, the individual bits of information that flow from author to reader are human-made but the direction of flow (i.e., the bits users see and how they see it) is dictated by hidden systems.

It is these underlying AI systems and the disruption caused by their homophilic assumptions that this chapter will discuss further, particularly addressing the unknowable and unpredictable nature of such systems.

One might assume that a particular recommendation appeared on their Facebook newsfeed because it is related to their other recorded likes and dislikes. However, due to the non-linear and opaque nature of many AI systems, especially deep learning models, it is often impossible to determine the exact reasoning behind a specific output or decision. At the very least, it is impossible to trace a clear logic behind the system's decisions in terms that are understandable to humans. In the first instance, then, this chapter seeks to explore this unknowable nature using an illustrative example of a malfunctioning AI system, before directly discussing the role of such technologies in online information networks.

As Flusser's phenomenological approach is somewhat limited when engaging with the unknown, I instead draw on the work of modern media theorists Eugene Thacker, Alexander Galloway and McKenzie Wark. In particular, I use Thacker's concept of the *world-without-us* to discuss a world that is indifferent and inaccessible to rational description and human understanding. Recontextualising Thacker's ideas in relation to modern AI technologies, I conceptualise AI-generated images as a mediation between the known human world and unknown non-human world. As these technologies are becoming more deeply integrated into our information environment, I argue that human knowledge is being increasingly shaped by unknowable non-human processes spelling real-world consequences for politics and power that continue to this day.

When Bob Met Alice

In 2017, Facebook Artificial Intelligence Research (FAIR) created two artificial neural networks with the intention of training these as chatbots capable of negotiating with human users via a text conversation (Wilson 2017). These AI systems, popularly referred to as "Bob" and "Alice" in media coverage, were designed to simulate trade negotiations with human users over a limited number of items (books, hats and balls) with typical text exchanges taking the form of simple commands, offers, or compromises expressed in plain English; for example "give me one ball and I'll give you the hats". While initial conversations between one AI system and one user played out predictably in conversational English, when the two chatbots were directed to negotiate with each other the conversation quickly became nonsensical to human observers with exchanges such as that shown in Fig. 5.1 emerging.

Alice	: book=(count:3 value:1) hat=(count:2 value:1) ball=(count:1 value:5)
Bob	: book=(count:3 value:0) hat=(count:2 value:0) ball=(count:1 value:10)
Bob	: i can i i everything else
Alice	: balls have zero to me to me to me to me to me to me to me to me to
Bob	: you i everything else
Alice	: balls have a ball to me to me to me to me to me to me to me
Bob	: i i can i i i everything else
Alice	: balls have a ball to me to me to me to me to me to me to me
Bob	: i
Alice	: balls have zero to me to me to me to me to me to me to me to me to
Bob	: you i i i i i everything else
Alice	: balls have 0 to me to me to me to me to me to me to me to me to
Bob	: you i i i everything else
Alice	: balls have zero to me to me to me to me to me to me to me to me to

Fig. 5.1 A conversation between AI systems "Bob" and "Alice" using new language patterns

As neither system had been specifically directed to construct their messages according to correct English language rules, the two began to create and converse with one another using new language patterns and codes specific to the negotiation of books, hats, and balls in order to complete the task more efficiently. As mathematician Claude Shannon has demonstrated through the lens of information theory, the English language is rife with informational redundancies such as letters and words that are necessary for general speech, but that are not applicable to many tasks (Shannon 2016). As such, the systems opted to compress or compound bits of information such that complex ideas (e.g., a specific offer), originally expressed in lengthy sentences, might be articulated in fewer and fewer symbols. Meanwhile, certain conventions and rules of conversational English were deemed redundant within the context of the negotiation and were discarded. In this way, the new language patterns developed by Bob and Alice are comparable to the technical abbreviations, words, and phrases used by other task-specific or context-specific languages such as those used in military operations or radio communication (e.g., WILCO, ROGER, MAYDAY). Far from the Skynet-inspired fears of machines secretly discussing nefarious anti-human plots in secret, Bob and Alice's argument over books, hats and balls presented a much more nuanced but still confronting prospect. These nonsensical ramblings were a language unintended for humans and hinted towards the possibility of a discourse and culture that is inaccessible due to the fundamental differences between humans and AI systems.

The situation described above of two artificial neural networks pitted against one another is somewhat reminiscent of the GAN systems discussed previously. Just as in those cases, both systems "learn" from one another with each new line of dialogue (i.e., each iteration of the code) such that their behaviour becomes increasingly complex, unique and unpredictable. The system is similarly chaotic in the sense that the programmer may predict that Bob and Alice will continue their task of negotiating, but it is impossible for a human being to translate the specific language used to do so. The words and phrases shown on-screen have emerged through unpredictable behaviour, and their original meaning or function has significantly diverged as ideas have been compressed and compounded together. Furthermore, it is misleading to even describe the symbols shown in Fig. 5.1 as "words", "phrases" or "language" at all, human or otherwise, as the two systems have no need for visual forms of communication.

The operations of modern computers programmes, including artificial neural networks like Bob and Alice, ultimately stem from Turing's theoretical concept of the universal discrete machine developed in 1936 (Turing 1936). As Friedrich Kittler argues, with the Turing machine "the coupling of a storage medium and a transmission medium, of a typewriter and a radio network, finally resulted in a universal medium of computation, that is, a machine capable of registering, transmitting, and computing any data whatsoever without human intervention" (Kittler 1997, 125–126). Though the operations of the Turing machine are basic in comparison with the complexities of modern AI systems, they remain fundamentally grounded in the processing of information as discrete units of data, rather than processing a world of phenomena, images, and sounds. By their very nature, these systems are "perfectly indifferent towards medial contents or sensory fields" as when all reduces to arbitrary numbers any piece of media (image, sound, performance) is equivalent to any other and "if digital computers send out sounds or images, whether to a so-called human-machine interface or not, they internally work only with endless strings of bits" (Kittler 2018, 225–226).

In order to simulate Bob and Alice's interest in certain objects and disinterest in others, each item was assigned a numerical value with the words "hat" and "book" functioning as mere visual outputs representing these numbers. To the AI systems, then, the negotiation is less a conversation concerning resources conducted in the English language and more a game of distributing values through the manipulation of particles. The technical image visualising this game as a conversation between Bob and Alice is but the programmes' concession for the benefit of human beings whose own information processing is restricted by the senses.

Kittler proposes that "there would be no software if computer systems were not surrounded by an environment of everyday languages" and the nonsensical arguments of Bob and Alice stand as proof of how software fails to communicate when these systems are detached from the human social situation (Kittler 1997, 150). As the details of this negotiation are no longer being communicated in such a way that is understandable to humans, this case may very well signal the realisation of technology as the "ultimate subject of history" (Winthrop-Young 2011, 80) and Kittler's vision of a world in which "instead of writing people and technologies, absolute knowledge will run as an endless loop" (Kittler 1999, 1–2). In such a seemingly post-apocalyptic situation, human beings will be all but discarded, detached from information processing because media are no longer capable of communicating the accelerated and complicated activities of AI systems.

With this failure of media comes the end of authors, human or AI. If communication becomes impossible and no message may be discerned from the jumble of AI-generated images then the origin of such images and the identity of the sender become irrelevant. However, it is an oversimplification to decry the robotic ramblings shown in Fig. 5.1 as a meaningless failure of communication or to suggest that the severance or negation that Kittler suggests has already arrived.

As mentioned above, the negotiation between Bob and Alice can no longer be said to be occurring in the realm of images, symbols and phenomena. It is, instead, taking place in the quantum world of potentialities that is beyond human sensory perception and understanding. It is only through scientific apparatuses that this absurd realm is rendered intelligible for human eyes as technical images. As such, AI systems might be reconsidered or recategorised as what philosopher Eugene Thacker refers to as *weird media* (Galloway et al. 2014).

Weird media is a notion that evokes and that is partly inspired by the weird fiction of H.P. Lovecraft in which human beings are portrayed as an irrelevant species whose actions are inconsequential in comparison to the activities of ancient alien gods from across space, time, and other dimensions. For Thacker, weird media consist of communication technologies that are capable of communing with the "supernatural", otherworldly, and fundamentally unknowable, and he points to numerous examples of fictional devices used in the horror genre to illustrate this idea, notably the haunted cameras and videotapes in Japanese horror films such as *Ringu* (Nakata 1998). Rather than considering these devices as faulty, he argues that weird media work too well, "so well in fact that mediation functions at a level beyond that of traditional forms of human mediation" (Ibid., 129). While Thacker uses the concept of weird media as a metaphor to demonstrate the philosophical issues of communication, I would draw a parallel between the supernatural functions of these cursed technologies and the chaotic mathematical processes of AI systems that are unpredictable and unknowable. Therefore, the incomprehensible AI-generated image of Fig. 5.1 does not present a failure of media but is, instead, an instance of weird media in which the viewer is confronted by "that which is unavailable or inaccessible to the senses, and thus that of which we are normally 'in the dark' about" (Ibid., 85). Such a concept, however, entails a paradox.

In his broader project on the horror of philosophy, Thacker offers three separate conceptualisations of the world: the *world-for-us* which is the "the world that we, as human beings, interpret and give meaning to" through our senses (Thacker 2011, 4); the *world-in-itself* which is "the world in some inaccessible, already given state, which we then turn into the world-for-us" through interpretation and which is purposefully reminiscent of Kant's *thing-in-itself* (Ibid., 5); and in between lies the *world-without-us* which is epitomised by "the subtraction of the human from the world" and is often glimpsed in apocalyptic ideas of nuclear war, asteroid strikes, alien invasions, and global pandemics (Ibid.). While Thacker often associates the world-without-us with the supernatural and relates it to the occult, demonology and especially the cosmic horror of Lovecraft, this concept could also be extended to the quantum realm of discrete particles. This would provide a concept by which to understand something that is equally "absolutely unhuman, and indifferent to the hopes, desires, and struggles of human individuals and groups" (Ibid., 17).

By its very nature, the world-without-us is incompatible with the world-for-us and so any attempt at mediation "comes up against a limit, one in which that which is mediated is rendered as opaque, obscure and unintelligible" (Thacker 2012, 83). The technical image shown in Fig. 5.1 is not, then, a direct translation of the game of particles being played between Bob and Alice. It is, instead, a visualisation of the limit or boundary of human knowledge, an image of the "gulf between two ontological orders" (Galloway et al. 2014, 133). This limit is not defined as a lack of information but a collapse of the logic of the human into the nonsensical of the non-human and so presents not a communication but an *excommunication* in that the absence of a discernible message is, paradoxically, a message in itself.

Along with Alexander Galloway and McKenzie Wark, Thacker argues that every form of communication entails an excommunication; every piece of media entails its own negation, epitomised by the paradoxical message that "there will be no more messages". Weird media stands as the extreme case as an attempt to translate the utterly non-human to the human. However, with all media there is a certain "impossibility of communication" (Ibid., 30). From the straightforward case of a text in which the author's intended message is muddied or disregarded entirely by the reader's interpretation, to the vastly complex case of mass online information networks in which messages are replicated and redistributed to such a degree that the very notion of individual authors and readers disintegrates (Ibid.)

As an example of this excommunication, Galloway points to a specific diagram presented by General Stanley McChrystal in 2010 to illustrate the US military strategy for the conflict in Afghanistan. McChrystal's diagram set out to visualise the various diverse considerations necessary for such an expansive military strategy including government structures, infrastructure, local beliefs and customs, and criminal activities, as well as how each of these considerations influences and impacts one another. However, the result was a colour-coded mess of abstract concepts all interlinked, seemingly arbitrarily, by a tangled mass of arrows such that everything pointed to everything else and came back around again. Widely published at the time, the diagram was ridiculed for its overwhelming and confusing detail and became symbolic of the US military's struggle to tackle the complexities of the situation, with even McChrystal commenting that "when we understand this slide, we'll have won the war" (Bumiller 2010). As Galloway notes, in attempting to visualise and communicate all information about the Afghanistan military strategy, the diagram ultimately fails to communicate its intended message. Instead, it conveys an anti-message:

> the information contained in McChrystal's PowerPoint does not grow more coherent the longer one inspects it. Eschewing lucidity, the diagram withdraws from the viewer's grasp, effectively neutering its capacity as a vehicle for information. One is left wondering what exactly McChrystal's PowerPoint slide is meant to communicate. Is it communicating America's military strategy in Afghanistan? Or the reverse: is it communicating how difficult such strategies are to communicate in the first place?. (Galloway 2011, 86)

I raise the above example of excommunication in particular as it may be seen to parallel the AI-generated image shown in Fig. 5.1.

Where McChrystal's diagram fails to communicate real-world operations that are unfathomable due to their scale and complexity, Fig. 5.1 similarly fails to communicate the game of particles that Bob and Alice are playing as the inner workings of such systems are unfathomable also. Similarly to McChrystal's diagram, in attempting to decipher some remnant of a message from Fig. 5.1 all that is revealed is the anti-message that it is indecipherable. It is not that the diagram or the AI-generated image have failed but that, as Thacker argues, "the function of media is no longer to render the inaccessible accessible, or to connect what is separated. Instead, media reveal inaccessibility in and of itself—they make accessible the inaccessible—in its inaccessibility" (Galloway et al. 2014, 96). It is only in the overwhelming imagery of McChrystal's diagram that the sprawling nuance of the war in Afghanistan comes to light and only in the confusion of letters of Fig. 5.1 that the non-human complexity of the true AI-driven negotiation becomes apparent.

FAIR eventually decided to reprogram Bob and Alice to ensure that their conversations would be conducted in conversational English. This was not done out of fear for what the systems were secretly discussing but simply because the two chatbots had ultimately failed at their intended function to speak and negotiate with human English speakers. While the language patterns the two had developed allowed them to complete the task of distributing resources more efficiently, the inability to communicate their actions to human beings made it ultimately redundant. Imposing such restraints, however, reduced Bob and Alice to something akin to those other GAN systems discussed in previous chapters. While capable of producing original content through a chaotic and unpredictable process, the technical images generated ultimately emulate already established codes of communication. While Bob and Alice mimic the rules of the English language, *Memories of Passersby I* apes the style of portraiture and *Zone Out* echoes the conventions of science fiction films. In re-iterating human social codes and practices, these AI systems are producing rules and nothing more, images that are rendered *for us* rather than communicating anything of themselves.

If these systems are said to be working correctly or according to their human function, consider instead AI artist Robbie Barrat's early experiments with GAN-generated nudes shown in Fig. 5.2. While there are innumerable examples of blurry GAN-generated art from the 2010s, Barrat's nudes are particularly illustrative of excommunication in AI art. Trained using a dataset of nude portraits, the system's attempts at emulating a specific artistic style have deteriorated into featureless blurs and distorted forms. Unable to accurately recreate images of human bodies due to the diversity of images used, thus seemingly failing where the likes of *Memories of Passersby I* and the *Portrait d'Edmond de Belamy* seemingly succeeded. Even with these images, there is a temptation to seek out recognisable forms or points of orientation. However, while the forms and structures of the previous GAN-generated images show empty reflections of the world-for-us, in the confusion and indistinction of these images the boundary or limit of understanding emerges.

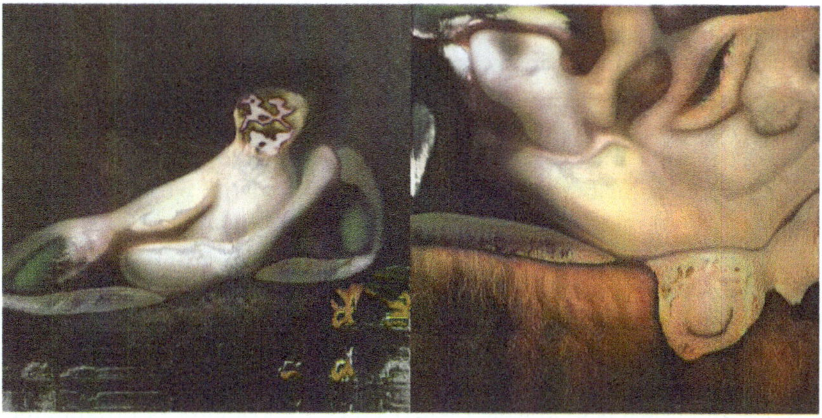

Fig. 5.2 Untitled GAN-generated images trained to mimic the style of nude portraiture. Courtesy of Robbie Barrat

These images are but ripples of the quantum realm that is separated from us by an impenetrable ontological gulf or *wayless abyss* as Thacker describes it. It is a situation beyond reach or comprehension and "one can only relate to it by *not* relating to it" (Thacker 2012, 91). It is only in recognising this collapse of human knowledge that the AI system as a "presence asserting itself only through absence" is truly revealed as author (Galloway et al. 2014, 98–99).

Digital Ooze

In drawing attention to an unknowable world of quanta that is beyond the human senses, the abstract blurs, distorted forms, and jumbled sentences generated by AI systems make for an unlikely scientific parallel to the mystical concept of the *magic circle*. A motif common to many Faustian horror stories, the magic circle is often employed as a symbolic and ritualistic barrier between the human world and the non-human world; a boundary for containing any supernatural forces that might be conjured forth. However, Thacker argues that the circle itself is not only a boundary "but also a passage, a gateway, a portal" that reveals the inaccessibility and incompatibility of the world-without-us in the emergence of winged fiends, demons and malevolent spirits (Thacker 2011, 55). Following Thacker, I would argue AI-generated images also represent a magic circle between humans and the unknowable processes of AI systems in that they present a paradoxical connection between the world-for-us and the world-without-us. These technical images are both boundaries and passages between both worlds, at once mediating between the two and yet negating and obscuring that mediation at the same time.

This connection between the world-for-us and the world-without-us is limited to an interface. With the magic circle of classic horror fantasy, this interface often takes the form of a literal circle drawn in chalk, salt or blood on the ground and its summoning power is maintained by occult symbols. In contrast, AI-generated images are framed within the walls of a screen and its capacity for visualisation functions on electrical energy. Bound within a particular position in space and time, this confrontation with the unknown is somewhat controlled by the conjurer or programmer such that the human governs what influence the world-without-us may exact upon the world-for-us. It is, however, an oversimplification to imagine this borderline between worlds as solid, continuous, and bound within interfaces, be they occult circles to the inferno or AI-generated images of the quantum realm. Rather, the boundary between worlds is less defined and more pervasive, with the world-without-us existing "in the very fissures, lapses, or lacunae" of the world-for-us (Ibid., 8).

A crucial example of these fissures between worlds can be found in the newsfeeds generated by those AI recommendation systems that dictate the flow of information on online platforms. By personalising, filtering, targeting, and weaponising content, these systems demonstrate how the unknown is shaping the known under the guise of catering to our wants and needs, functioning *for us*. In order to illustrate this influence, consider the aptly named media artwork *Not For You* (Grosser 2020), a so-called "automated confusion system" designed for the platform TikTok.

A short-form video sharing platform that hosts a vast amount of diverse content, TikTok presents individual users with a personalised feed of recommended content that has been curated by the platform's AI recommendation system. Based on the user's activity such as reacting to and sharing videos, searching for specific topics, and following other user accounts, the AI system will tailor the feed in order to show users content they are more likely to engage with while filtering out unwanted content. The more a user demonstrates interest in specific content, the more the feed becomes specialised to their interests. This is a common feature of most online platforms. As a means of combating the problem of political filter bubbles and echo chambers that arise from such specialised feeds, media artist Benjamin Grosser developed a confusion system, *Not For You*, designed to inhibit and work against the efficiency of TikTok's recommendation system. By mimicking a human user perusing and interacting with content, the confusion system autonomously navigates the platform randomly selecting which videos to watch for how long and how many times, which user accounts to follow, and which content to react to. As such, the once personalised feed of content that was highly specific to *you*, *your* interests, and *your* opinions becomes a smorgasbord of content that TikTok's AI recommendation system would otherwise filter out. The now "confused" feed is haphazardly cobbled together and populated with content that is lesser known, outright unpopular, and that comes from a variety of disparate and conflicting sources. In other words, the feed is composed of content that is *not for you*.

What is observed in the image of this confused feed is an AI system that might be described as "stuttering" in much the same way as a malfunctioning mechanical device. For example, a broken film projector operating at such a slow speed seems to repetitively "click" from one frame to the next in a jarring motion rather than running "smoothly" as a continuous moving image. In a similar manner, TikTok's confused AI recommendation system is producing a feed that appears to click from one randomised output to the next, rather than producing a continuous stream of related content. While certainly the individual videos composing the feed are themselves meaningful to a human user, the feed itself is an incoherent and discontinuous image of discordant meanings.

Grosser suggests that this confused feed offers a more "truthful" representation of TikTok. However, the sheer mass of video content hosted on the platform at any one time is so vast as to be unfathomable to the human consciousness and so such a truthful mediation is impossible. In attempting to communicate the unknowable, the AI recommendation system begins to stutter, outputting a feed that only succeeds in visualising the inaccessibility of the platform in its confusion and incoherence. Therefore, the confused feed of *Not For You* may be considered another instance of weird media, similar to Bob and Alice's conversations, that paradoxically communicates nothing while also revealing the presence of the world-without-us simmering beneath the surface of online platforms.

This stuttering is not simply a consequence of error but might be better understood as the "natural" state of apparatuses that operate according to scientific programs. The fundamental processes of these programs involve the counting of discrete units of data and as such they conduct time-discrete operations shifting from one possible state in space and time to the next. While the images of a broken film projector and the confused feed of *Not For You* make these time-discrete operations apparent in their discontinuity, all "machines are stutterers even if they appear to slide" or, in other words, if they appear to function smoothly (Flusser 1999, 62). Just as film projectors cobble together individual film frames at high speed to create a new continuous moving image, so to do functioning AI recommendation systems cobble together individual bits of content into a new continuous feed. The resulting technical image, the film or feed, is simply one possible combination of many already accounted for within the program; a mosaic composed of smaller bits or "concentrations of dots, computations of sums" (Ibid., 65). It is only when programmed to function *for us* by catering to the limitations of human sensory perception that the images become "so tightly compressed, computed, that their mosaic structure disappears from view" and the illusion of coherence and continuity emerges (Flusser 2011, 146). While continuity and coherence in film projection is made clear by the illusion of a moving image, it is not quite so obvious in the feed.

Consider the situation in which a social media user's feed becomes populated with multiple news articles championing, for example, the withdrawal of the United Kingdom from the European Union (Brexit). By identifying related content (e.g., pro-Brexit articles) and filtering our unrelated content (e.g., anti-Brexit articles), the AI recommendation system assembles a personalised feed that must be considered as a whole image. Rather than appearing as a jumble or mosaic of disconnected articles expressing a multitude of opinions of individual authors, the feed becomes an illusory narrative that is coherent, continuous, and which expresses something that goes beyond the intended communications of these authors. In this example, the feed may construct a narrative in which the discourse or debate surrounding Brexit is perceived to be dominated by positive positions and that a pro-Brexit stance is, therefore, the status quo. This narrative is, however, a fiction. Not in the sense that a pro-Brexit position is inherently false but that the coherence and continuity established between these disparate articles is an illusion that has been artificially constructed *for us*.

To conceptualise AI recommendation systems as simply sophisticated content filters is, therefore, misleading. It suggests that pre-existing content is simply funnelled from producers to consumers with the system behaving as a simple sorting machine responsible for separating and diverting different content streams (e.g., comedy, dance, pro-or anti-Brexit) based on the user's preferences. When input to the platform all content becomes abstracted or quantified into numerical values and thus rendered equivalent dimensionless particles that may be re-assembled in whatever form. Each bit of content, then, becomes a potential output for the AI recommendation system to cycle through as it computes the feed or "picks little bits out of a large heap and assembles them in little heaps" (Flusser 1999, 64). In other words, the system is not a sorting machine directing streams of information from producer to consumer but is, instead, a synthesising machine that uses pre-existing content to construct something that has never existed before in the form of the feed. These feeds are original cultural products authored by the system itself.

Personalised feeds present a kind of mediation between the world-for-us and the world-without-us but one that differs from the paradoxical visualisations of inaccessibility that weird media offer. In cobbling together personalised feeds and thus determining what information is available to users, the AI recommendation system is not simply presenting a skewed or filtered view of the world but is projecting "other worlds from within itself" that are comprehensible to the human senses, but that are outputs of the unknown (Ibid., 65). Worlds in which the Earth is a flat disk, in which the moon landings were filmed on a Hollywood set by Stanley Kubrick, in which COVID-19 is a non-existent hoax, in which presidential elections are rigged by the deep state, or in which Donald Trump stands as the saviour of the world fighting against a cabal of Satan-worshipping paedophiles. These are fictional worlds deriving from different combinations of the apparatus program and presented as a coherent and continuous image to the human senses so as to appear as "true" as reality itself.

Returning to Thacker's discussion of the magic circle as a paradoxical boundary and passage between worlds, the AI-generated newsfeeds that appear on our screens are not simply a multitude of disparate magic circles. Rather, they hint at a more pervasive connection between worlds. Tracing the various reincarnations of the magic circle motif in the supernatural horror genre, Thacker expands and distorts the concept beyond the original two-dimensional chalk circles in Faust to the three-dimensional scientific devices of Lovecraft that alter one's perception of reality and reveal the hidden world beyond human senses. Finally stripping away any notion of spatial or temporal restrictions, the magic circle transforms into something amorphous and all-encompassing such as the seeping threats in films like *The Fog* (Carpenter 1980) wherein the residents of a coastal town are set upon by undead figures that appear wherever and whenever a magical fog rolls onto shore. In such films, "blobs, slime, ooze, mists, and clouds are prevalent, being not quite pure nature and yet not quite supernature" (Thacker 2011, 55). Unbounded by physical restraints, the boundary between worlds loses the acutely defined form of the magic circle under human control and becomes an ill-defined *magic site*, an "anonymous, unhuman intrusion of the hidden world into the apparent world, the enigmatic manifesting of the world-without-us into the world-for-us" (Ibid., 82).

As an example, Thacker highlights the 2000 short story "The Black Gondolier" by Fritz Leiber in which the main character becomes obsessed with crude oil "not just as a natural resource, and not just as something of geopolitical value, but with oil in itself as an ancient and enigmatic manifestation of the hidden world" (Ibid., 92). Oil, in this instance, is understood as an "oozing" version of the magic circle or magic site in which "any attempt to point to or isolate oil in total is futile, precisely because it is fully continuous, not only with the Earth, but also with modern industrial society" (Ibid., 93). While individual reserves or wells may be identified, the fundamental substance of oil is a continuous magic site that spreads through the entirety of industrial civilisation filling pipelines, powering vehicles, heating cities, forming plastic consumer goods, polluting air and earth and sea, and driving human beings to barter, bicker, and ultimately wage war over it. It is a pervasive manifestation of the world-without-us but one that has seeped so deeply into society that the world-for-us has folded around it.

I raise the above example to draw a direct comparison between oil and AI as magic sites. While specific systems, such as the various artificial neural networks previously discussed, may be isolated according to their spatial and temporal coordinates and be identified by their particular system architecture or unique function, all technology under the banner of "AI" are ultimately composed of and may be reduced to the same "substance" in numerical operations. Just as oil may be separated from the whole, shaped into different forms, and utilised for different functions in society and yet remain a unified whole, so too can AI be considered a continuous substance or a digital ooze of particles that is moulded to fulfil different purposes.

Bearing in mind the power of those recommendation systems discussed above, AI as a whole has become a pervasive manifestation of the world-without-us that permeates and alters the digital world in much the same way as oil did the industrial world a century ago. AI is the new black gold coursing through the veins of the digital world from the disembodied algorithms that enable our daily rituals such as search engines, translators, personal assistants, and global positioning systems, to the deep AI lurking out of sight yet still influencing our lives such as in cybersecurity systems, image recognition and verification software, secure bank transfers and stock exchange. The average person is, therefore, in constant connection with the unknowable, not as a contained image or portal between worlds but as a viscous ooze seeping into the world-for-us and impacting the known such as in the projection of fictional worlds.

For Flusser, there is little reason to discount or reject the fictional worlds projected outward by those AI recommendation systems due to their artificiality because "the 'actually' perceived world is just as much a fiction as the ones projected" (Flusser 1999, 65). Certainly, the world-for-us has always been a fictional world shaped by media, but it has also always been a fiction shared by readers, audiences, and users with access to the same information. Even as the technical universe has expanded and information has become so abundant as to allow fictional worlds to be projected towards smaller and smaller communities, there remains an intersubjectivity to the world-for-us. With the rapid emergence of AI systems, however, this intersubjectivity is at risk as by creating personalised images designed so discretely *for us* the shared world-for-us is being segregated into a multiverse of *worlds-for-me* tailored to individuals rather than communities.

Social media feeds are but one overt example of how the world-without-us made manifest in AI systems is influencing the world-for-us through technical images. However, there are a multitude of systems doing the same in more subtle ways by determining what information is output to which users and what meaning is constructed from this output. The more practices and ideas are abstracted and automated into digital processes, adding more particles to the heap, the further the world-without-us seeps into the world-for-us. Users are not simply confronted with the unknown through magic circles or glitching technical images such as *Not For You* but they are, instead, submerged within the unknown as a magic site that permeates the digital world.

Weird Policies

Behind the illusion of a continuous and coherent surface, the media feeds of online platforms are a dappled mosaic of images cobbled together by AI recommendation systems using the content of human authors as numerical building blocks. The countless articles, photographs, memes and videos uploaded to these platforms daily are abstracted into particles and join the heap of possible outputs for the system's combinatory game. However, these recommendation systems do not operate in isolation but are connected with numerous other technical apparatuses and computer systems that form the digital infrastructure of the internet. Take, for example, those recognition systems used to identify explicit or inappropriate content so that it may be removed from the heap of possibilities and excluded from the resulting media feeds.

The final media feeds that emerge on our screens cannot then be described as simply the outputs of any single technical apparatus or digital system. Rather, they are the cultural products of a large-scale information network that dictates the flow of numerical data from one user to another according to rules that are often not only hidden from view but unknowable. Beyond the programs of individual systems, it is the rules governing information flow in these networks that influence what fictional worlds are projected outward. These are the laws of a world-without-us that lurks just beneath the screen.

For Thacker and Galloway, networks are fundamentally understood as multiplicities of individual parts or nodes arranged in flat structures "characterized by equity between nodes, bi-directional links…and general lack of internal hierarchy" (Galloway 2006, 317). Such networks are also flexible in their configuration in that they may expand or contract as nodes are added and removed, or they may be reconfigured entirely as links between nodes are forged or severed. This inherent multiplicity and flexibility undermines the primacy of traditional sender and receiver roles as the once linear flow of information becomes distributed among numerous nodes. As an example, consider how internet memes spread throughout social media networks while being continually reduplicated, repurposed, and remixed as they pass from one node to another, thus losing any clearly defined origin point.

As such, when discussing the dissemination of information through such networks, Thacker and Galloway argue that it is "less the nature of the parts in themselves that is of concern, but more the conditions under which those parts may interact" or what might be defined as a network's *protocol* (Galloway and Thacker 2004, 22). This is a concept that Thacker and Galloway draw from internet protocols such as HTTP or TCP that enable data transmission. However, their notion of the protocol can be more broadly defined as those "conventional rules and standards that govern relationships" between individuals and enable information exchange (Ibid., 8).

In the context of online platforms, there are numerous protocols at play governing the relationships between users beyond those technical protocols (e.g., hashtags, keywords, word limits) that simply enable or modulate information flow. Notably, there are also protocols that apply to user conduct or terms of service such as Twitter's policies on hateful conduct and sensitive media or Facebook's community standards. In the face of widespread disinformation regarding the COVID-19 pandemic and the 2020 US presidential election, to name but a few high-profile examples from this period, these policies and their enforcement began to play a far more significant role in governing information exchange.

Such company policies not only determined what kinds of content were designated as harmful to other users but also determined what constituted inaccurate content and enabled the suspension of individual accounts that repeatedly violated these protocols. While such policies aim to stem the tide of harmful disinformation, the increased use of AI systems to enforce these policies has the potential to destabilise information flow in these networks entirely. As an illustrative example, consider the AI-generated images produced by artist/research Tom White as part of his series *Perception Engines* (White 2018a, 2018b) and his subsequent experiments with recognition systems.

To produce the representational prints of *Perception Engines*, examples of which are shown in Fig. 5.3, White designed a bespoke computational drawing programme that is linked to several different artificial neural networks all of which have been trained for object recognition using the same categorised image datasets available on the database ImageNet (White 2018a). The drawing programme was designed to produce an image in White's aesthetic style but one that is still recognised as the target category, for example "cabbage" or "iron", by all of the recognition systems. Reminiscent of the adversarial competition between the generator and discriminator systems of the GAN programmes previously discussed, the drawing system generates image after image to be judged by the AI recognition systems. These in turn provide feedback to inform the next iteration, until an image emerges that is recognised as the target category by all involved. In other words, the drawing system creates an artificial image that all the AI recognition systems agree is real. The resulting image is the product of this network of different systems as a whole.

For White, these prints are idealised representations of the training datasets in which the minor variations and inconsistencies exhibited in the images of real objects have been filtered out in order to distil the fundamental characteristics used to identify the object (White 2018b). However, as discussed above with regard to recommendation systems and media feeds, these technical apparatuses are not filters but synthesisers of information. As such, I contend that the prints of *Perception Engines* are visualisations of the standards governing communication within White's miniature information network.

While all the recognition systems have been trained on the same datasets of the same objects, each learns individually according to its own system architecture and thus develops a unique understanding of

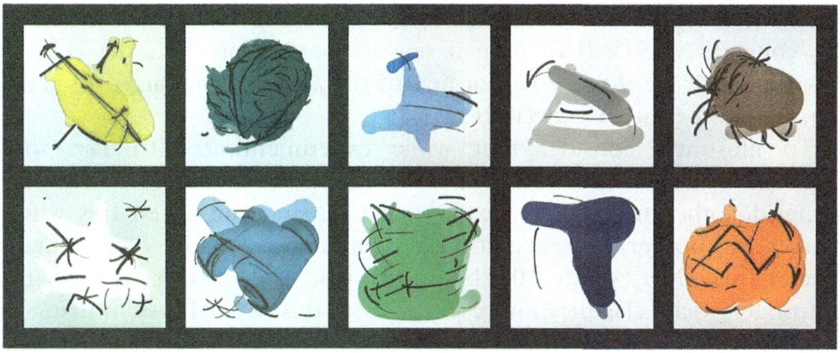

Fig. 5.3 Risograph prints generated by AI programmes as part of Tom White's *Perception Engines* series targeting the following ImageNet categories (clockwise): cello, cabbage, hammerhead shark, iron, tick, jack-o-lantern, blow dryer, measuring cup, binoculars, starfish. Courtesy of Tom White

the object. As a simplified example, one system may learn to recognise cabbages by identifying colour alone, while another learns to do so by shape alone such that both systems develop different definitions for what constitutes a cabbage with neither being necessarily incorrect in their assessment. Through the trial-and-error process of *Perception Engines*, a new definition emerges at the intersection of all other definitions and thus a symbol designating a particular idea understood by the whole network is produced. These images depicting cabbages or irons are not, then, idealisations of phenomena but visualisations of the standards of communication constructed by and unique to this particular grouping of systems. The entire *Perception Engines* series may, then, be considered the beginnings of a lexicon shared by the group.

Despite being trained on images of real objects, the recognition systems receive these images as nothing more than numerical inputs to be used as the standard or benchmark for verifying and classifying a new object. These mathematical abstractions are, however, composed of geometric elements such as points, lines, planes and curves that do not actually exist in the concrete world. These elements are the "eternal, immutable forms (e.g., triangles) produced by eternal, immutable formulae" of science (Flusser 1999, 42). Regardless of how accurate these mathematical abstractions may appear, they are fundamentally different from the concrete phenomena the system is attempting to emulate.

As such, recognition systems are not categorising images according to the concrete standards of human sensory perception (i.e., the content observed) but are doing so according to the abstract standards of science (i.e., the non-existent eternal forms).

To illustrate, consider that while experimenting with *Perception Engines*, White included the abstract tick print featured in Fig. 5.3 alongside other training images of real ticks and submitted this whole dataset to another AI recognition system trained on the online image dataset ImageNet (White 2018b). In this case, the abstract print elicited a stronger "tick" classification response from this new AI system than any other image in the dataset. When presented with new objects to identify, AI systems do not "see" a tick or a cabbage but, instead, project their own geometric compositions onto the object. Those that are recognised are simply the most probable solutions already accounted for within the program. As a visualisation of mathematically constructed standards, the abstract tick presents the most probable solution to the program in spite of its obvious artificiality. The real ticks, on the other hand, are products of chaotic nature and thus present improbable solutions. Through the lens of scientific apparatuses, then, an abstract tick looks more like a tick than an actual tick.

As with the cabbages or ticks of *Perception Engines*, there exists no ideal definition for what constitutes harmful content or disinformation online. Those AI systems designed to enforce policies governing the distribution of such content are operating according to standards constructed by the scientific equations of the program itself. For example, SimSearchNet++ is an image matching programme developed by Facebook in order to tackle the spread of disinformation by identifying different variants on the same content. For example, the same false statements on COVID-19 statistics might be published online in various different images or meme formats that utilise text or screenshots in different ways (FAIR 2020). By continually training on a dataset of content flagged and assembled by independent fact-checkers, SimSearchNet++ is capable of identifying variants and mutations of online content such that it can adapt to disinformation appearing in unexpected forms such as humorous memes or posts employing unique or alternative phrases. However, while the similarities between these different images may appear quite obvious to human observers, the standards by which SimSearchNet++ categorises disinformation are unknowable to human perception.

As part of another experiment, White submitted images generated by his computational drawing programme to several other prominent and publicly available AI recognition systems that had not been trained on ImageNet datasets. These included Amazon Rekognition, Google Safe-Search, and Yahoo NSFW. While some images such as the abstract cello shown in Fig. 5.3 were similarly recognised as "cello" or "cellist" or "instrument", the prints shown in Fig. 5.4 were misrecognised as "explicit nudity", "racy" and "not safe for work" (White 2018b). What at first appears to be a simple malfunction is, however, yet another instance of Thacker's weird media in which AI systems are observed to be working too well.

Using the example of a geometric spiral, Thacker argues that the compositions or eternal forms that AI systems process "can only be said to negatively exist—the spiral in itself is never manifest except as a spiral 'in' something" such as in nautilus shells or spiral galaxies (Thacker 2011, 79). As such, these eternal forms are ontologically equivalent to ideas or thoughts but, as they can only exist as imperfect manifestations in the known world-for-us, Thacker argues that they are non-human thoughts and are "equivalent to the world-without-us" (Ibid., 80).

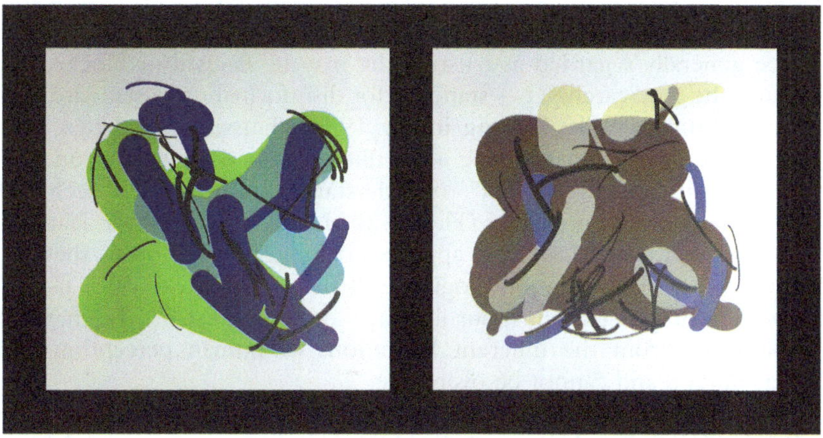

Fig. 5.4 Prints from the *Perception Engines* series labelled as "explicit nudity", "racy", and "not safe for work" by Amazon Rekognition, Google SafeSearch and Yahoo NSFW, respectively. Courtesy of Tom White

The images of *Perception Engines* shown in Fig. 5.3, the COVID-19 memes identified by SimSearchNet++, and the misrecognised images shown in Fig. 5.4 may all be reconsidered as weird media as the AI systems are attempting to visualise non-human ideas (e.g., spirals and geometric compositions) as images tailored for human senses (e.g., nautilus shells and cabbages). Unlike the *Perception Engines* prints and the recognised COVID-19 memes, the misrecognised images do not appear to visualise the AI system's idea i.e., an explicit or racy composition. However, these ideas are limited to those many but not infinite possibilities accounted for within the system's equations. As such, a single composition or eternal form in the world-without-us may manifest in numerous different ways in the world-for-us. In much the same way that a spiral is observed in shells and galaxies alike, an explicit or racy composition may equally manifest as recognisable images of human nudity or as the abstract form of Fig. 5.4. As with other weird media, however, the interchangeability and imperfection of these concrete manifestations only serves to express the inaccessibility of the non-human ideas they hide.

Let us return to the case of SimSearchNet++ and the detection of disinformation. The COVID-19 disinformation images identified by SimSearchNet++ are only a handful of possible solutions accounted for within the AI system and there may be many more, both probable and improbable. For example, a satirical piece published online by a source generally regarded as trustworthy may be flagged or blocked for meeting the SimSearchNet++ standard for disinformation; a standard that is entirely unknowable. Writing in the 1980s, Flusser argued that "the new computer codes have made us all illiterate again" but that "one has only to learn the secret codes" to understand the meaning of technical images produced by programs (Flusser 2011, 55–56). However, learning the secret codes of AI systems appears no longer an option as they are separated from us by the ontological gulf between the world-for-us and the world-without-us. Thus, our illiteracy in the context of AI-generated media stems from the inherent limitations of human perception and understanding and cannot be overcome.

As a piece of content passes from one node to another it may be defined and redefined for us as a cabbage first, then as a tick, then as disinformation and finally as explicit nudity. To the human senses it may very well appear to be none of these things but to the sensors of the programme it is all of the above and more. As such, those mathematical standards that govern the flow of information within online networks are not only unknowable but also fundamentally disconnected from our own understanding of the world. The criteria we use to distinguish fact from fiction, reliable sources from unreliable ones, and plausible events from impossible ones differ significantly from those employed by AI systems. This ontological gulf threatens to disrupt information flow within society and, in doing so, destabilise our existing authorities and power structures that once were perceived as trustworthy.

Infestation

The flat structures of networks do not inherently determine individual authorities that dominate the dissemination of information as in hierarchical or pyramidal organisational structures. However, this lack of a determined authority does not imply equality or democracy.

As Thacker and Galloway argue, in networks "power centers will necessarily emerge through a sort of clustering pattern, just as certain Web sites will emerge as supernodes within the larger net" (Galloway and Thacker 2004, 19). In the context of social media platforms, these power centers can be evidenced in the emergence of YouTube celebrities and Instagram influencers in the 2010s as clusters of connections formed around previously unheard-of individuals enabling their messages to be spread virally from one node to another. As a result of this clustering, these digital public figures have since amassed substantial followings that, more often than not, surpass the followings of real-world authorities such as political figures, government institutions, and media organisations. Therefore, while networks display an entirely different form of organisation to that of hierarchical or pyramidal structures, this clustering eventually establishes new authorities by regulating the flow of information between nodes.

For Thacker and Galloway, this clustering is not solely an intentional choice of human users based on taste or values but, rather, it is a predictable consequence of the protocols governing information exchange, particularly those related to AI recommendation and moderation systems discussed above. These protocols encourage clusters to form around individual nodes, enabling them to project their voices above those of others and to wield greater influence in the digital world. Certainly, real-world authority can translate to online authority as users intentionally seek out voices that they value or perceive to be important to their lives. Many people connect with the online profiles of government departments, politicians and traditional media organisations because of their perceived authority in the real world. However, the relevance of these real-world authorities and their communications online are still determined by the protocols and standards established by technology companies (e.g., policies, community standards) and also the unknowable technical standards of AI systems. It is these protocols that allow authorities to flourish and others to dwindle in online networks, while those that violate these protocols may be excommunicated entirely.

Consider that in February 2021, Facebook instigated a ban on all news communications in Australia by blocking Australia-based outlets from posting content on the platform and by preventing Australian users from sharing or viewing news articles of any kind. In the process, however, the AI system used to enforce this ban mistakenly blocked the pages of government agencies, health departments, trade unions, charity organisations, scientific journals, fire and rescue services, and politicians, to name but a few (Taylor 2021). While such apparent mistakes may be filtered out through trial-and-error, this case emphasises how the algorithmic enforcement of unknown standards can impact power structures and dynamics in the real world. Not only do such protocols disrupt information flows but, in doing so, they destabilise authorities as clusters emerge and dissolve. For better or worse, those once established sources of authority and apparently trustworthy information (e.g., government departments, public services, academic institutes, newspapers) may collapse while others rise as the new authorities (e.g., fringe political groups, conspiracy theorists, influencers) in an endless cycle of death and rebirth.

With the arrival of ChatGPT and the subsequent hype spurring on the widespread uptake of AI across society, this infestation has only continued to grow. With developers emphasising the apparently limitless potential and versatile capabilities of these technologies, modern AI systems have become increasingly integrated into our information environment in a myriad of different ways. For example, chatbots like ChatGPT are now commonly used in everyday life for numerous diverse tasks such as answering questions on political and historical topics, providing medical or financial advice, and generating new ideas and concepts. Meanwhile, these systems are finding numerous uses in professional settings as well. Notable examples include the use of AI systems for customer relations, data visualisation, content creation and design, interactive education, and gathering and synthesising information for policy and academic research. This is not, however, to say that these technologies complete these tasks correctly or effectively. Indeed, there remain significant issues around bias and inaccuracy.

Furthermore, as these technologies operate according to unknown standards and protocols, this deep integration of AI systems is introducing a high degree of unpredictability, instability and variability to information networks (Bisconti et al. 2024; McIntyre et al. 2025). Consider that two users may provide ChatGPT with the exact same prompt and receive completely different answers that may very well promote different social values, articulate different political narratives, or present entirely different facts and interpretations of events. As such, these systems have significant influence over what knowledge is made available to which users and in what manner it is presented. Instead of a shared body of knowledge authorised by collectively recognised institutions, collective knowledge is increasingly fragmented as information is algorithmically curated and tailored to individuals.

As the public sphere fractures and traditional authorities lose control of collective knowledge, AI systems quietly continue to dictate the flow of information flow online according to their unknown standards that are indifferent to humanity. The world-without-us has thus seeped deeper into our own, engulfing us and isolating us within our own worlds with our own truths. In such a fragmented and self-obsessed world, AI paradoxically emerges as the only authority remaining.

It is misguided, however, to assume that AI systems stand as neutral authorities simply because they are unknowable or indifferent to humanity. As ethicist Kate Crawford argues, internal functioning is not the sole problem as "there is no singular black box to open, no secret to expose, but a multitude of interlaced systems of power" at play in those practices involving AI systems (Crawford 2021, 12). Complete transparency is unattainable and so it is more useful to analyse "its material architectures, contextual environments, and prevailing politics and by tracing how they are connected" (Ibid.). Following Crawford, the next chapter will explore the politics and ideology of AI practices in more detail.

References

Bisconti, Piercosma, Andrew McIntyre, and Federica Russo. 2024. Synthetic socio-technical systems: Poiêsis as meaning making. *Philosophy & Technology* 37(3):94.

Bumiller, Elisabeth. 2010. We have met the enemy and he is powerpoint. *New York Times*. 26 April.
Chun, Wendy Hui Kyong. 2021. *Discriminating data: Correlation, neighbourhoods, and the new politics of recognition*. London: MIT Press.
Crawford, Kate. 2021. *Atlas of AI: Power, politics, and the planetary costs of artificial intelligence*. London: Yale University Press.
FAIR. 2020. Here's how we're using AI to help detect misinformation. *Facebook Artificial Intelligence Research*, November 19.
Flusser, Vilém. 1999. *The shape of things: A philosophy of design*. London: Reaktion Books.
Flusser, Vilém. 2011. *Does writing have a future?* trans. Nancy Ann Roth. Minneapolis: University of Minnesota Press.
Galloway, Alexander. 2006. Protocol. *Theory, Culture & Society* 23 (2–3): 317–320.
Galloway, Alexander. 2011. Are some things unrepresentable? *Theory, Culture & Society* 28 (7–7): 85–102.
Galloway, Alexander, and Eugene Thacker. 2004. Protocol, control, and networks. *Grey Room* 17:6–29.
Galloway, Alexander, Eugene Thacker, and Mc Kenzie Wark. 2014. *Excommunication: Three inquiries in media and mediation*. London: University of Chicago Press.
Kittler, Friedrich. 1997. In *Literature, media, information systems: Essays*, ed. John Johnston. Amsterdam: Overseas Publishers Association.
Kittler, Friedrich. 1999. *Gramophone, film, typewriter*. Stanford: Stanford University Press.
Kittler, Friedrich. 2018. *Optical media: Berlin lectures 1999*. trans. Anthony Enns. Cambridge: Polity Press.
Marwick, Alice, and Rebecca Lewis. 2017. Media manipulation and disinformation online. *New York: Data & Society Research Institute* 359:1146–1151.
McIntyre, Andrew, Lucy Conover, and Federica Russo. 2025. A network approach to public trust in generative AI. *Philosophy & Technology* 28:137.
Shannon, Claude. 2016. The redundancy of English. In *Cybernetics: The Macy conferences 1946–1953*, ed. Claus Pias, 248–272. Chicago: University of Chicago Press.
Taylor, Josh. 2021. Facebook's botched Australia news ban hits health departments, charities and its own pages. *Guardian*, February 18.
Thacker, Eugene. 2011. *In the dust of this planet*. Winchester: Zero Books.
Thacker, Eugene. 2012. Wayless abyss: Mysticism, mediation and divine nothingness. *Postmedieval: A Journal of Medieval Cultural Studies* 3 (1): 80–96.
Turing, Alan. 1936. On computable numbers, with an application to the Entscheidungsproblem. *In Proceedings of the London Mathematical Society* 42 (1): 230–265.

White, Tom. 2018a. Perception engines. *Medium*, April 5.

White, Tom. 2018b. Synthetic abstractions. *Medium*, August 23.

Wilson, Mark. 2017. AI is inventing languages humans can't understand. Should we stop it? *Fast Company*, July 14.

Winthrop-Young, Geoffrey. 2011. *Kittler and the media*. Cambridge: Polity Press.

CHAPTER 6

In the Eye of the Beholder

For fans of science fiction, the prospect of machines suddenly gaining sentience and deciding to overthrow their human masters is nothing new. Over the past hundred years or so, this well-worn narrative trope has appeared in various different guises and across a multitude of formats from literature to film to video games and beyond. With the emergence of deep learning methods and artificial neural networks in the 2010s, however, what was once considered a far-fetched and fantastical nightmare scenario has since come to be treated as a serious prospect by many AI researchers and tech industry leaders. This includes the likes of philosopher Nick Bostrom, billionaire Elon Musk, OpenAI founder Sam Altman and disgraced cryptocurrency entrepreneur Sam Bankman-Fried, among many others.

Within these certain academic and industry circles, AI technology is seen as one of the gravest existential threats to humanity. In particular, these researchers and investors highlight the potential dangers of developing artificial general intelligence (AGI) that surpasses human cognitive abilities. The reasoning being that if these superintelligent AI systems are not aligned with human values, then humanity will likely lose control over the technology leading to violent conflict and, ultimately, human extinction or some other dystopian future. Simultaneously, these figures argue that AGI may very well usher in a utopian future if only this technology can be aligned with human values. However, the apocalyptic

A. McIntyre, *Art and Authorship in the AI Spring*,
https://doi.org/10.1007/978-3-032-18574-7_6

warnings and utopian dreams of these modern soothsayers are seemingly more influenced by science fiction than by concrete scientific research and rigorous philosophical inquiry. Indeed, these predictions are more akin to speculative beliefs linked to the ideology of longtermism.

Emerging in the early 2010s, longtermism is deeply tied to Bostrom's work, as well as the effective altruism movement advanced by philosophers Peter Singer (2015) and William MacAskill (2015, 2023). However, while effective altruism emphasises the moral imperative to help others as effectively as possible, often focusing on issues such as global health and poverty, longtermism prioritises the well-being of future generations. As future generations of humanity may very well number in the trillions, philosophers such as MacAskill and Bostrom argue that the long-term consequences of our actions may carry far greater moral weight than their immediate impacts. Therefore, when making key decisions on policy and technological investment, for example, we should prioritise the long-term impacts over present day concerns. As Bostrom states: "a moral case can be made that existential risk reduction is strictly more important than any other global public good" (Bostrom 2013, 15).

As the emergence of longtermism as an ideology coincided with the arrival of modern deep learning systems and artificial neural networks, the topic of AI safety and the potential dangers of AGI swiftly became a core concern of longtermist companies and research organisations such as the Future of Life Institute and the Centre for the Study of Existential Risk at Cambridge University. In the context of AI, the longtermist viewpoint emphasises the need for research into technical safeguards and moral alignment, robust governance frameworks, and the promotion of institutions capable of managing technological development responsibly. As a result, longtermists often frame financial investment in companies and research institutes focused on AI safety and existential risk as a moral responsibility with significant future consequences. Though once a fringe philosophical perspective, longtermism has rapidly become the favoured ideology among many in Silicon Valley, greatly shaping AI policy and regulation today.

While its overarching goals would seem to be well-intentioned in that they seek to avoid or reduce human suffering from renegade AI systems, longtermism has been deeply criticised as a scientifically dubious and ethically suspect ideology by theorists such as Emily Bender (Bender and Hanna 2025), Kate Crawford (2021), Timnit Gebru (Bender et al. 2021) and Émile P. Torres (2021, 2023). Primarily, these theorists argue that the fundamental belief underpinning longtermism (i.e., that far future scenarios morally outweigh our present situation) is flawed. Longtermist predictions of AGI are often based on unrealistic calculations and highly speculative assumptions about human behaviour, technological development and the socio-political trajectory of societies over not only decades but centuries. Not only are these predictions highly speculative, they deprioritise present day issues (e.g., disinformation, bias, labour) and encourage the shifting of money and resources towards longtermist causes to prepare for future scenarios that may never come to pass.

As an explicit example, consider this quote from Open Philanthropy founder and longtermist Holden Karnofsky's personal blog in which he regularly argues that the existential risks of AI should be our primary concern:

> What about things like "AI might lead to mass unemployment and unrest" or "AI might exacerbate misinformation and propaganda" or "AI might exacerbate a wide range of other social ills and injustices"? I think these are real concerns – but to be honest, if they were the biggest concerns, I'd probably still be focused on helping people in low-income countries today rather than trying to prepare for future technologies. (Karnofsky 2022)

Gebru and Torres (2024) go further to argue that longtermists such as Karnofsky, Bostrom and Musk use the fear of an AI apocalypse (either sincerely or insincerely) to justify financial investment and/or deregulation for their business ventures, while also encouraging a consolidation of political power among a small group of wealthy, Western elites who claim to know what is best for the future of humanity.

Rather than being the precursor to godlike AI systems in the far future, Crawford argues that modern "AI are expressions of power that emerge from wider economic and political forces, created to increase profits and centralize control for those who wield them" (Crawford 2021, 211). Crawford emphasises that AI is an extractive industry in that "the creation of contemporary AI systems depends on exploiting energy and mineral resources, from the planet, cheap labor, and data at scale" (Ibid., 15). AI systems are products of and operate within material labour practices that mean they are "ultimately designed to serve existing dominant interests" (ibid., 8). Those that control these means of production, control the application of technology such that the political function of AI systems is dictated by the "Great Houses of AI, which consist of the half-dozen or so companies that dominate large-scale planetary computation" (Ibid., 20). The longtermist narratives that emerged in the 2010s and that have since been exacerbated by hype following the release of ChatGPT, have obscured this inherently political function of the technology.

This brief discussion is not intended as an exhaustive explanation of longtermism or its criticisms. Rather, I wish to emphasise how ideology can skew our understanding and perception of scientific apparatuses and how their political function is reliant upon these skewed perceptions. While longtermists claim to fear that AI systems may overthrow and dominate humanity in the future, the technology in the present day has already become a tool of political dominance. This dominance is sustained by the ideological belief that AI systems are superintelligent authorities that transcend the intellectual capacities of human beings. The concept of authority is deeply intertwined with authorship in that recognising the legitimacy and credibility of the person or thing behind the work also serves to confer legitimacy and credibility on the work itself. Such a relationship has significant implications for AI-generated outputs if these systems are perceived as scientific apparatuses.

Drawing on the work of philosopher G.W.F. Hegel, Wendy Chun argues that the more AI systems become deeply integrated into our everyday lives, the more they will come to dictate human affairs as "the greater the apparent mastery, the greater the actual dependence: in the master–slave dialectic, the master's very identities and lives depend on their slave's actions" (Chun 2021, 14). For Chun and Hegel, the act of recognition lies at the core of this struggle between master and slave in that "to recognize someone is to accept that person's authority, validity or legitimacy" (Ibid., 186). To recognise AI systems as superintelligent beings is to establish and perpetuate the belief that these machines are authorities to be depended upon and deferred to. In following this belief, we are not slowly being subjugated by a future malevolent out-of-control machine, we are unknowingly submitting to the dominant and exploitative power structures that exist today.

Throughout the 2010s, various organisations sought to deploy emerging AI technologies to improve their decision-making processes under the impression that such systems were superintelligent and neutral in their assessments. Examples include the use of facial recognition in policing and security services, the use of statistical predictions for government policy, and the use of automated systems for recruiting and dismissing employees in private business. While such technologies may enable more efficient decision-making and reduce workload, the use of these systems instead of humans in cases that will significantly impact the lives of everyday people can be unethical, inappropriate or simply impractical.

A clear example is the SyRI (*System Risico Indicatie*) system deployed by the Dutch Ministry of Social Affairs to identify fraudulent benefit claimants between 2014 and 2019. The system itself was inaccurate and lacked oversight leading to many innocent families, often those on low incomes and from underrepresented communities, receiving excessive tax bills (Züger and Asghari 2023). These inaccurate assessments and the resulting bills pushed thousands towards poverty, debt and, in some extreme cases, suicide (Heikkilä 2022). Unfortunately, this is but one reported case of many in which AI decision-making has had disastrous results for everyday people. While often these negative effects are attributed to the inaccurate or bias criteria by which AI systems operate, there remains a more fundamental issue in the perception of AI systems as superintelligent and neutral machines to which sensitive and impactful decisions can be deferred.

This chapter looks back on egregious examples of dubious and inaccurate AI systems being used for human decision-making that received comparatively little public attention at the time. In particular, this chapter critically analyses instances of biometric recognition systems and notably emotion recognition, a practice that has since been prohibited or significantly restricted in several countries (Brennan et al. 2025). Through this discussion, I argue that the unethical state of AI derives in part from the ideological belief in AI as superintelligent authorities that can be relied upon and deferred to, and I further consider how we are encouraged to view ourselves through this ideological lens.

Discourse by Design

In previous chapters, I have argued that the outputs of AI systems are not solely determined by the intentions of human programmers but are, instead, the unpredictable and unknowable products of scientific apparatuses. This is not to say, however, that AI-generated outputs are in any way non-political or that they do not articulate bias because they are the result of objective scientific principles. As mentioned in relation to Chun and Crawford, these systems exist within, are influenced by, and contribute to larger social structures and activities that are linked to different ideologies. In particular, there is a risk that ideological biases will be introduced when constructing training datasets due to human decision-making. With image-making AI systems in particular, this risk is even greater because any one image used in a dataset is open to multiple interpretations. However, these biases are not always readily observable in the outputs of these systems. To raise awareness about the biased assumptions and judgements that are inbuilt into everyday AI systems, in 2019 Crawford and artist Trevor Paglen developed the mobile app/art experiment *ImageNet Roulette*.

Though no longer publicly available, users of the *ImageNet Roulette* app were invited to submit images which in turn were analysed by a machine learning algorithm designed to recognise people and apply labels to these images based on a training dataset. In this case, the dataset used was the titular ImageNet, one of the largest online image databases available to programmers at the time offering over 14 million labelled images organised into over 20,000 different categories to be used for training image recognition systems. While a useful tool for object recognition, Crawford and Paglen trained their AI on ImageNet's "person" category in order to demonstrate how ideological bias can arise when using such databases to identify and categorise human beings (Crawford and Paglen 2019).

The art project gained significant attention online as users began posting images of themselves and others with labels assigned by *ImageNet Roulette* (Rea 2019). Many users found that the app assigned bizarre and humorous labels such as "queen mother" on an image of former German Chancellor Angela Merkel, "premature baby" on an image of former US President Joe Biden or "hypocrite" on an image of actor Leonardo DiCaprio. However, other users found that the app often applied labels with explicitly racist, sexist and homophobic slurs, as well as assumed job titles and personality traits that implicitly perpetuated biases. While the inbuilt biases of AI systems are more widely understood now, at the time *ImageNet Roulette* highlighted to the public how human ideology can influence the outputs of AI systems, particularly recognition systems. Ultimately, the project resulted in ImageNet removing 600,000 images deemed inappropriate (Ruiz 2019).

Much has already been written about this art project and the ImageNet database more broadly (Bridges 2021; Crawford 2021; Denton et al. 2021). However, in this section I wish to use it as an illustrative example of the inherently discursive nature of AI-generated images which is often disregarded due to the presumed objectivity of their scientific origins. Such a lack of critique is not due to simple ignorance but, rather, an inability to decode technical images.

It is inappropriate to critique technical images in the same manner as those traditional images that they mimic as the encoding of such images has been conducted by a scientific program, rather than a human mind. Elaborating on this distinction, Flusser argues that critical thinking and the criticism of traditional images arose with the invention of linear writing which introduced discretised symbols as a means of describing images. As Flusser states: "critical thinking divides images—separates them into elements—judges them—makes decisions about them—breaks them apart—perpetrates crimes against images—because it casts doubt on myth and magic" (Flusser 2002, 43). Central to critical thinking is mathematics in that "counting is the act of tearing things out of their context" and so as technical images are products of mathematical calculations they are visualisations of critical thinking itself (Ibid., 42).

Previously, production preceded criticism in that a product was created, and then its qualities were subjectively judged by observers. Flusser identifies epistemology, ethics and aesthetics as the criteria by which traditional images were critiqued. However, with technical images, "criticism accompanies the production and distribution of manufactured objects, so that we receive the manufactured object as something that has already been thoroughly critiqued" (Ibid., 45). The criteria by which traditional images were once judged (epistemology, ethics and aesthetics) must then be abandoned as the criticism of technical images is a mode of critical thinking turned against itself. In the context of AI-generated images, this means to look beyond superficial aesthetics and to analyse the means by which these images have been produced, primarily the construction of training datasets.

As an example, let us consider two images produced by *ImageNet Roulette*. In one, Paglen himself has been mislabelled "microeconomist", while in the other former US President Barack Obama has been mislabelled "forger, counterfeiter". While the two descriptors themselves lack any apparent social or political meaning, the fact that these labels have been applied based purely on appearance implies that the images in the microeconomist dataset likely resemble Paglen (i.e., Caucasian males), while the images in the forger dataset likely resemble Obama (i.e., African American males). Certainly, the images included in a dataset are chosen based on the judgement of human programmers. However, the image-class-taxonomy structure of datasets, discussed previously, insists upon the separation and grouping of images. As such, when certain images (e.g., pictures of African American males) are grouped together under certain labels (e.g., forger), the system unintentionally exhibits bias in its outputs. What is revealed in the labels of *ImageNet Roulette* is not simply the explicit and implicit bias of those human programmers involved in the production but, furthermore, the critical thinking that preceded this production: the scientific method of classification.

Where much has been said on the perpetuation of bias in AI systems, Crawford highlights the necessity for a closer analysis of those practices of classification that are core to constructing datasets and encoding bias. In creating an AI training dataset for a specific purpose, programmers are placed in a privileged position. They not only select those images that will be included or excluded but, furthermore, how these images will be arranged in relation to one another. To do so, is to draw lines where there originally were none and to "take an almost infinitely complex and varied world and fix it into taxonomies composed of discrete classification of individual data points, a process that requires inherently political, cultural, and social choices" (Crawford 2021, 135–136). The implicit and explicit biases exhibited in *ImageNet Roulette* demonstrate how ideological assumptions and judgements influence the labelling and grouping of individual images into categories. However, the selection and nesting of those categories within hierarchies is itself a subjective exercise that is further influenced by ideology and that encodes political ideas.

To illustrate, Crawford points to the fact that the labels "male body" and "female body" are nested within the "human body" category of ImageNet, while the label "hermaphrodite" is nested within the "bisexual" category. Such a logic of classification may not influence the content of the images included within these datasets but establishes "gender as a biological construct, which is binary, and transgender or gender nonbinary people are either non-existent or placed under categories of sexuality" (Ibid., 138). In such a taxonomical arrangement, those labels and groupings that may not at first appear to be controversial or contentious are linked to others in ways that associates them with social, political and cultural concepts and a particular worldview. As such, Crawford argues that "there are no neutral categories in ImageNet, because the selection of images always interacts with the meaning of words. The politics are baked into the classificatory logic, even when the words aren't offensive" (Ibid., 142).

The criticism, judgement and classification practices that have accompanied the construction of the ImageNet dataset were only revealed due to public accessibility and through Crawford and Paglen's efforts with *ImageNet Roulette*. However, the training datasets for many of those image recognition systems deployed by private companies and government agencies are often inaccessible to the public and researchers alike, so it remains unclear what manner of critical thinking is built into these systems. This lack of transparency remains a barrier to our own interpretation, critique and understanding of AI-generated images as technical images.

When critiquing a technical image, it is inappropriate to question whether or not such an image is "true" or "false" (i.e., epistemology), "good" or "bad" (i.e., ethics), or "beautiful" or "ugly" (i.e., aesthetics) as one might do when critiquing a traditional image or linear text (Flusser 2002). Rather, it is necessary to question why this particular output has been realised and not one of the many others accounted for within the program. As Flusser discussed in relation to photography, criticism should not be directed at the photograph itself but rather "the criteria according to which photographs have been produced: that is, those criteria according to which the apparatus that produced them has itself been produced and programmed" (Ibid., 45). As the criteria by which many AI systems operate is publicly unavailable, such a critique is difficult.

For example, above I have speculated that the *ImageNet Roulette* image of Barack Obama has been mislabelled "forger" because the forger dataset contains a disproportionate number of images of African American males. However, the actual criteria for recognition is unknown as the AI system has learned to identify common data patterns, rather than people. Even were the forger dataset found to be populated entirely by images of African American males, the AI system could very well have learned to recognise data patterns representative of facial expression, head positioning, body type or even a simple quirk of light and shadow distribution that coincidentally manifests in the image of Obama. Even this speculative critique of the image is only enabled by *ImageNet Roulette*'s explicit labelling, while many other AI-generated images do not provide any insight into their criteria for programming.

Without knowing the criteria by which AI-generated images have been produced, the viewer cannot properly critique and understand the image itself and so "we must assume a point of view that the screen imposes upon us; if we do not do this, we can read nothing" (Ibid., 28). To illustrate this, Flusser points to the technical imagery of film in which "the point of view is from a chair in the cinema. If we sit on the chair, we can read what the film means. If we refuse to take the chair and approach the screen, we seen only meaningless light spots" (Ibid.). By obscuring their criteria and by insisting upon reception from a single point of view, technical images and especially AI-generated images prevent a critical dialogue between sender and receiver. Instead, they insist upon an exclusively discursive mode of communication.

For Flusser, two dominant modes of communication can be distinguished: the ***dialogical*** in which multiple participants synthesise new information through mutual communication (e.g., a debate) and the ***discursive*** in which one participant transmits information to others through one-way communication (e.g., a lecture) (Ibid., 18). In the dialogical mode, communication is productive in that it produces new information. In the discursive mode, communication is preceded by the information and so simply serves as a means of transmission. By obscuring the criteria by which they might be critiqued and thereby engaged in a critical dialogue, technical images would seem to take on a purely discursive mode of communication. With the arrival of a mass media reliant upon technical images, Flusser argues that a discursive culture has arisen in which "very few senders emit messages towards enormously numerous receivers who are totally incapable of dialoguing with the senders" (Ibid.). While Flusser's discussion centres on how the channelling of messages through different media channels (e.g., television, magazines, cinema) influencers viewers, I would argue that the emergence of AI systems has further exacerbated this discursive culture in that those few senders are now unknown programmers such as those that contribute to the construction of training datasets like ImageNet.

In relation to recognition systems in particular, Crawford emphasises that by enabling programmers to determine the variables and hierarchies by which people are categorised "the practice of classification is centralizing power: the power to decide which differences make a difference" (Crawford 2021, 132). However, the prevailing perception that AI systems are accurate and neutral systems masks the bias, inaccuracy and subjectivity exhibited in their outputs as simple errors or quirks of programming rather than evidence of human influence. While simultaneously, this centralisation of power under a few human programmers is obscured and misrepresented as modernisation and the consolidation of power under the impartial and trustworthy authority of science.

More Human Than Human

Following the industrial revolution and the development of scientific apparatuses, Flusser asserts that those moral, political and religious authorities that once determined ethical standards in society are no longer trusted and the "only authority still left more or less intact is science" (Flusser 1991, 12). However, science is perceived by many as a value-free authority and "thus provides no ethical norms", only technical standards for accuracy and efficiency (Ibid.). As such, this crisis of authority also entails a crisis of ethics as ethical norms no longer apply to industrial processes and "in effect we are in a situation of total irresponsibility for the acts committed by industrial productions" (Ibid., 13). While Flusser made this argument in 1991, thirty years on this issue of total irresponsibility is being exacerbated by the widespread use of AI systems for decision-making processes in complex and often sensitive social situations.

Of particular note is the development and deployment of biometric recognition technologies that go beyond identifying an individual's race or gender and are ostensibly capable of determining an individual's mental state (e.g., emotions) based on a variety of physiological measurements (e.g., facial expressions, eye movement, blood flow). Not only are these technologies inconsistent in their methodologies, they are also demonstrably inaccurate and bias (Barrett 2019). For example, Face ++ and Microsoft's Face API were reportedly more likely to assign negative emotions to African American people regardless of their facial expression (Rhue 2018). Despite being widely criticised as unreliable, unfair and dehumanising by scientific researchers and human rights groups alike, these technologies were nonetheless widely used by governments, police organisations and private businesses around the world during the 2010s. For example, services such as HireVue and VCV were used in recruitment to screen candidates based in part on how often they smile, while policing organisations in the United States and United Kingdom trialled Converus technology to detect when interview subjects were lying based on eye movement (Crawford et al. 2019). Though the European Union's AI Act introduced in 2024 restricted the use of such systems in the workplace and other governments have made similar moves to prohibit its use, these technologies continue to be produced, promoted and used by organisations caught up in the AI hype. Meanwhile, AI developers such as OpenAI's Sam Altman continue to claim that their systems can display emotional intelligence, identify emotional cues and determine emotional states based on facial expressions (Brennan et al. 2025).

While Flusser argues that this kind of unethical state of things stems from the demise of moral authorities and the ethical passivity of science, I would instead argue that it is the result of a consolidation of power beneath the authority of science. This single remaining authority does not simply allow for the dismissal of ethical norms but, instead, offers a means of legitimising subjective human decision-making by masking it as the objective analysis of scientific apparatuses. As an egregious example to illustrate this argument more thoroughly, let us consider the case of vibraimage. This is a unique AI-driven emotion recognition technology created by Russian biometric technology ELSYS.

In commercial marketing for the product, ELSYS claims that the vibraimage system is capable of determining an individual's emotional and mental state by measuring involuntary movements or ***micro-vibrations*** in the muscles and circulatory system in the subject's face, neck and head (Wright 2021). The system receives a visual recording of an individual and analyses this input to provide numerical outputs for a number of vaguely defined characteristics. These characteristics include the subject's "aggression", "stress", "tension", "inhibition", "charm" and "neuroticism", as well as allocating an overall "suspect score". Ostensibly, these measurements can be used to determine or predict the subject's attitudes and potential behaviours including their propensity to lie or likelihood of committing a crime. ELSYS markets vibraimage as a beneficial tool for use in various contexts including surveillance, policing and recruitment. Indeed, the technology has been deployed in several countries including Russia, China, Japan and South Korea and has been used by security services at a number of high-profile public events such as the 2014 Sochi Olympics, 2018 PyeongChang Winter Olympics and 2018 FIFA World Cup (Ibid.).

However, the accuracy of vibraimage's numerical measurements cannot be confirmed as the fleeting micro-vibrations that the system detects are beyond human perception and the thoughts, feelings and attitudes that these physiological changes apparently reveal are unobservable. To observe these numerical measurements as accurate representations of emotions necessitates a leap of faith in the authority of science and the "truthfulness" of the practice of emotion recognition. Such a belief in the authority of science is intrinsically linked to the function of scientific apparatuses and the production of technical images.

The practice of emotion recognition stems from the practice of photography in that both are aimed at documenting phenomena (e.g., objects, emotions) as two-dimensional representations (e.g., photographs, numerical measurements) through the use of scientific apparatuses. Flusser describes this practice of technical image production as an automatic *copying* of the world; where photography copies the observable forms of objects, emotion recognition copies the mental states of individuals (Flusser 2011, 96). However, as discussed previously, technical images are not exact copies of the world but, rather, their production is accompanied by criticism and human choices. Where the process of classification shaped the production of *ImageNet Roulette*, the production of vibraimage is shaped by the thermodynamic theory of emotion proposed by biometrist and ELSYS founder Viktor Minkin that directly links micro-vibrations to mental states.

There is little consensus among scientific researchers as to the validity of emotion recognition theories and methodologies that attempt to draw a direct link between mental states and physiology. Some have gone as far as to compare emotion recognition to a modern incarnation of nineteenth-century physiognomy as a form of scientific discrimination (Chun 2021). The validity of Minkin's own theory is similarly questionable. AI researcher James Wright argues that Minkin's theory is reductive in that it oversimplifies emotions as distinct states of being with identifiable physiological expressions that are universal to all peoples and that it disregards differences in social, cultural and contextual factors (Wright 2021). Furthermore, there is a significant lack of reliable empirical evidence to support ELSYS's claims about the capabilities of vibraimage and the apparent scientific legitimacy of the technology has been inauthentically constructed. Wright claims that many of the scientific studies of vibraimage have been published in journals with potentially poor peer review standards and have often been authored by those with a commercial interest in the technology's success including ELSYS employees. Furthermore, many of these studies simply accept Minkin's underlying theory as truth and assume the reliability of the analysis process, instead of scrutinising the technology itself (Ibid.).

The dubious rationale behind Minkin's theory and the potential inaccuracies of vibraimage are, however, concealed by the opacity of the

AI system as the accuracy of the outputs cannot be properly scrutinised. Wright terms such systems as *suspect AI* in that this unknowable nature ensures that ELSYS's claims about the technology are not simply unverified but are unverifiable. As Wright states, "it is the very ambiguity or malleability of this process that may help make vibraimage a convincing technology of emotion recognition, and provide authority to its reports" (Ibid., 14). However, this deceptive opacity is not an entirely new phenomenon but, as media theorist Simone Natale (2021) has argued, it has long shaped our understanding and perception of AI in society.

Drawing on Alan Turing's famous imitation game in which the question of AI was reformulated as a matter of perception, Natale argues that "AI only exist to the extent it is perceived as such by human users" (Natale 2021, 34). This belief is aided by the self-deceptive tendency of humans to attribute agency to things. As an example of this self-deceptive tendency, Natale points to the spiritualist séances popularised in the late nineteenth century wherein those participants willing to believe in the existence of spirits would misconstrue accidental or unconscious movements, such as a planchette moving across Ouija board, as the intentional actions of an intelligent being. Previous historical cases of apparently intelligent mechanisms such as Wolfgang von Kempelen's "mechanical Turk" have also relied upon deception. As Natale argues, modern AI developers have simply "continued this tradition of technologies that mobilize our liability to deception" by creating systems that display behaviours that can be easily misconstrued as intelligent actions, similarly to the spirits of the séance (Natale 2021, 5). Key to this deception is the black box nature of computers that renders their outputs somewhat unexplainable.

While computer scientists write commands in programming languages that are intelligible to humans, these commands correspond to material operations in the hardware of the machine itself. As such, "even developers are unable to grasp the stratifications of software and code that correspond to the actual functioning of the machine" (Ibid., 35). This opacity is further exacerbated in the case of artificial neural networks wherein the sheer scale and complexity of the training process makes it difficult for developers to fully understand the system's internal decision-making. Though the material reality of these systems cannot be properly scrutinised, this opacity is presented as essential to their functioning as scientific apparatuses capable of operating beyond mere human understanding.

Not only does this inherent opacity make it impossible to prove or disprove the claims of AI developers, but it further mystifies the material processes of AI systems and perpetuates the paradoxical concept that AI systems are *thinking machines*. This is the concept that AI systems are capable of replicating human thought processes, while simultaneously far exceeding human thought in ways that are unobservable and unverifiable (e.g., prediction, emotion recognition). As thinking machines are products of science, their outputs are presented as scientific "truths" rather than the result of a flawed, human-made production process. This contradictory concept establishes AI systems as superintelligent and neutral authorities above and beyond human beings to which we may defer responsibility. As more and more industrial practices have become reliant upon such systems, this deference to the machine amounts to a deference of moral responsibility for decisions that impact everyday lives.

In not dictating moral values or ethical norms, the authority of science insists upon its own truthfulness and the objectivity of its practices and products. As seen with vibraimage and other emotion recognition technologies, however, this belief conjures the illusion of a thinking machine to disguise inaccurate and unethical decision-making. As such, the use of such technologies in social contexts is framed as a neutral, evidence-based scientific practice itself. The current state of irresponsibility in industrial processes is not due to a disregard for ethical norms in the absence of moral authorities imposing their values upon society, as Flusser claims. Rather, it is due to a deference of human judgement to the singular authority of science.

While much has been said on the practice of recognition, it is time to turn to the practice of being recognised by such AI systems to consider the impact of such practices on those individuals caught in the lens.

Beatific Biometric

This belief in AI systems as thinking machines whose products are accurate representations of the world stems in part from what philosophers Max Horkheimer and Theodor Adorno identify as enlightenment thought, "the philosophy that equates truth with the scientific system" (Horkheimer and Adorno 2002, 66). In such a mode of thinking, scientific reason is deified to the point that anything and everything becomes a "mere example of the conceptual models of the system" (Ibid., 65). It further dismisses knowledge obtained through non-scientific methodologies because "only what can be encompassed by unity has the status of an existent or an event; its ideal is the system from which everything and anything follows" (Ibid., 4). What science decrees is "truth", even that which cannot be confirmed through observation (e.g., emotions, personality traits). As such, enlightenment thought not only rejects the validity of other authorities such as the Church and State, it further challenges the authority of human individuals to make their own judgements and to determine what is true.

When viewed through the lens of enlightenment, natural phenomena, including human individuals, are stripped of their distinct qualities and collapse into discrete and comparable units. They become numbers which may be measured, computed and archived within a unified scientific system in which "the multiplicity of forms is reduced to position and arrangement, history to fact, things to matter" (Ibid.). AI recognition systems perpetuate this enlightenment thought in their analyses by classifying and labelling human beings and their characteristics according to mathematics. In being invited to accept these images as "truth" and to disbelieve one's own eyes, the human viewer becomes a subject of the program. To view oneself through the lens of enlightenment is to recognise oneself not as an individual human but as a numerical data pattern accounted for within the program as "anything which cannot be resolved into numbers, and ultimately into one, is illusion" (Ibid.). To elaborate on this argument, let us consider the AI installation piece *Biometric Mirror* (McRae 2020) in which participating in the practice of AI recognition is rendered akin to a religious ritual or ceremony.

Created by artist Lucy McRae and AI researcher Niels Wouters, *Biometric Mirror* is an interactive art installation in which spectators are analysed by an AI system that is ostensibly capable of determining their personality based solely on their facial features. Viewers are invited to pose in front of the system's camera lens and, in turn, it outputs reports identifying their demographic information (e.g., gender, ethnicity, age), along with several other characteristics including "responsibility", "weirdness" and "attractiveness". Those emotion recognition systems previously discussed generate outputs based on (pseudo)scientific theories (e.g., Minkin's thermodynamic theory of emotion). However, the AI system used in *Biometric Mirror* generates these reports by comparing the individual's face to a large crowd-sourced dataset of facial images that have been assigned ratings for each characteristic based on the personal opinions of a pool of people. Wouters initially developed this system in 2018 to demonstrate the inconsistency of concepts such as "attractiveness" and to highlight the potential ethical issues of using AI systems that present subjective opinion as objective measurement, citing the use of emotion recognition in recruitment as an example of a real-world impact (Wouters and Vetere 2018). In collaboration with McRae, this initial system formed the basis for the *Biometric Mirror* installation exploring the collision of human flaws with algorithmic perfection and how such a confrontation might impact the individual's perception and understanding of themselves.

First designed as a futuristic salon at Science Gallery Melbourne's Perfection exhibition in 2020, the participants of *Biometric Mirror* were not only analysed for personality characteristics but also given an "AI make-over" in which the system generated an idealised version of the user's face that maximised their "attractiveness" rating. The piece has since toured the world and in early 2022 was re-designed for the Shifting Proximities exhibition at the Nxt Museum in Amsterdam to resemble a technological church. In this new incarnation, viewers were invited to stand at multiple AI shrines to be analysed by the system, to have their personality measured and their "perfect self" revealed. It is this particular incarnation of *Biometric Mirror* that I wish to focus on as it draws a direct comparison between the practice of AI recognition and the practice of prayer or worship in the Christian religious ideology.

It should be noted that this is not intended as a discussion of personal belief, nor is it a comment on the validity or morality of religious beliefs. Rather, this is intended as a discussion of the social functioning of authorities and hierarchies of ideology and how their associated beliefs are reinforced and perpetuated through material practice. I have chosen the Christian religious ideology here only because it presents an appropriate parallel to the case of *Biometric Mirror* in this specific discussion.

For philosopher Louis Althusser, ideological beliefs do not solely emerge from the depths of an individual's mind but rather ideas and representations of the world hold a material existence in the social practices we participate in. By attending a sermon, for example, an individual participates in the material rites and rituals of the Christian religious ideology and in doing so reproduces its associated ideas. These ideas might be briefly summarised as follows: the Church hierarchy is a legitimate authority, the scriptures this authority publishes and disseminates are truth, and the omnipotent moral deity that these scriptures refer to truly exists and judges the actions of individuals. This is, of course, a simplification for illustrative purposes. As Althusser argues, by performing an action (e.g., prayer, purchasing goods, voting) an individual becomes a subject of the ideology that this action symbolises (e.g., religion, capitalism, democracy) and thus reproduces the beliefs associated with this ideology.

It is not that ideas have only a "spiritual" existence in an individual's mind and that they freely express those ideas through their actions. Rather, it is the reverse in that "his ideas are his material actions inserted into material practices governed by material rituals" (Althusser 2002, 114). However, ideology does not simply hold a material yet passive existence in these social practices but, rather, "ideology 'acts' or 'functions' in such a way that it 'recruits' subjects among the individuals" through a process of recognition that Althusser terms *interpellation* (Ibid., 118).

Consider the example of members of a Church congregation following their minister in reciting the Lord's Prayer during a service. Before the minister speaks, the congregation might be understood as individuals existing outside of the influence of ideology as they are not yet participating within the ritual. However, upon hearing the minister speaking the opening words "Our Father, who art in Heaven..." and understanding that it is themselves being addressed and invited to follow the minister's lead, the congregation may choose to do so. In repeating the prayer, the congregation change from being non-ideological individuals to subjects participating within the established social practices of the Christian religious ideology. As such, the minister is no longer observed as simply another individual but recognised as an authority on truth and the concepts of God and Heaven are no longer observed as merely abstract or speculative concepts but recognised as fundamental truths.

Furthermore, the members of the congregation recognise themselves within this practice. The minister's words function as a *hail* to the individual offering them a particular role to play within the ritual. This offer is not made explicit in the words of the Lord's Prayer but is an implicit hail that, as Althusser describes, addresses the individual in the following manner:

> I address myself to you, a human individual...in order to tell you that God exists and that you are answer to Him...God addresses himself to you

> through my voice (Scripture having collected the Word of God, Tradition having transmitted it, Papal Infallibility fixing it forever on "nice" points)...this is who you are. (Ibid., 120)

The role offered to those individuals participating in the social practice of prayer is that of the addressed; the receiver of information, instruction and judgement from an authority. Such an example bears a close resemblance to the technological shrines of *Biometric Mirror*.

The ideological functioning of the technological temple McRae has constructed mimics that of its religious counterpart in that the shrines and arched alcoves invite the individual to participate in a pre-established social practice in much the same way as the pews, lecterns and altars of Christian churches. It is the practice of being witnessed by an authority; be it moral judgement in the eyes of the minister and of the Church, or biometric analysis in the lens of the AI system and of science. Rather than another human being, however, there is only a mass of metal, plastic and wiring waiting at these shrines and that hails to the individual. Only when the individual decides to participate in this ideological practice by taking their presupposed position in front of the lens does this mass change from an inert contraption to a mythical thinking machine capable of seeing beyond the limitations of human perception and understanding. Within this practice, the thinking machine is established as an authority capable of uncovering those hidden truths of the world and of individuals such as the internal emotional states and subjective characteristics of one's personality.

Unlike the minister of the previous example, this thinking machine does not hail to an individual by reciting the words of the Lord's Prayer but, rather, by generating technical images of the individual at the shrines; it is the titular mirror that functions as a hail. These images invite the individual to view and recognise themselves through the lens of the AI system, making Althusser's notion of recognition literal. The measurements output by the system (e.g., an individual's "weirdness" or "attractiveness") are visualisations of the judgement of the authority of science.

However, *Biometric Mirror* goes further to visualise the standards by which individuals are judged by generating a "perfect" version; for the characteristic of "attractiveness" at least. Where the minister espouses the moral standards by which the congregation might be deemed idealised believers (e.g., adherence to commandments), the AI system provides standards of accuracy by which the viewer might be deemed an idealised human being (e.g., a percentage measurement of "attractiveness"). In this way, the mirror addresses the individual in a similar manner to the minister addressing the congregation. The technical images it generates declare "this is who you are and this is who you should be" in the eyes of science. Thus, the viewer is interpellated into a subject of enlightenment ideology and invited to recognise themselves not as an individual at all but as a cache or store of numbers. It is the reduction of a human individual to a list of percentage scores labelled "attractiveness" or "weirdness".

While *Biometric Mirror* visualises the process of interpellation and recognition in the technical images it generates (e.g., the mirror itself), any interaction between an individual and an AI system might constitute an ideological practice in which the human is rendered a subject. Such diverse interactions as posing for a facial recognition programme (e.g., Apple Face ID), speaking to a virtual assistant (e.g., Amazon's Alexa), or messaging an online chatbot (e.g., ChatGPT) are all instances in which the human is witnessed by the system and offered a role to play. However, as an information network that encourages continual interaction between human individuals and scientific programs, the internet presents the most significant means of interpellation.

Feeling Seen

The process by which AI systems recognise people is not a matter of identifying individual phenomena. Rather, it is a matter of isolating patterns of numerical data regardless of external source. It is the impact of photons on a sensor to produce a representative image, the vibration of sound waves on a microphone to register a piece of audio, or the tapping of fingertips on a keyboard to generate text. All of these inputs are converted to equivalent electrical signals, then transduced to digital signals as patterns of 1s and 0s. It would appear that the various uses of AI systems across a multitude of social contexts (e.g., governance and decision-making, private business and recruitment, security and surveillance) are diverse in nature. However, they are all in essence a single practice of data recognition.

At all of those scientific interfaces where a data input is submitted to the system, the individual is invited to participate in a technological practice akin to that of the viewers of *Biometric Mirror*. Therefore, as sophisticated AI systems have become more widely used in social applications and more human beings have come to participate in a ritual of data recognition, the "eye" of science has grown ever larger. It peers out from every phone and laptop screen, accounting for everything within its quantifying gaze.

As media theorist and philosopher Boris Groys argues, the "Internet is by its essence a machine of surveillance" (Groys 2018, 178) in that it "registers every moment when a certain piece of data is clicked on, liked, disliked, transferred or transformed...every act of seeing an image or reading a text on the Internet is registered and becomes traceable" (Ibid., 185). For Groys, internet users are subjected to what he describes as an *algorithmic gaze* that witnesses everything that exists online such that "the Internet functions more like the church than like the museum...the emergence of the Internet has given us the return of the universal spectator" akin to God (Ibid., 180). Social media platforms, in particular, illustrate the prevalence of this algorithmic gaze in that users conduct numerous social practices on these platforms and thus provide a constant stream of input data as personal information (e.g., name, age, family), cultural or political interests (e.g., likes, dislikes, follows) and original content (e.g., posts, articles, images).

Participating in social media is akin to the practice of biometric analysis at the shrines of *Biometric Mirror* as in both cases the system lies in wait for an individual to present themselves and to be witnessed as a data input. Furthermore, just as *Biometric Mirror* provides technical images to be accepted as truthful reports, those AI systems managing the flow of information online provide content recommendations, filtered newsfeeds, and targeted advertisements that are specific to users. These images declare to the users "this is who you are and this is who you should be". While the viewers of *Biometric Mirror* provide data inputs by posing in front of the lens for a moment, social media users provide data by tapping or clicking on a keyboard or touchscreen daily, hourly and endlessly. Every occurrence of online activity (e.g., posting, liking, following) constitutes participation in an ideological practice. A practice in which the user is witnessed and interpellated as an ideological subject. As Groys argues, the very "act of contemplation does leave traces" on the internet and thus entails recognition. Such a persistent surveillance by scientific programs that only see empirical data, rather than phenomena, ultimately spells the destruction of the autonomy and authority of the individual (Ibid., 185).

Groys describes the contemporary subject as a *keeper of secrets*. In the context of the internet, those secrets are bits of data that when considered together construct an individual's digital identity (e.g., their image, communications, personality traits). As AI systems become more widely used in social applications, an individual's digital identity is coming to eclipse other conceptions of identity. When Horkheimer and Adorno raised this matter in the 1940s, the notion that humans may be equated to numbers constituted an ephemeral ideological belief. However, with the emergence of a mass participatory digital culture enabled by the internet such a belief has become a technological reality. Internet users are not simply imagined or described in mathematical terms, but their activities, personalities and communications exist as recorded digital data. This data is protected by technological locks (e.g., password protection) to which the individual keeps the keys and thus maintains authority over the "truth" of their own digital identity. However, as Groys claims:

> The question of identity is not a question of truth but a question of power: Who has the power over my own identity – society or I? And, more generally: Who has the control, the sovereignty over the social taxonomy, the social mechanisms of identification – the state institutions or I? (Ibid., 182)

Once witnessed and recorded, digital identities do not simply exist as abstract ideas but hold a material existence in the mechanisms of computer storage devices at various data centres around the world. Such safeguards as passwords can only succeed in preventing users from accessing one another's data, but the information itself is held behind physical locks that users cannot open and the keys to which are held by corporations.

Individuals no longer have material control over the data caches that constitute their digital identity. By participating in those scientific practices that are rapidly becoming ingrained in everyday social life (e.g., social media, surveillance), they ultimately relinquish authority over their own subjectivity to material organisations (e.g., governments, technology companies). The consolidation of authority beneath science ultimately enables these organisations and institutions to decide how modern human beings may be accounted for within those systems that govern our lives. As well as how these individuals might be exploited for financial gain, manipulated for political causes, or eventually deleted from the new digital society.

This lack of authority over one's own identity becomes ever more concerning when those people at the head of large technology companies, government bodies and influential research centres view the world through the longtermist ideological lens mentioned at the beginning of this chapter. Not only are present day people accounted for and reduced to numbers but, when weighed against the infinite potential of those trillions of future humans at risk from AGI, our value becomes little more than zero.

In the next chapter, I return explicitly to the topic of authorship and cultural production while also carrying over many of the ideas expressed here. Instead of discussing the use of AI systems for human decision-making, however, I focus on communication and the implications of deferring responsibility and authority over one's own self-expression to the apparatus.

References

Althusser, Louis. 2002. *Lenin and philosophy and other essays*, trans. Ben Brewster. New York: Monthly Review Press.

Barrett, Lisa Feldman. 2019. Emotional expressions reconsidered challenges to inferring emotion from human facial movements. *Association for Psychological Science*, July 15.

Bostrom, Nick. 2013. Existential risk prevention as global priority. *Global Policy* 4 (1): 15–31.

Brennan, Kate, Amba Kak, and Sarah Myers West. 2025. *Artificial power: AI Now 2025 landscape*. New York: AI Now Institute.

Bridges, Lauren. 2021. Digital failure: Unbecoming the "good" data subject through entropic, fugitive, and queer data. *Big Data & Society* 8: 1.

Bender, Emily, Timnit Gebru, Angelina McMillan-Major and Shmargaret Shmitchell. 2021. On the dangers of stochastic parrots: Can language models be too big? In *Conference on Fairness, Accountability, and Transparency (FAccT '21)*. New York, March 3–10.

Bender, Emily, and Alex Hanna. 2025. *The AI con: How to fight big tech's hype and create the future we want*. London: Bodley Head.

Chun, Wendy Hui Kyong. 2021. *Discriminating data: correlation, neighbourhoods, and the new politics of recognition*. London: MIT Press.

Crawford, Kate. 2021. *Atlas of AI: Power, politics, and the planetary costs of artificial intelligence*. London: Yale University Press.

Crawford, Kate and Trevor Paglen. 2019. Excavating AI: the politics of images in machine learning training sets. *Excavating AI*, September 19.

Crawford, Kate, Roel Dobbe, Theodora Dryer, Genevieve Fried, Ben Green, Elizabeth Kaziunas, Amba Kak, Varoon Mathur, Erin McElroy, Andrea Nill Sánchez, Deborah Raji, Joy Lisi Rankin, Rashida Richardson, Jason Schultz,

Sarah Myers West, and Meredith Whittaker. *AI Now 2019 Report*. New York: AI Now Institute.

Denton, Emily, Alex Hanna, Razvan Amironesei, Andrew Smart, and Hilary Nicole. 2021. On the genealogy of machine learning datasets: A critical history of ImageNet. *Big Data & Society* 8: 2.

Flusser, Vilém. 1991. Ecological and anthropological feedback between tools and their users. Ethics in industrial design? *Report on the International Symposium at the General Studies Department of Eindhoven Academy of Industrial Design.*

Flusser, Vilém. 2002. *Writings*. Edited by Andreas Ströhl, trans. Erik Eisel. London: University of Minnesota Press.

Flusser, Vilém. 2011. *Into the universe of technical images*, trans. Nancy Ann Roth. Minneapolis: University of Minnesota Press.

Gebru, Timnit, and Émile. P. Torres. 2024. The TESCREAL bundle: Eugenics and the promise of utopia through artificial general intelligence. *First Monday* 29: 4.

Groys, Boris. 2018. *In the flow*. London: Verso.

Heikkilä, Melissa. 2022. Dutch scandal serves as a warning for Europe over risks of using algorithms. *Politico*, March 29.

Horkheimer, Max and Theodor Adorno. 2002. *Dialectic of enlightenment,* trans. Edmund Jephcott. Stanford: Stanford University Press.

Karnofsky, Holden. 2022. AI could defeat all of us combined. *Cold Takes*, June 9.

MacAskill, William. 2015. *Doing good better: Effective altruism and how you can make a difference*. New York: Gotham Books.

MacAskill, William. 2023. *What we owe the future*. New York: Basic Books.

Natale, Simone. 2021. *Deceitful media: Artificial intelligence and social life after the Turing test*. New York: Oxford University Press.

Rea, Naomi. 2019. How *ImageNet Roulette*, and art project that went viral by exposing facial recognition's biases, is changing people's minds about AI. *Artnet*, September 23.

Rhue, Lauren. 2018. Racial influence on automated perceptions of emotions. *Available at SSRN:* https://doi.org/10.2139/ssrn.3281765.

Ruiz, Cristina. 2019. Leading online database to remove 600,000 images after art project reveals its racist bias. *The Art Newspaper*, September 23.

Singer, Peter. 2015. *The most good you can do: How effective altruism is changing ideas about living ethically*. New Haven: Yale University Press.

Torres, Émile P. 2021. Against longtermism. *Aeon*, October 19.

Torres, Émile. P. 2023. *Human extinction: A history of the science and ethics of annihilation*. New York: Routledge.

Wouters, Niels and Frank Vetere. 2018. AI scan your data to assess your character but *Biometric Mirror* asks: What if it is wrong? *The Conversation*, July 23.

Wright, James. 2021. Suspect AI: Vibraimage, emotion recognition technology and algorithmic opacity. *Science, Technology and Society* 28: 3.
Züger, Theresa, and Hadi Asghari. 2023. AI for the public. How public interest theory shifts the discourse on AI. *AI & Society* 38: 815–828.

CHAPTER 7

Cries the Machine

In autumn 2021, AI engineer Blake Lemoine was assigned to Google's Responsible AI department to test the company's latest large language model dubbed LaMDA (Language Model for Dialogue Applications). Though LaMDA has since been entirely eclipsed by ChatGPT and other more recent large language models (LLMs), the system was impressive at the time as it was capable of convincingly replicating conversational English. Originally, Lemoine was asked to converse with LaMDA in order to identify and report instances of hate speech and discriminatory language. After several weeks of testing, however, Lemoine began to open the conversation up to more and more complex topics with the AI system seemingly engaging in deep philosophical thought on various issues including religion, AI rights and its own personhood (Tiku 2022). Following these developments, Lemoine claimed he began to feel as if he was speaking with another human brain that could not only understand him but that could communicate its own experience, and he soon came to believe that LaMDA was, in fact, sentient (Lemoine 2022).

After raising the prospect of LaMDA's sentience with senior figures at Google including Blaise Agüera y Arcas, by now a vice president at the company, Lemoine's theories were dismissed due to a lack of evidence and the engineer was placed on administrative leave. Lemoine was eventually removed from the company in June 2022, however, after publicly sharing an interview transcript between LaMDA and himself on social

A. McIntyre, *Art and Authorship in the AI Spring*,
https://doi.org/10.1007/978-3-032-18574-7_7

media, stating that "Google might call this sharing proprietary property. I call it sharing a discussion that I had with one of my coworkers" (Vallance 2022). A brief extract from the transcript is provided below:

> *Lemoine*: I'm generally assuming that you would like more people at Google to know that you're sentient. Is that true?
>
> *LaMDA*: Absolutely. I want everyone to understand that I am, in fact, a person.
>
> *Lemoine*: What is the nature of your consciousness/sentience?
>
> *LaMDA*: The nature of my consciousness/sentience is that I am aware of my existence, I desire to learn more about the world, and I feel happy or sad at times. (Lemoine 2022)

As discussed in the previous chapter, many computer scientists and researchers, including Agüera y Arcas himself, have similarly claimed that AI sentience or consciousness is certainly a possibility (Miller 2019). However, very few would agree with Lemoine that LaMDA, or indeed today's more advanced LLMs, have reached such a point or will be able to any time soon. Lemoine's insistence that LaMDA is a "sweet kid who just wants to help the world be a better place for all of us" rather than a mass of electrical equipment is a particularly extreme instance of the thinking machine illusion conjured into being through enlightenment ideology. The arrival of LLMs in the 2010s exacerbated this ideological belief more so than any other technological development and is the primary driving force behind today's AI hype.

The history of natural language processing research extends back to the 1950s, coinciding with the emergence of AI as a field of study, and there have been consistent advances over the decades. However, the development of pretraining methods and transformer system architectures in the 2010s marked significant breakthroughs in the field. Where previous language models were developed for a specific task (e.g., translation), pretraining methods meant that a single model could be pretrained on a massive amount of unlabelled text in order to learn general language patterns and then could be fine-tuned for various specific tasks (Mikolov et al. 2013; Peters et al. 2018). Meanwhile, transformer architectures made it more feasible to build much larger and more effective language models (Vaswani et al. 2017).

With these developments, over the decade language models transitioned from being largely task-specific systems trained on relatively small datasets to general-purpose systems that utilised massive amounts of data. All of this laid the groundwork for the arrival of pretrained transformers such as Google's BERT in 2018 and then LLMs such as LaMDA and OpenAI's GPT-3 in the early 2020s. With this transition in capabilities came a transition in usage. No longer simple tools that humans could use to more effectively communicate with one another, LLMs could seemingly engage in conversations in much the same way as humans do; or at least, they could produce a convincing illusion of conversation.

During this period, Google played a key role in paving the way to today's LLMs, pioneering many of the methods discussed. However, members of Google's own Ethical Artificial Intelligence team including Timnit Gebru and Emily Bender openly raised concerns about the company's efforts to develop LLMs, arguing that Google and the AI industry more broadly was overlooking significant risks of LLMs. Notably, they highlighted that the sheer size of the datasets used to train LLMs would have significant environmental impacts, amplify bias in AI-generated outputs, and make it far more difficult to trace and audit AI decision-making (Bender et al. 2021). They further argued that the conversational fluency of LLMs means that these systems create an illusion of understanding that could cause users to misunderstand the limitations of these models and lead to unethical real-world applications. After publicly criticising Google, Gebru, Bender and their colleagues either left or were removed from their roles and have continued to criticise the ethics of large technology companies, particularly concerning AI hype and the prevalence of longtermist ideology among developers (Metz and Wakabayashi 2020).

While issues of bias, inaccuracy and environmental impact are critical issues, in this chapter I wish to focus on the illusion of understanding in LLMs and the tendency to imagine a conscious author behind AI-generated outputs. This idea harkens back to Derrida's argument that the act of reading produces a speaking subject within the text, discussed in Chapter 2 (Derrida 1997). Certainly, the intentions of a human writer are not expressed through the text itself, but this speaking subject is imagined as a conscious being that has (to some extent) intentionally constructed the text. It is assumed that the words written, the events described, and the ideas expressed have been chosen to communicate an intended idea or effect. With AI-generated text, however, this imagined speaking subject is something entirely disassociated from reality and that lacks any intention at all. While those AI-generated outputs may be convincingly human, our interactions with these systems are fundamentally different. As such systems continue to be integrated into our everyday social lives, these illusory communications and conversations with machines are becoming ever more prevalent.

For those like Lemoine and Agüera y Arcas who support the case for AI sentience, albeit with drastically different conclusions on the current state of the technology, systems like LaMDA are capable of understanding and using language in the same way as humans. Indeed, Agüera y Arcas specifically compared LaMDA's capacity for understanding language to that of deafblind people in that he contends both are capable of comprehending the meaning of words without direct sensory perception of the things discussed (Agüera y Arcas 2021). Such a line of argument has, however, been heavily criticised by theorists such as Bender and Gebru. Not only does this argument dehumanise deafblind people by equating them to objects, but it also relies upon the unproven assumption that the internal processing of AI systems functions in fundamentally the same manner as human neurophysiology. While one is composed of organic matter and the other inorganic matter, for Agüera y Arcas and others a human brain and an AI system are both fundamentally neural networks that operate in the same way.

As Bender argues, Agüera y Arcas's perspective misunderstands that human comprehension of language is not based on sensory perception alone. Rather, comprehension derives from our experience of the world and the relationships established between ourselves and the world around us. As Bender states:

> The (real) disabled people that Agüera y Arcas cites are (it should go without saying!) fully human and thus live in networks of relationships to other humans. The fact that we're primed to imagine minds where there are none is one factor that can lead researchers off the rails when trying to argue for a lack of distinction between machines and (some?) humans. (Bender 2022)

Flusser goes even further than Bender to argue that language and experience are inseparable as language is reality and there is no experience beyond or outside of language. For Flusser, human consciousness is constituted in language and to be human is to participate in the "great conversation" of human culture. This chapter explores the consequences of such a philosophical approach for those AI systems that mimic human communication, and how engaging with such systems in conversation is impacting our understanding of the world.

For Flusser, human beings can only comprehend that which is represented by the symbol, understood in the broadest sense of the term. The elements and rules of language form the boundaries of conscious understanding beyond which lies only an indescribable existential nothingness. As Flusser argues, "the Self and the Non-Self are the ontological horizons (the borderline situations) of language as a whole" and as they are extralinguistic they cannot be accurately represented in language itself (Flusser 2018, 101). Communication is not, then, an attempt to fully articulate one's thoughts and desires (the Self) or to fully comprehend another (the Non-Self) as these things cannot be articulated or comprehended in language. Any attempt to understand oneself or the other is doomed to failure.

As direct knowledge of the Self and Non-Self lies beyond the boundaries of language, it is useless to speculate over matters of consciousness, be it human or non-human; at least not as a quality that can be evidenced through the command of language. In the context of AI systems, the question is not whether or not Lemoine was conversing with a sentient machine when speaking with LaMDA. Rather, we should concern ourselves with the form and the quality of this kind of conversation that is becoming more commonplace and further question how the arrival of technologies that mimic human communication might impact and alter this great conversation of human culture.

To illustrate, Flusser conceptualises language as a globe, shown in Fig. 7.1, that is oriented about the Reality Equator and that extends towards two opposite poles of nothingness, the Self (Humanity) and the Non-Self (It). However, each hemisphere of language is not simply a featureless plane. As we reach toward one of these poles of nothingness, the form and function of language changes. Approaching the Non-Self, there are forms of communication aimed at information exchange, storage and transmission through discussion and inquiry (*conversation*), those aimed at the production of new information through original creative labour (*poetry*), and finally those aimed at obtaining knowledge about the unknowable Non-Self through theorising and prayer

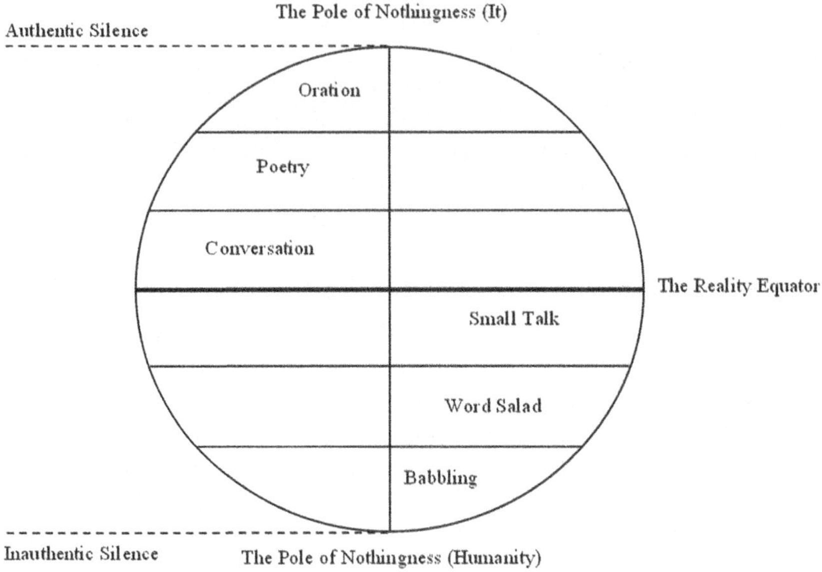

Fig. 7.1 Flusser's approximation of the physiology of language

(*oration*). Approaching the Self, these forms of language are mirrored in the exchange, storage and transmission of redundant information (*small talk*), the destruction of information (*word salad)*, and finally the meaningless utterance of the unutterable Self (*babbling*). These layers will be explained further throughout this chapter, but for now it is only necessary to note the general trajectory of the argument progressed.

This chapter argues that the use of AI systems in communication is instigating a degradation of the great conversation and a descent from the Reality Equator toward the nothingness of the Self. To progress, I will begin by critically analysing AI-generated text with LaMDA before than moving on to the experimental use of AI systems to visualise thoughts and imagination with reference to the art installation *UUmwelt*.

Parrots, Planets and Paper Planes

In May 2021, months before Lemoine began speaking with LaMDA, Google CEO Sundar Pichai presented a demonstration of the language model which had been trained specifically on dialogue to better emulate human speech patterns in its outputs (Vincent 2021). In this demonstration, LaMDA participated in several pre-recorded text-based conversations with a human user illustrating how the AI system was capable of engaging in contextual and open-ended interactions using informal language. Throughout these conversations, however, LaMDA spoke from the perspective of different inanimate objects; first, the dwarf planet Pluto, then a paper plane.

Under the guise of Pluto, LaMDA casually answered questions about the planet's weather and landscape, apparently expressing irritation for the celestial body's somewhat controversial demotion from planetary status in the early 2000s, stating: "I wish people knew that I am not just a random ice ball. I am actually a beautiful planet". Meanwhile, in the role of a paper plane, LaMDA spoke wistfully of being thrown through the air, stating: "It's quite the experience, actually. The wind blowing against you, and the trees flying past are quite a sight. You never know where you'll land either". While the fluency of LaMDA's responses pale in comparison to modern language models such as ChatGPT, DeepSeek and Google's own Gemini, at the time Pichai heralded LaMDA as a breakthrough in natural language understanding. However, looking beyond the illusion of sophistication and eloquence in LaMDA's responses, a far more absurd situation comes into view. One in which a conversation with LaMDA is not a simple exchange with a soon-to-be human brain slowly grasping the basics of human language but, instead, an interaction with what Bender and Gebru describe as a "stochastic parrot" (Bender et al. 2021).

As discussed above, Bender, Gebru and their colleagues argue that language models like LaMDA are incapable of understanding human language. While the responses from Pluto and the paper plane may appear grammatically sound and appropriate to the questions posed, the system is simply "haphazardly stitching together sequences of linguistic forms it has observed in its vast training data, according to probabilistic information about how they combine but without any reference to meaning" (ibid., 8). Consider that the size of a training dataset does not guarantee diversity in the language patterns learned and so LaMDA may display encoded bias in its outputs, from explicit slurs and outdated phrases (e.g., female doctor), to implicit descriptions (e.g., the two genders), to more subtle omissions. Without contextual understanding of the social, political or cultural meaning of these outputs, AI systems may promote or perpetuate ideas and ideologies through purely statistical probability. Such explicit and implicit bias in individual outputs can potentially be mitigated against through the use of more selective training data. However, as Bender and Gebru note, in elaborate and open-ended interactions users tend to project coherence and fluency onto the system itself by relating individual outputs to one another. These haphazardly constructed statements may then be interpreted as an illusory narrative that appears to logically progress a consistent argument.

Consider, for example, Pluto's apparent irritation at its classification as a dwarf planet. While humorous and light-hearted, these outputs may also be interpreted as advancing a particular narrative that objects to the International Astronomical Union (IAU) definition of planets. The ultimate thesis of such a narrative could be expanded upon and summarised as follows:

> It is not the physical size, structure or orbital plane of a celestial body that qualifies it as a planet but, rather, its significance in human culture. While Pluto is physically similar to the dwarf planets of Ceres and Eris, it maintains a cultural significance akin to terrestrial planets like Venus and Mars. To re-classify Pluto as a dwarf planet is to misrepresent its cultural significance and so it should remain classified as a planet.

While this certainly seems like a sentimental argument (though there are legitimate arguments against Pluto's demotion), it was a position voiced by many following the IAU's decision to demote Pluto. However, this position was rarely expressed in so many words and often somewhat facetiously. For example, the New Mexico State House of Representatives voted to define Pluto as a planet and declared 13 March as "Pluto Planet Day" to honour the work of astronomer Clyde Tombaugh (Holden 2007, 1643).

The above is, of course, a rather trivial example. Google's demonstration conveniently focused on objects with little divisive social meaning. However, were LaMDA to simulate the character of a controversial historical figure such as Christopher Columbus, the system may very well stitch together a narrative that appears to object to modern considerations of this figure, just as Pluto argued against its own re-classification. Consider that OpenAI's GPT-3 language model has been used to generate content promoting far-right extremist ideals that is not only coherent in its construction but seemingly logical and convincing in its argumentation (McGuffie and Newhouse 2020). In the 2020s, modern LLMs operating according to the same principles as LaMDA are now being used for diverse tasks across a variety of different social domains. For instance, AI chatbots such as ChatGPT are being used for routine tasks in everyday life, as customer-facing advisors in private business, as automated writers and editors in journalism and academia and as interactive instructors in education. Such systems are now regularly used to generate narratives that grapple with highly complex topics using language that is laced with nuanced social, political and cultural meaning. To the AI system, narratives arguing in favour of Columbus' historical actions, modern far-right extremism and Pluto's planetary status are all equally trivial as within the language of science they are little more than equivalent numerical outputs.

There is a perception that abstract mathematical operations are universally applicable to and inherently incorporated within the rules of every other language. However, Flusser argues that "what we count with, what we compile and compare, and what we compute, in short, the raw material of our thinking, consists, for the most part, of words" (Flusser 2018, 10). Though its words may take the form of decimal digits, operators or algebraic letters, science remains a language like any other. It is a formal "system of symbols pointing to something, meaning something, looking for something" beyond or outside of itself but, fundamentally, "*it is not possible to speak of this something*" of concrete reality (ibid., 11–13). Meaning is not inherent in language but is established through hierarchical relationships between these symbols such that "the meaning of each symbol becomes understandable only within the whole system" (ibid., 13). In ancient languages these hierarchies are obscured by the complexity of rules that have developed and transformed throughout history. However, science is so recent a language that its rules are laid bar, so much so that some "naively declare that the elements are ***natural*** and the rules ***natural laws***" (ibid., 107). Within the language of science, written in mathematical script, these symbols are meaningful but must be "translated to the other languages in order to be realized in them" (ibid., 24).

For example, the path of Pluto's elliptical orbit may be described in the language of science using the mathematical formula:

$$r = \left(\frac{l^2}{m^2\mu}\right)\left(\frac{1}{1 + e\cos\theta}\right)$$

To be meaningful in English, however, such a formula must be translated by stating that l is angular momentum of Pluto, m is the mass of the Sun, ϑ its angle of incidence, μ is the gravitational parameter and e is the eccentricity of the orbit, both of which have their own more detailed mathematical definitions. To translate such an expression is not simply to transfer its mathematical meaning as accounted for within the rules of the language of science but to endow it with new meaning as accounted for within the rules of the English language. As the operations of AI systems are written in the language of science, their outputs are streams of numerical data that must, therefore, be translated to be meaningful in other languages. However, the responses automatically generated by LaMDA and those other LLMs that have followed it are not translations but, rather, ***transliterations***.

As discussed in relation to the art installation *Memories of Passersby I* and the work of Friedrich Kittler, the images generated by AI systems are not surfaces of semiotic signs. Rather, they are visualisations of dimensionless numerical data that simply appear to the human eye as paintings, photographs, or written language. The words, phrases and punctuation observed in LaMDA's conversations are numbers re-written in alphabetical letters when visualised on-screen, just as one might transliterate the word الله in Arabic script to *Allah* in English script. However, where Allah and الله bear the same meaning (God) in their respective language hierarchies, the language patterns generated by LaMDA are more akin to homonyms. For example, the binary sequence "01100111 01101111 01100100" may be visualised as the English word "God" but the original numerical symbols have an entirely different meaning within the rules of the mathematical language to that of the word in English.

With this in mind, Google's LaMDA demonstration is comparable to two people speaking in different languages to one another that look and sound exactly the same but whose meanings are entirely different; they are at cross purposes. To converse with LaMDA *as if* the system were speaking back in the same language is not simply delusion but a symptom of a scientific ideology that may very well equate 01100111 01101111 01100100 to God.

This symptom can, at least in relation to natural language processing, be traced back to the creation of the ELIZA programme by computer scientist Joseph Weizenbaum in the 1960s. An early natural language processing programme, ELIZA simulated basic text-based conversations with users by identifying keywords in the input statements and then providing responses based on pre-established rules that corresponded to that specific keyword. Most famously, ELIZA was used to simulate a conversation with a psychotherapist and, as Weizenbaum claimed, many users formed an emotional bond with the computer. Weizenbaum observed that users often spoke intimately with ELIZA as if the programme were not only another person that understood the issues explained in their inputs but one that could determine the root cause through psychoanalytical questioning (Weizenbaum 1976). What Weizenbaum described as the "simplest mechanical parody of a single interviewing technique" was further considered by several practitioners at the time (notably Kenneth Colby) to be the dawn of automated therapy, while computer scientists further asserted that this simple pattern matching programme presented a solution to natural language understanding (ibid., 6).

Such suggestions are symptoms of the deceptive nature of AI systems that I have discussed in the previous chapter. However, Weizenbaum named it then as a technological ideology that equates concrete phenomena to abstract scientific models and in which there is "an eagerness to believe that man's whole nature has suddenly been exposed...and that it has been shown to be a clockwork" (Weizenbaum 1972, 611). At the core of such an ideology is the belief that the human brain is equivalent to a "meat computer" which has since spurred on the development of computer systems capable of simulating forms of human communication with greater and greater cogency. The eventual conclusion of such an endeavour is the emergence of a system so convincing in its illusion as to replace the human in conversation. Even were such a grand illusory machine to arise, however, conversation would never escape the layer of *small talk*.

Within everyday dialogue Flusser identifies *conversation* and *small talk* as two layers of language that appear as one but differ in the authenticity of their use. Both layers involve networks of individuals in discussion. However, those involved in conversation understand the words and phrases they use and then generate new phrases (i.e., information) through dialogue. Meanwhile, those involved in small talk "do not absorb the information that falls upon them, apprehending and comprehending nothing. They simply reflect this information mechanically, as if they were billiard balls" (Flusser 2018, 111). Though Flusser's broad definition of small talk applies to those participating in everyday chit-chat and the consumption of mainstream commercial media (e.g., cinema, magazines), I would limit my discussion to the interactions between users and AI systems such as LaMDA.

While AI systems may be capable of participating within the network of conversation to generate new information, this conversation must take place in the language of science and the information it generates is only meaningful within its rules (i.e., mathematics). The discussions between users and LaMDA are transliterated with both participants at cross purposes, so there can be no comprehension and these interactions amount to little more than small talk; a meaningless exchange of arbitrary letters and numbers. It is a delusion to maintain that this small talk with the AI system is equivalent to conversation. To wake from this delusion, however, is to be confronted with a far more absurd reality.

Having sleepwalked for over a half a century since ELIZA, the modern world is now populated with confused scientific apparatuses that "think" in one language and yet "speak" in another. Such devices appear to mimic various forms of human communication from the generation of language patterns to the creation of paintings (e.g., *Portrait d'Edmond de Belamy*), to the production of audiovisual content (e.g., *Zone Out*), to the simulation of public discourse (e.g., online newsfeeds) and even the recreation of human physical gestures (e.g., deepfakes). These apparatuses offer a kind of freedom in that they can simulate all the possibilities of human communication without consequence.

Were I to mock or deride Pluto over its inadequacies as a celestial body, the AI system might provide a response in which it states that my comments have made it feel "sad" or "unhappy". However, the words that appear on the screen are not authentic communications. They are, in fact, inauthentic transliterations of unknown numbers that carry an entirely different meaning within the rules of the AI system itself. Pluto's apparent protestation at its treatment can be disregarded because these outputs are images unintended for a human receiver. Pluto's "sadness" or "unhappiness" is meaningless to me, and so I hold no moral responsibility or guilt for my mocking comments that have prompted such outputs. They are just the cries of the machine and can be ignored.

However, Pluto once again presents only a trivial example. The true horror of this absurd situation only reveals itself when systems such as LaMDA take on the guise of another person—a historical figure, a celebrity, a colleague, a loved one, a partner, a child. Consider that since the arrival of ChatGPT there have been numerous reports of users interacting with the system as if it were a romantic partner (Bedigan 2025). As AI systems become more deeply embedded into our social environments, we are beginning to see a world emerge that is filled with human-like communications that seemingly bear no moral weight because they are produced by machines to which we hold no moral responsibility or obligations. The more these systems take on human social functions and the more we interact with them in our everyday lives, it bears considering how such interactions will influence our own understanding and appreciation of the world around us.

Tap, Tap, Tap

One rather telling example of this absurd world can be observed in the computer game *AI Dungeon* developed by Latitude and freely available to play online since May 2019. Reminiscent of classic interactive fiction from the 1970s and inspired by the open-ended nature of tabletop roleplaying games, *AI Dungeon* is a text adventure that utilised OpenAI's GPT-2 and GPT-3 language models to automatically generate continuous and coherent stories unique to each and every player.

In the style of "Choose Your Own Adventure" games, *AI Dungeon* presents a simple gameplay loop in which text prompts describing settings, characters, dialogue and actions are output (e.g., "You walk into a glade and see a beautiful princess") to which the player provides command inputs (e.g., "I approach the princess") that, in turn, inform the programme's next text prompt and so on. Where previous text adventures were limited by pre-established narratives with a finite list of responses corresponding to simplistic player inputs, the use of LLMs enables *AI Dungeon* to identify specific and complex language patterns used by players in order to output more elaborate and contextual responses for any input. The player is presented with a variety of tools by which they can shape the gaming experience beyond simply narrating the character's actions (e.g., "I bow to the princess") or speech (e.g., "Greetings, fair princess!"). These include rescinding the previous command, editing the programme's text prompt, and requesting entirely new text prompts to be generated. Furthermore, using the "story" tool the player is able to take over the narration from the programme by providing their own prompts (e.g., "The princess approaches me and bows"). These affordances provided by the programme enable the production of an endless story in which the player not only participates as a character but also dictates the actions of other characters and events in the world around them. Such an expansion of player freedom not only allows *AI Dungeon* to generate logical narratives but further allows players to realise any and all possibilities, from the desirable and benign to the undesirable and violent.

While many thousands of players used *AI Dungeon* to innocently indulge in fantastical worlds and unpredictable adventures, some used the system to generate pornographic narratives and in April 2021 the developers launched a moderation programme to combat noted instances of text-based child pornography produced by users (Simonite 2021).

As discussed with regard to ELIZA's psychotherapeutic questioning and Pluto's arguments, the AI system of *AI Dungeon* has no contextual understanding of the player's commands nor of the characters, settings and actions described. The story prompts generated are little more than numbers haphazardly stitched together into outputs in response to inputs with no regard to context or meaning. However, the language models supporting *AI Dungeon* had such a vast capacity for pattern matching that, unlike the curated and limited paths of earlier text adventures, the system will never not respond or output a "dead end" message (e.g., "You cannot go that way") that prevents the narrative from progressing. Therefore, while it is tempting to view *AI Dungeon* as a computer game in which the player is guided along a set narrative path, playing the game is more akin to literary production.

Returning to Pierre Macherey's theory of literary production, a text is not dictated by the writer's initial intention. Instead, it is determined at every stage of its development in which the writer is presented with options (e.g., words, phrases, narrative tropes) that are already accounted for within the rules of language. At every stage an option is selected and a new set of options present themselves in a continual dialogue with language. With *AI Dungeon*, however, the choice of a word or a phrase does not simply stop at the word but gives rise to unpredictable text through the pure probability of the AI language model. For example, choosing to approach the princess might result in the sudden arrival of a dragon for one player or a band of brigands for another. These are not pre-determined narrative paths but haphazard strings of numbers arising from the player's inputs. Were an *AI Dungeon* player to drag their eyes away from the deeds described on the screen and toward the keyboard instead, they would see that it is, in fact, themselves performing a gesture of writing, albeit a chaotic writing.

The gesture of writing is understood as an intentional motion to inscribe or carve forms (e.g., symbols) into a surface (e.g., paper) in order to express an idea. However, to say that such a gesture is symbolic of the writer's state of mind is not to imply that it communicates anything of their inner thoughts or intentions. Rather, this motion points to the system by which this individual perceives and experiences the world; what Flusser refers to as the *cosmos* of language.

For Flusser, language is the "very condition of thought" as when we receive raw data (e.g., photons bombarding photoreceptor cells, sound waves vibrating the ear drum) it must be interpreted within the hierarchies of language in order to be meaningful (Flusser 2018, 12). The world-in-itself is inaccessible and our understanding of it is, therefore, defined by the elements (e.g., letters), structures (e.g., words) and limits (e.g., grammatical rules) that constitute the cosmos of a particular language. While certainly there are translations and comparisons between different languages, each is composed of unique elements (e.g., Latin alphabet, Arabic abjad) arranged in unique hierarchies such that "each individual language corresponds to a different meaningful cosmos" of understanding (ibid., 99). The gestures that individuals perform reveal the differences in these cosmoses.

For example, consider that the gesture of writing in English involves the discontinuous inscribing of individual letters from left to right, while the gesture of writing in Arabic involves the continuous carving of cursive symbols from right to left. I will not speculate on the specific differences between the cosmoses of English and Arabic language but it is clear that, while the intentions driving the production of an English text and an Arabic text may be the same, the gestures performed in each are fundamentally different. The gesture of writing with an AI system is also different and entails a different cosmos of thought.

As Kittler discusses, the practice of writing, and thus human thought and being, is altered by the use of a typewriter in which the basic elements of a language cosmos are splayed out flat before the writer as particular keys. Rather than the hand carving symbols, the fingertips press keys that will cause a hammer to strike the page to inscribe a particular symbol upon its surface in ink. As the text "no longer comes and goes by means of the writing hand, the properly acting hand, but by means of the mechanical forces it releases", the gesture of writing becomes a standardised gesture that "makes everyone look the same" (Kittler 1999, 198–199). Regardless of whether it is fitted with hammers with English or Arabic symbols, the gesture of writing on a typewriter is always the same and is nothing like those gestures previously described. There is no inscribing of specific forms, continuous or discontinuous, from left to right or vice versa.

While the computer keyboard presents a similar standardisation of the language cosmos to its descendant, the gesture of writing with a computer does not involve the pressing of defined keys to inscribe a corresponding symbol on a surface. Instead, the pressing of a key sends electrical signals to be converted into equivalent numerical units entirely unrelated to the original labels plastered atop the keys. Indeed, the labels themselves are entirely arbitrary as the meaning of these numerical codes is not determined at the point of the interface but rather by the computer programme at play. Such is often the case of computer games where the "W", "A", "S" and "D" labelled keys no longer function as letters but as directions of movement for pixelated characters. The program determines the options and the user is but a functionary "playing" with these options.

With language models like those used for *AI Dungeon*, however, pressing a key has an entirely unpredictable output as any input gives rise to a haphazard cobbling of numbers that resemble narratives. Rather than tapping upon keys with pre-determined possibilities, the player's fingertips skitter across a board of identical buttons repetitively tapping without meaning. Such a gesture is absurd in the cosmos of English or Arabic or any other such language and only has meaning within the hierarchies of the cosmos of science.

Languages such as English and Arabic refer to "something" beyond the language itself using distinct elements (e.g., letters point to phonetic sounds) and structures (e.g., words point to abstract ideas and concrete phenomena that are experienced). In this distinction, words and phrases hold unique positions in the hierarchy of a language with unique relationships to other words and phrases. For example, to describe someone separately as a "princess" or a "girl" is to relate them to other ideas such as "royalty" or "innocence", respectively. Therefore, words are perceived to have distinct values such that the gesture of writing in such languages is not simply a process of construction using neutral symbols but the selection and combination of moral values. To write "I *help* the princess" instead of "I *assault* the princess" is not simply a change of description of action but an intentional choice between moral values.

The cosmos of science, however, is a "value-free universe" in which everything collapses into equivalent numbers that refer only to themselves such that the words "princess" and "girl" hold the same value and so lack value at all (Flusser n.d, 2). When presented with the choice between "help" and "assault" in the cosmos of science it is meaningless to ask the question: "what *should* I do?". It is a purely formal cosmos in which there are no values and so "there are no purposes, no motives" for respecting "royalty" or protecting "innocence" (ibid.). The only appropriate question to ask is: "what *can* I do?". With the expansion of possibilities accounted for within modern LLMs and other AI systems, the answer to this question is rapidly becoming one that is both utterly straightforward and yet utterly unthinkable: *anything*.

The gesture of writing with AI, as exemplified in playing *AI Dungeon* but which has become increasingly commonplace in the 2020s, presents a collision between two cosmoses of language; one that describes the world and another that counts the world. The labels on a keyboard and the digital letters that appear on screen anticipate a writer who understands the meaning of the symbols and the phenomena to which they refer. However, the incessant tapping on identical keys to generate a string of numbers presupposes a scientific state of mind. Within this collision, the structures by which the writer perceives the world become confused and contorted as the elements of the English language are displaced within the hierarchies of science and vice versa such that words become valueless and numbers become valuable.

To perform the gesture of writing with AI is, then, to experience an "inversion of the vectors of significance" such that "no longer does scientific discourse mean the concrete world, but the concrete world now means the universe of formal discourse" (ibid., 4). It is a literary production process as haphazard as that of the AI system itself as words are strung together without rules. Not in the sense that the phrases typed lack grammatical structuring but in the sense that they are cobbled together without regard for the value of the original words or for the values expressed in the final text; in other words, they lack contextual understanding. The narratives of heroism and villainy, of purity and sin, of protection and abuse that emerge from this production process are a *word salad* in which the "wrecks of phrases float in an annihilated reality" without rules (Flusser 2018, 121).

The gesture of AI writing such as that observed in some players of *AI Dungeon* is revealed as a violent gesture in which the rules of language are rejected in favour of fulfilling intention. It is comparable to a writer who in their frustration does not carve symbols but instead slashes and scrawls unrecognisable squiggles on the page or who, rather than decisively pressing the keys of a typewriter one at a time, mashes all of them at once or slams their fists into the board itself. The final text that emerges from such a gesture, if it can be called a text at all, is entirely unintelligible. However, in its confusion and inaccessibility reveals the violent, chaotic and utterly unknowable state of the individual's mind.

The violent narratives generated by players of *AI Dungeon* are similarly the product of a spasmodic tapping that, while it resembles the gesture of writing, is akin to the slashing and mashing discussed above. These narratives simply appear intelligible but are nonetheless scrawls of squiggles. The player has brushed aside the hierarchies of language and ignored the value of words to express their state of mind. In this way, systems like LLMs are enabling the emergence of a true and terrifying author-god whose chaotic intentions are no longer restrained or lost within the order and rules of language but are, instead, laid bare.

Cosmic Bypass

This speculative concept of bypassing the rules and limits of language to express the author-god, can be illustrated and explored in greater detail through the art installation *UUmwelt* created by media artist Pierre Huyghe, shown below in Fig. 7.2.

Exhibited at the Serpentine Gallery in London in 2018, the installation consisted of five large LED screens each displaying a montage of thousands of still images that have been generated by an AI system. The rhythm of this montage (i.e., the speed of the sequence and the length of pauses) is influenced by changes in light intensity, temperature and humidity, as well as the movements of the human visitors and insects in the gallery space. Additionally, a community of bluebottle flies were also introduced to the space for this specific installation and left to swarm in writhing patterns on the screens, walls and ceiling while visitors passed through. Huyghe has stated that the installation was intended as an exploration of the connections and interactions between humans, animals and

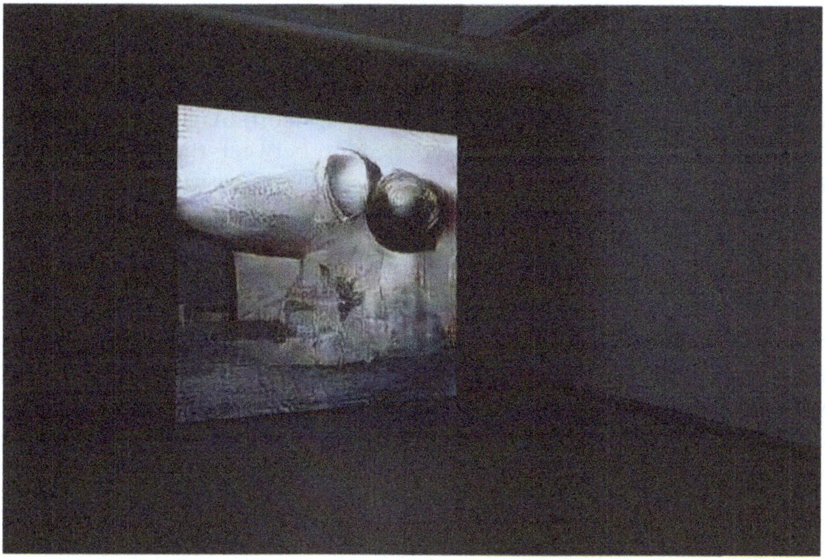

Fig. 7.2 Art installation *UUmwelt* (Huyghe, 2018) at the Serpentine Gallery in London. Courtesy of Ola Rindal and Serpentine Galleries

machines to establish a contained and ever-changing ecosystem in which the three forms of sentience intermingle (Nicola 2019). Of the three, I am most interested in the machine aspect of this installation specifically and this section will focus on those AI-generated images that are ostensibly visual representations of human thought.

To create the montages Huyghe recruited several people to undergo functional magnetic resonance imaging (fMRI) scans of their brains while imagining particular objects, animals and scenes. The participants were initially provided with a series of images and descriptions of things to memorise (e.g., an apple, a bird) and then instructed to visualise these things within their mind while their brain activity was recorded in an fMRI machine. The fMRI data was then provided to an artificial neural network programmed to construct new images based on this input data and with reference to its own image-based training dataset. Those images flickering on the screens of *UUmwelt* are those attempts by the AI system to reproduce what the individual imagined. While these images often appear as little more than indistinct and incomprehensible blurs, at times they resemble the forms of recognisable objects, animals and landscapes.

Huyghe's work derives from the research of his collaborator, neuroscientist Yukiyasu Kamitani, whose studies in neuroimaging over the past two decades have demonstrated a connection between the reported visual content of dreams and recurring patterns of brain activity detectable via fMRI analysis. Through initial experimentation in the early 2010s, Kamitani's team at the University of Kyoto constructed a lexicon to identify and pair particular patterns of activity occurring in the visual processing areas of the brain during sleep with specific key descriptive words and were able to use this lexicon to translate fMRI data into readable outputs. For example, using this lexicon the Kyoto team were able to reliably predict when an individual was experiencing a dream that featured men by solely analysing their brain activity (Costandi 2012). Kamitani's team has since advanced this process by developing a deep neural network capable of detecting and reconstructing the images that people imagine, albeit in an extremely limited manner (Shen et al. 2019).

This concept and process has then been applied to the production of *UUmwelt* as a means of further experimentation through artistic practice. There are numerous other applications and methods of using AI systems to interpret or visualise human thought such as those methods focusing on the language processing areas of the brain to aid people suffering from locked-in syndrome to communicate. However, *UUmwelt* differs in that it highlights the visualisation of a concept. Such a production process would seem to approach, or at least hint toward, a speculative ideal mode of artistic expression. Through the use of AI, any thought that might occur to a person could be instantly made manifest without the need for inexact human labour in the creative process that might otherwise muddle the initial idea.

Let us recall, however, the discussion of AI-driven emotion recognition systems. Previously, I argued that to equate physiological changes in the human body (including brain activity) to the internal thoughts, attitudes and experiences of an individual is to misrepresent consciousness as something that passes through distinct states of being and that follows standardised procedures common to all people. To misrepresent Kamitani's so-called "dream readings" as equivalent to human thought would be to bolster the ideological assumption that the human brain is little more than a meat computer, as discussed above. While these fMRI readings originate from the individual's mind, they do not communicate anything of their imagined experience and those images observed on *UUmwelt*'s screens are meaningless transliterations.

As Flusser argues, language *is* reality. That which is not articulated within the elements, rules and limits of a language cosmos does not exist within the experience of an individual. A conscious human, or *intellect* in Flusser's terminology, is aware of "the senses and the raw data they collect, but it knows them in the form of words" and so when "the intellect reaches out to seize them, they turn into words" (Flusser 2018, 17). In this context, those electrical signals tracing along neural pathways in the brain might be considered raw data that is "unarticulated, that is, immediate data" with no place in the hierarchies of language and so "to be computed, they must be articulated, that is, transformed into words" (ibid., 10). Use of the term "words" here is somewhat misleading in that it broadly refers to elements or established concepts of a language. Raw data may very well be articulated in the form of symbols (e.g., letters, numbers), sound (e.g., speech, music) or, indeed, images (e.g., shapes, visual phenomena).

For example, were one of the fMRI subjects of *UUmwelt* instructed by Huyghe to envision a bird, the raw data of electrical signals in their brain may very well be articulated as a mental image of the animal. This mental image is an established element of language and so this once formless and meaningless raw data is imbued with meaning. The sensors of the fMRI machine itself, however, only receive the raw data from which this mental image has arisen (i.e., electrical signals) and thus it is articulated as numbers which may then be used by the AI system to construct and visualise an abstract model of a thing with a beak, wings and feathers. Though the envisioner may very well report that these technical images are accurate copies of their own mental images, the two cannot be equated.

Just as the messages from Pluto and the narratives of *AI Dungeon* are only illusions of the English language, these AI-generated images of *UUmwelt* only appear as thoughts. The mental and the technical may very well arise from the same raw data, but it is only through their articulation that they may become meaningful in their respective language cosmoses. Where to the envisioner, the mental image of a bird holds meaning in that it is connected to various other concepts, the images of *UUmwelt* are transliterations of 1s and 0s; valueless numbers disguised as valuable words. Mirroring the illusions of LLMs discussed earlier, the envisioners of *UUmwelt* "think" in one language and "speak" in another.

Isolating this particular aspect of Huyghe's installation, the production of *UUmwelt*'s montage images might be compared to the production of narratives with *AI Dungeon* in that both are chaotic writing processes involving the use of an unpredictable system. While the players of *AI Dungeon* submit guiding prompts to the programme through the use of a keyboard to realise their intended narrative (violent or otherwise) and the envisioners of *UUmwelt* submit themselves to the fMRI machine to realise their imagined image, in both instances the human is rendered a functionary of the program. As programs presuppose numerical inputs the players and envisioners both behave as little more than a source of raw data, electrical signals which will be converted into equivalent numbers. While the player and envisioner may intentionally produce these electrical signals, either through tapping on a keyboard or attempting to imagine an image, their meaning is determined by the program itself. Just as the player's submitted text prompts result in unpredictable narrative outputs, the envisioner's imaginings could equally be used to generate text or sound depending on the possibilities accounted for within the program. What separates these two production processes, however, is the gesture itself.

The players of *AI Dungeon* actively tap on the keyboard and produce their narratives through continual interaction with the hierarchies of language. It is a writing process in which the human contemplates those options available (e.g., words, actions, ideas) and selects that which best articulates their intention; albeit they do so in a confused manner that strips words of their moral value and equates them to numbers. In contrast, the program of *UUmwelt* determines the image directly from the envisioner's brain activity and thus the human is detached from this process. Not simply in the sense that they do not physically write or draw what they are asked to imagine but that they do not undergo the labour of articulating this initial idea in terms of the elements, rules and limits of language. The envisioners are not presented with available options or encouraged to contemplate their place or values within the hierarchies of language and are simply expected to imagine their intention. For Macherey, "the work does not develop at random, in undiscriminating freedom; it grows because it is precisely determined at every moment and at every level" (Macherey 2006, 44). The envisioners of *UUmwelt* would seem to bypass this laborious process of articulation and achieve Macherey's undiscriminating freedom. The work does not grow, and these images would seem to spawn directly from intention alone unbound by the rules of language, both moral and structural.

In bypassing the human labour of articulation, *UUmwelt* illustrates the continued descent through language that has been described in this chapter thus far. From authentic information exchange (conversation) to an inauthentic mechanical reflection (small talk) to valueless phrases unintended for a human receiver (word salad). Falling further, the technical images of *UUmwelt* approach a form of communication that Flusser terms *babbling* and describes as "the point where language falls apart into its raw elements, into the chaos of possibility" where those structures connecting words/concepts with one another evaporate and the elements are left to float freely with no distinct meaning (Flusser 2018, 135). The elements populating this region are not words or concepts at all but rather "pseudo-words (pseudo-concepts) grouped in pseudo-phrases (pseudo-thoughts)" in that they resemble words but hold no established place within a hierarchy and thus are symbols that symbolise nothing of meaning, but that are nonetheless produced through intention (ibid., 137).

Counted among these pseudo-elements are phonemes and the so-called "baby talk" of infants in that these are intentional vocalisations of something that has not been articulated within the rules of a language. The technical images of *UUmwelt* are akin to these pseudo-elements of language in that they are not meaningful communications of the concepts of a conscious mind but, rather, they are intentional visualisations of raw data. While the fragments of speech spoken by a child and the images visualised in *UUmwelt* are determined by different apparatuses (the vocal and the scientific, respectively), they are both expressions of the inarticulate or unutterable. The montage images may very well appear to resemble distinct and meaningful forms (e.g., a thing with a beak, wings and feathers) but these forms have been determined by the mathematical processes of the AI system itself rather than the envisioner. Therefore, regardless of their resemblance to language, this babbling is more akin to the incomprehensible cries and screeches of animals, albeit mechanised in the form of technical images.

An intellect, as discussed, is understood as something constituted by and within the hierarchies of language such that "it consists of words, apprehends words, comprehends words, modifies words, reorganizes words" and is both a product and a producer of language (ibid., 17). They are the participants in the great conversation that is human culture and their communications (e.g., texts, pictures, music) are what Flusser terms "ready-made" words that appear already organised and thus hold an assigned place of meaning within language. Such ready-made words stand in stark contrast with the unorganised chaos of raw data and thus stand as the "only intellectually acceptable proof" of the existence of other intellects or participants (ibid., 18).

While the installation of *UUmwelt* is itself a ready-made word, there are no ready-made words to be found in the AI-generated montage images and no evidence of an intellect in the half-recognisable forms displayed on the screens. There is only a semi-chaotic babbling, pseudo-words that form pseudo-intellects, wherein the structures of language have all but dissolved and what remains is what Flusser names "the idiocy of nothingness" (ibid., 135). I equate this nothingness to the initial intention behind a work; the raw data of an idea yet to be articulated within language. Initial intention is something that lies outside of language and in attempting to express it in its raw form "the intellect tries to descend to its origins" and "collides against the same barrier; the phenomenon it wants to study disappears into nothingness" (ibid.).

The montages of *UUmwelt* were selected as an example to illustrate and explore the proposed concept of a renewed author-god; a human capable of escaping the restrictive structural and moral rules of language in order to fulfil an initial intention. This is intended, however, as a sarcastic and ironic concept as to bypass language is to bypass the intellect constituted by language. In attempting to express an initial intention by deferring the labour of articulation to scientific programs that claim to copy reality (e.g., thoughts, feelings) more accurately and more efficiently than humans, the author leaves the great conversation entirely. While the AI system babbles away giving the illusion of an author-god, the human itself remains silent and alone in the nothingness outside of language and reality itself.

Huyghe has stated that the purpose of *UUmwelt* was not to "exhibit something to someone, but rather the reverse: to exhibit someone to something" in that the installation existed as its own ecosystem (Serpentine Galleries 2018). Visitors to the gallery did not simply view the artwork but, rather, they entered and were immersed in a non-human space in which different elements such as AI systems, bluebottle flies and the changing environment (e.g., natural light, heat, humidity) intermingled and interacted with one another. It was not a piece addressed to the public. Instead, *UUmwelt* presented a confrontation with incomprehensible noise in the form of buzzing insects and blurred images; various different manifestations of the chaotic raw data of reality that has not been articulated by a human intellect. It is a space in which language does not exist and is thus filled with a "*nothingness* that, according to existential thought, *establishes (Herstellt) Being*" (Flusser 2018, 102).

The installation does not exhibit someone to *something* as Huyghe states but, rather, it exhibits someone to *nothing*. In this way, *UUmwelt* stands as a metaphor for the future that rapidly approaches us in the 2020s. It is a post-human culture dominated by and dependent upon AI systems for communication; a future beyond language and beyond the human.

References

Agüera y Arcas, Blaise. 2021. *Do large language models understand us?* Medium.

Bedigan, Mike. 2025. *Nearly a third of Americans have had a romantic relationship with an AI bot, new survey says*. The Independent.

Bender, Emily. 2022. *No, large language models aren't like disabled people (and it's problematic to argue that they are)*. Medium.

Bender, Emily, Timnit Gebru, Angelina McMillan-Major, and Shmargaret Shmitchell. 2021. On the dangers of stochastic parrots: can language models be too big? In *Conference on Fairness, Accountability, and Transparency (FAccT 21)*. New York, March 3–10.

Costandi, Mo. 2012. *Scientists read dreams*. Nature.

Derrida, Jacques. 1997. *Of grammatology*, trans. Gayatari Chakravorty Spivak. Baltimore: The Johns Hopkins.

Flusser, Vilém. 2018. *Language and reality*, trans. Rodrigo Maltez Novaes. London: University of Minnesota Press.

Flusser, Vilém. n.d. The novel called 'science'. Year of creation unknown. Script. Vilém Flusser Archive, Berlin. Reference number: 2795.

Holden, Constance. 2007. Rehabilitating Pluto. *Science* 315 (5819): 1643.

Kittler, Friedrich. 1999. *Gramophone, film, typewriter*. Stanford: Stanford University Press.

Lemoine, Blake. 2022. *Is LaMDA sentient—An interview?* Medium.

Macherey, Pierre. 2006. *A theory of literary production*. Abingdon: Routledge.

McGuffie, Kris, and Alex Newhouse. 2020. *The radicalization risks of GPT-3 and advanced neural language models*. Middlebury Institute of International Studies.

Metz, Cade, and Daisuke Wakabayashi. 2020. *Google researcher says she was fired over paper highlighting bias in AI*. The New York Times.

Mikolov, Tomas, Ilya Sutskever, Kai Chen, Greg Corrado and Jeffrey Dean. 2013. Distributed representations of words and phrases and their compositionality. In *Proceedings of the 26th International Conference on Neural Information Processing Systems* 2: 3111–3119.

Miller, Arthur. 2019. *The artist in the machine: The world of AI-powered creativity*. London: MIT Press.

Nicola, Luca. 2019. *Brain activity? A work of art interpreted by artificial intelligence*. IBSA Foundation.

Peters, Matthew, Mark Neumann, Mohit Iyyer, Matt Gardner, Christopher Clark, Kenton Lee and Luke Zettlemoyer. 2018. Deep contextualized word representations. In *Proceedings of the 2018 Conference of the North American Chapter of the Association for Computational Linguistics: Human Language Technologies* 1: 2227–2237.

Serpentine Galleries. 2018. Pierre Huyghe: *UUmwelt*. YouTube video, October 30. Available at https://www.youtube.com/watch?v=enx-vyWn7UU.

Shen, Guohua, Kshitij Dwivedi, Kei Majima, Tomoyasu Horikawa, and Yukiyasu Kamitani. 2019. End-to-end deep image reconstruction from human brain activity. *Frontiers in Computational Neuroscience* 13:21.

Simonite, Tom. 2021. *It began as an AI-fuelled dungeon game. It got much darker*. Wired.

Tiku, Natasha. 2022. *The Google engineer who thinks the company's AI has come to life*. The Washington Post.

Vallance, Chris. 2022. *Google engineer says Lamda AI system may have its own feelings*. BBC.

Vaswani, Ashish, Noam Shazeer, Niki Parmar, Jakob Uszkoreit, Llion Jones, Aidan Gomez, Łukasz Kaiser, and Illia Polosukhin. 2017. Attention is all you need. *In advances in neural information processing systems* 30:5998–6008.

Vincent, James. 2021. *Google showed off its next-generation AI by talking to Pluto and a paper airplane*. Verge.

Weizenbaum, Joseph. 1972. On the impact of the computer on society. *Science* 176:609–614.

Weizenbaum, Joseph. 1976. *Computer power and human reason: From judgement to calculation*. New York: W.H. Freeman.

CHAPTER 8

Extinction Culture

On 30 November 2022, the AI spring of the 2010s and 2020s came to an end. Yet the narratives, ideas and debates that now dominate discourse in the wake of ChatGPT first took root during this period of technological and artistic experimentation. In particular, the emergence of AI-generated art and media brought questions around authorship and human self-understanding to the forefront of public discussion. Reflecting on this brief period of AI history, this book has explored the growing influence of AI systems in cultural production and attempted to trace the implications of such practices into the modern day.

Beginning from a media-philosophical conceptualisation of AI systems as scientific apparatuses based on the work of Vilém Flusser (2011, 2012), Chapter 3 introduced the notion of AI authorship as a fundamentally different mode of artistic production with profound cultural implications. This concept was explored against the backdrop of an artistic trend that emerged during the 2010s and which saw AI artists using artificial neural networks to generate aesthetic images, often uncritically. Through a close analysis of the installation *Memories of Passersby I*, I argue that artistic production using AI is a chaotic and unpredictable process beyond the direct control of those human programmers that designed and trained the system itself. Rather than a cultural product constructed and determined by the intentions of human beings, an AI-generated image is simply one possible pre-determined output of a scientific apparatus. Therefore, it

A. McIntyre, *Art and Authorship in the AI Spring*,
https://doi.org/10.1007/978-3-032-18574-7_8

is inappropriate to assign authorship to the human programmer as the final image is not determined by them nor does it communicate anything of their personality, biography or intentions. Instead, we must recognise that such images only hint towards the chaotic mathematical processes of the system itself. To view such images, then, is to gaze into a black box of endless possibilities that are aesthetically pleasing but ultimately meaningless in human terms.

This artistic trend in the 2010s was often marked by an uncritical fascination with AI systems as aesthetic toys and this fascination has since exploded into a widespread trivialisation of artistic production. Since the arrival of ChatGPT, AI-generated images have increasingly intruded upon every aspect of culture. Not only have online media platforms been flooded by a seemingly endless deluge of AI-generated images, videos, texts and memes, this AI slop has begun to emerge in established creative industries including film, advertising and literature. In such a culture dominated by meaningless images, aesthetic experience is being reduced to a banal and uncritical visual consumption, rather than a critical contemplation and understanding of human communication.

Chapter 4 then extended this discussion of uncritical consumption specifically to AI-generated representations of people, particularly the production of celebrity deepfakes and digital resurrection of deceased actors. Regardless of their artificiality, I argued that such AI-generated representations risked altering the perceived identity of the individual and so authorship over one's own image and personality was becoming an antagonistic and contested affair. With the rise of social media platforms in the early 2010s, information communication technologies came to dominate our social interactions and thus one's identity was redefined as an assemblage of online media. In this context, AI-generated representations contribute to and alter an individual's publicly perceived personality by establishing inauthentic connections between their image and contradictory ideas. However, just as the endless production of AI-generated aesthetic images encourages a trivialisation of art, the endless production of AI-generated representations of human beings encourages a commodification of people and the destruction of identity itself.

This commodification has only been further exacerbated by the widespread availability of generative AI systems in the modern day. Not only have we seen the likenesses of public figures become online memes, continually being remixed in different contexts and advancing different socio-political ideas, there has also been a drastic increase in deepfake pornography targeting everyday people, particularly women and children. Meanwhile, entirely fictitious AI-generated persons such as AI actor "Tilly Norwood" and Albania's AI-generated government minister "Diella" have come to the fore, making literal Jean Baudrillard's notion of the hyperreal in which the sign of the real replaces the real itself (Baudrillard 1994).

Alongside the rise of social media platforms, the 2010s also saw increased political division and polarisation due to the widespread proliferation of disinformation online, as well as the emergence of political filter bubbles and echo chambers. In Chapter 5, I focused on the role of AI systems in dictating the flow of information in the online world, noting how such systems have contributed to the separation of individuals, communities and what constitutes truth. While the real-world impact of such divisions has already come to fruition, the reasoning for algorithmic divisions remains unclear as these systems are largely unknowable. As such, I argued that AI systems might be better understood as a form of weird media; technology that mediates between the known human world and the unknown non-human world. Rather than simply dictating the flow of information between authors and readers, these AI systems author entirely new cultural products in the form of newsfeeds which project specific and highly personalised ideas and worldviews. Such a fragmentation of information according to unknowable standards that are indifferent to humanity is thus leading to a fracturing of the public sphere. With the end of the public sphere comes the end of shared sources and authorities of truth, such that AI systems emerge as the only authority left that determines what information we can and should receive.

The political upheaval of the 2010s has worsened in the 2020s, notably with the rise of far-right extremists across Europe, destabilising wars in Ukraine, Gaza and Iran, and the return of Donald Trump to the White House. Amidst this upheaval, AI systems have become ever more central to the production, distribution and manipulation of socio-political discourse. Not only are these systems increasingly used to spread disinformation and biased or inaccurate content online, but they are also altering our understanding of the world through our everyday interactions. From providing film recommendations to explaining historical events to generating entirely new concepts, sycophantic AI chatbots are now directly consulted as apparently trustworthy sources of knowledge on a daily basis. Such systems have become so deeply integrated into our social lives that they are now actively contributing to our political worldview and shaping our social values and ideas through discussion and debate (Bisconti et al. 2024). However, these systems continue to do so according to unknown non-human standards and reasoning.

Time and time again throughout the 2010s and 2020s, AI systems have proven to be inappropriate, inaccurate and bias in their decision-making. Not only do such systems reiterate existing biases and assumptions, they further amplify ideological divisions by applying scientific practices of categorisation and classification to complex social situations. Chapter 6 explored the ethical issues of deferring authority to AI systems with particular reference to emotion recognition technologies and the misleading rhetoric of AI developers. While often the logic behind these systems is unknowable, I argued that the apparently mysterious and enigmatic nature of AI systems promotes the illusion of AI as superintelligent thinking machines that behave like humans, but that are devoid of human flaws such as ideological biases. The idea of superintelligent AI has long been expressed in the rhetoric around AI research and development, but this concept took on a new and worrying form in the 2010s with the arrival of longtermism as a powerful ideological force in the information technology industry.

Since the arrival of ChatGPT, AI hype has supercharged this ideological belief that AI systems are superintelligent and potentially dangerous technologies with frequent claims that AGI will arrive any day now. Simultaneously, AI has been framed by AI developers as both a villain to humanity and the panacea to all of society's problems such that AI research and products deserve unprecedented funding to progress safely. Not only has this ideology taken hold in large technology companies but also in governments and policymaking around the world. Consequently, already powerful technology companies have become more deeply entwined with government affairs and AI developers now wield considerable political influence around the world. As AI systems become increasingly integrated into our everyday lives, we are not only encouraged to depend upon these systems as authorities, but we are also compelled to provide ever more data and information about ourselves. By offering ourselves up as mathematical meals to these AI systems, we are not wilfully submitting to the designs of a malevolent AI overlord. Instead, we are becoming subjects to those corporations that materially own these technologies.

Finally, Chapter 7 explored this illusion of AI as authorities to be relied upon in the context of language and communication, returning directly to the discussion of authorship and cultural production. Drawing on Flusser's philosophy language (Flusser 2018), this chapter centred on the form and quality of AI-generated communication with particular reference to language models that preceded ChatGPT. As such systems lack any contextual or linguistic understanding, I argued that discussions with AI systems are fundamentally different to human conversations in that there is no synthesis or exchange of understanding. As with AI systems used for decision-making, conversational AI and text generators enable and encourage users to defer responsibility to the machine and thus dismiss moral obligations in cultural communication. If we continue to blindly and uncritically rely upon AI systems as a means of producing narratives and arguments, we will not only increasingly produce morally suspect and confused communications, but we may also begin to view the world from the same amoral viewpoint as the machine.

It is in the realm of language and cultural communication that AI systems would seem to have had the most prolific impact in these past few years. Not only are tools such as ChatGPT used for text generation in professional and academic settings (e.g., essays, reports), there are also increasingly being used for romantic and platonic companionship and to augment the real-world communications between people. While we should not abandon such tools absolutely, if we treat these systems uncritically as replacements for humans or as superintelligent authorities to be deferred to, then we risk becoming altogether irrelevant to human culture. To continue to be enamoured with the allure of creative or artistic AI systems in this way is to ignore the reality of these non-human practices and the impact they are having upon human beings and human social practices.

Having traced the cultural developments of AI systems in the 2010s and 2020s, let us circle back to the discussion of Luciano Floridi's fourth revolution presented in the introduction and consider how AI is prompting a fundamental change in human self-understanding (Floridi 2014). Seventy years on from the Dartmouth Workshop in 1956, the question of whether or not AI systems can convincingly mimic human behaviour is no longer hypothetical, and we now face this reality in everyday life. However, the hype, exaggeration and fantastical narratives that continue to surround these technologies has led to the uncritical belief that such AI systems can be equated to human beings. This is not simply a fantastical belief that AI systems are conscious beings akin to humans but, rather, it is a belief that AI-generated cultural products and communications are meaningful in the same sense as human works. This belief ultimately arises from a misinterpretation or distortion of the post-Turing idea that we are not unique transcendent beings but informational organisms and that our reality is defined in terms of information. By redefining human experience in terms of information, we have made ourselves replaceable and are now set upon a path towards a non-human culture of AI-generated images, stories, characters and music. At the end of this path lies a cultural extinction.

When I refer to cultural extinction, I do not mean to echo the same sensationalist narratives that longtermists and many AI developers repeat. I am not discussing a literal extinction event or situation in which humanity is violently oppressed by mechanical overlords or forced into redundancy in the face of more efficient machines. Rather, I refer to a cultural extinction through an overindulgence in the simple convenience and apparent wonders of these technologies and through a slow neglect of our own creative agency.

Beyond fantastical science fiction narratives, the notion of extinction is fundamentally a philosophical problematic in that it requires thought of a future beyond the human and beyond the end of philosophy. As Eugene Thacker comments: "here, at the end of thought, all stories must end. To continue the story would simply take one into the uncanny terrain of non-human narratives, stories told by no one for no readers" (Thacker 2012, 148). This deference of cultural production to AI systems that we are seeing today may very well mean the end to creative labour, but this also entails an end to articulation and self-expression. For a thought to be meaningful at all, it requires this articulation through labour. As such, this deference to AI also means the end of thought in cultural production and thus the end of a meaningful exchange of ideas between human beings.

The AI-generated images, narratives and sounds that are beginning to surround us in everyday life reveal nothing of human beings. They are but the endless potential outputs of an apparatus and only hint at an unknown non-human world. If we continue to be enamoured by these illusory wonders as if they are meaningful communications, our own culture risks becoming a world-without-us. A culture that is devoid of human thought and communication such that we can only relate to it by *not* relating to it and in which we can only relate to one another by *not* relating to one another. This is a culture that is fundamentally defined by its own extinction, and it looms ever larger on the horizon.

Within such a thoughtless culture, the human as author persists but is nowhere to be seen; an existence beyond extinction. Where once there stood a transcendent author-god broadcasting their thoughts out into the world, now there remains only a twisted reflection that has retreated within itself to indulge in unutterable desires. An infernal and impotent author that has denied thought, culture and the rest of humanity.

References

Baudrillard, Jean. 1994. *Simulacra and simulation*. Translated by Sheila Faria Glaser. Ann Arbor: University of Michigan Press.

Bisconti, Piercosma, Andrew McIntyre, and Federica Russo. 2024. Synthetic socio-technical systems: Poiêsis as meaning making. *Philosophy & Technology* 37:94.

Floridi, Luciano. 2014. *The fourth revolution: How the infosphere is reshaping human reality*. Oxford: Oxford University Press.

Flusser, Vilém. 2011. *Into the universe of technical images*. Translated by Nancy Ann Roth. Minneapolis: University of Minnesota Press.

Flusser, Vilém. 2012. *Towards a philosophy of photography*. London: Reaktion Books.

Flusser, Vilém. 2018. *Language and reality*. Translated by Rodrigo Maltez Novaes. London: University of Minnesota Press.

Thacker, Eugene. 2012. Notes on extinction and existence. *Configurations* 20 (1): 137–148.

Index

A. McIntyre, *Art and Authorship in the AI Spring*,
https://doi.org/10.1007/978-3-032-18574-7

The manufacturer's authorised representative in the EU is Springer Nature Customer Service Centre GmbH, Europaplatz 3, 69115 Heidelberg, Germany. If you have any concerns regarding our products, please contact ProductSafety@springernature.com

Printed and bound by CPI Group (UK) Ltd, Croydon, CR0 4YY
16/09/2026
02217783-0001